Social Closure and International Society

Laying the foundations of a theory of 'international social closure,' this book examines how actors compete for a seat at the table in the management of international society and how that competition stratifies the international domain.

In a broad historical survey from the 'Family of Civilised Nations', through the Great Powers' club, to the G7 and G20 today, Naylor investigates the politics of membership in the exclusive clubs that manage international society and ensure its survival, providing us with a new way to think about how status competition has changed over time and what this means for international politics today. With its sociologically grounded theory, this book advances English School scholarship and transforms the study of contemporary summitry, providing a ground-breaking approach rooted in archival research, elite interviews, and ethnographic participant observation.

This book is of interest to international relations scholars interested in the 'expansion' and globalisation of international society, the history of international summits, and transformations in international order, as well as to those examining concepts including stratification, hierarchy, and networked governance. With its emphasis on non-state actors in global governance, scholars and practitioners alike working on/for civil society will also find this research of great value.

Tristen Naylor is a Fellow in International Relations at the London School of Economics. He was previously the Lecturer in Diplomatic Studies at the University of Oxford, where he was named 'Most Acclaimed Lecturer' in the Social Sciences. Prior to his academic career, Dr. Naylor worked in foreign policy for the Government of Canada. He is a recipient of the Canadian Public Service Award of Excellence.

Global Governance
Series Editor: John J. Kirton, University of Toronto, Canada

Global governance is growing rapidly to meet the compounding challenges of a globalized 21st-century world. Many issues once dealt with largely at the local, national or regional level are now going global, in the economic, social and political-security domains. In response, new and renewed intergovernmental institutions are arising and adapting, multilevel governance is expanding, and sub-national actors are playing a greater role, and create complex combinations and private-partnerships to this end.

This series focuses on the new dynamics of global governance in the 21st century by:

- Addressing the changes in the structure, operation and impact of individual intergovernmental institutions, above all their innovative responses to the growing global challenges they confront.
- Exploring how they affect, are affected by and relate to non-state actors of global relevance and reach.
- Examining the processes of cooperation, competition and convergence among international institutions and the many global governance gaps where global challenges such as terrorism, transnational crime and energy do not confront powerful international institutions devoted to their control.
- Dealing with how global institutions govern the links among key issues such as climate change and health.

In all cases, it focuses on the central questions of how global governance institutions and processes generate the effective, legitimate, accountable results required to govern today's interconnected, complex, uncertain and crisis-ridden world.

The G7, Anti-Globalism and the Governance of Globalization
Edited by Chiara Oldani and Jan Wouters

Social Closure and International Society
Status Groups from the Family of Civilised Nations to the G20
Tristen Naylor

For more information about this series, please visit: https://www.routledge.com/Global-Governance/book-series/ASHSER1420

Social Closure and International Society
Status Groups from the Family of Civilised Nations to the G20

Tristen Naylor

Taylor & Francis Group
LONDON AND NEW YORK

First published 2019
by Routledge
2 Park Square, Milton Park, Abingdon, Oxon OX14 4RN

and by Routledge
605 Third Avenue, New York, NY 10017

First issued in paperback 2021

Routledge is an imprint of the Taylor & Francis Group, an informa business

© 2019 Tristen Naylor

The right of Tristen Naylor to be identified as author of this work has been asserted by him in accordance with sections 77 and 78 of the Copyright, Designs and Patents Act 1988.

All rights reserved. No part of this book may be reprinted or reproduced or utilised in any form or by any electronic, mechanical, or other means, now known or hereafter invented, including photocopying and recording, or in any information storage or retrieval system, without permission in writing from the publishers.

Trademark notice: Product or corporate names may be trademarks or registered trademarks, and are used only for identification and explanation without intent to infringe.

Publisher's Note
The publisher has gone to great lengths to ensure the quality of this reprint but points out that some imperfections in the original copies may be apparent.

British Library Cataloguing-in-Publication Data
A catalogue record for this book is available from the British Library

Library of Congress Cataloging-in-Publication Data
Names: Naylor, Tristen, 1984– author.
Title: Social closure and international society: status groups from the family of civilised nations to the G20 / Tristen Naylor.
Description: Abingdon, Oxon; New York, NY: Routledge, 2019. | Series: Global governance | Includes bibliographical references and index.
Identifiers: LCCN 2018040168 | ISBN 9780815369462 (hardback) | ISBN 9781351252423 (e-book)
Subjects: LCSH: International organization—History. | International cooperation—History. | International relations—Sociological aspects.
Classification: LCC JZ1318 .N424 2019 | DDC 306.2—dc23
LC record available at https://lccn.loc.gov/2018040168

ISBN 13: 978-1-03-209410-6 (pbk)
ISBN 13: 978-0-815-36946-2 (hbk)

Typeset in Times New Roman
by codeMantra

To everyone who encouraged me to write a book,
I may someday forgive you.

Contents

List of figures ix
Acknowledgements xi

1 The closure games 1
2 International social closure 19
3 Institutions and mobility 36
4 Exclusion 53
5 Inclusion 72
6 Incorporation 114
7 Conclusion 151

Annex: methods 159
Bibliography 173
Index 209

List of figures

2.1 Exclusion strategies 28
2.2 Inclusion strategies 29

Acknowledgements

In a book about inclusion, exclusion, and status, the trickiest bit to write might well be the acknowledgements. To those I've mistakenly left out and those who feel I haven't celebrated enough, please accept my apologies. Take solace in the fact that very few people will actually read this and the unintentional slight won't be noticed by anyone much at all.

Academics generally read the Acknowledgements section to get a sense of an author's intellectual pedigree (and then form biases and prejudices accordingly). As no one has shaped my thinking more than my family and friends, I can't not acknowledge them first. Those of you only interested in pigeonholing me as a scholar should just skip down a few paragraphs.

I've worked on this project for eight years, and in that time an incredible cast of characters has coloured my life. I'm faced with an embarrassment of riches – there are too many of you to name, but please know that I'm grateful to each of you for the innumerable ways in which you've made so many days (and nights) happy ones. I'm lucky enough to be able to call the world's brightest, funniest people my friends. I'm especially grateful to those of you who supported me during this manuscript's final months, particularly for your patience. I'll forever be grateful for the steady stream of reassurance, coffee, beer, and wine with which you sustained me. Each of you know who you are and what you mean to me. I'll always be there for you as you have been for me, likely with a bottle of red in hand.

I also happen to have the greatest family in the world. I hope this book helps you even just a little bit understand what I do, why, and how. At the very least, you now have something to show your friends when they ask what I do with my time despite not having a regular job like a normal person.

If there are any ideas in this book that are worthy of merit, Edward Keene is responsible. As a DPhil supervisor, he was peerless; as a colleague and friend, he is equally so. Eddie, I'll never be able to thank you enough. I am also especially indebted to Andrew Hurrell and Iver B. Neumann for the advice they gave as this project (and my academic career) developed. Jennifer Welsh, Kalypso Nicolaidis, Yuen Foon Khong, David Hine, Michael Bloomfield, John Gledhil, Jörg Freidrichs, Ivan Manokha, Corneliu Bjola, Tarak Barkawi, Kate Millar, Yuna Han, Chris Rossdale,

Gustav Meibauer, and Cindy May also have my thanks for all sorts of help over the years. George Lawson's and Emma Saint's advice and encouragement over the past year has especially helped turn this work into a better piece of scholarship than it otherwise would have been. And I can't fail to thank Mark B. Salter for being the reason why I'm an academic at all.

Thanks must also be given to John Kirton and Madeline Koch of the G7 and G20 Research Groups at the University of Toronto. Much of what forms the empirical basis of this book would not have been possible without them and their incredible team of researchers. It was John who suggested that my research might be a good fit for Routledge, and I'm grateful to the editorial team of Rob Sorsby, Claire Maloney, and Natalie Hamil for shepherding this book along (not to mention their patience with delays). Christopher Frattina helped prepare the final manuscript. While he gave the manuscript the closest, most thorough reading, I'd like to be able to blame remaining errors on him; but, of course, what errors remain are mine and mine alone. I likewise am grateful to Andrew Liu for his help in putting together the index.

I must also thank my students at both Oxford and the London School of Economics (LSE). Be it in our lectures, seminars, or tutorials, you have played a critical role in shaping how I approach the discipline, think about the world, and relate those thoughts to others. I'm fortunate to now count many of you as friends. Teaching has been the most rewarding dimension of being an academic, and I can't thank you enough for being the reason why I have the greatest job in the world.

Research is not cheap. My thanks goes to the Clarendon Fund; the Social Sciences and Humanities Research Council of Canada; the Department of Politics and International Relations at Oxford; University College, Oxford; and the Department of International Relations at the LSE for supporting this project financially. My family have also been generously supportive over the years. I'd like to say that I'll someday repay them, but we all know the choice I made when I decided to do a doctorate was to forgo present income in order to forgo future income.

Finally, to whomever might someday read this book: I hope that what follows is useful. And I hope that you're able to take what I've done and produce something better.

November 2018
The King's Arms, Oxford

1 The closure games

Order and international society

This book is about how international actors compete for a 'seat at the table' in the management of international society and how that competition stratifies the international domain. It helps develop a theory of 'international social closure' to equip international relations (IR) to better capture these dynamics, explain why actors adopt particular strategies in their pursuit or maintenance of status positions, and understand how these things are significant in the maintenance of international order. This book examines how competition for inclusion in the management of international society has changed over time and what this means for contemporary politics by examining three different status groups throughout the history of the particular international society that has come to encompass the globe: the Family of Civilised Nations, the Great Powers' club, and G-summitry (the G7 and G20). I argue that the same dynamics of social closure that operated during the globalisation of Western European international society continue to stratify international order today.[1]

'International order' can be understood in two ways: as a social ranking and as an institutionalised set of norms, ideas, values, beliefs, and practices – order as position and order as disposition. This book is concerned with both of these expressions. It examines their interaction and aims to deepen our understanding of how particular forms of order are reproduced – and on occasion, transformed – so as to improve the English School's account of international society and how it interacts with the broader international domain.[2] While the English School offers many valuable insights, there are holes in its approach. Existing scholarship provides rich accounts of particular instances of international social closure: in analyses of the globalisation of Western European international society, the entries of outsiders into that society, and the exclusion of others from it (and thereby in each case, instances of the reproduction of specific forms of international order bound up in the idea of a society of states).[3] The School lacks a general theory that captures how inclusion in the management of international society is denied, sought, and granted. What is necessary is a theoretical perspective that allows us to see how the various elements of the politics of status groups – exclusion, entry, and incorporation – relate to one another. Such a theory would allow us to conceive of international society as a status group in the wider international domain and analyse how inclusion in this status group works (along with other status groups embedded in it). We need a theoretical toolkit that allows us to answer questions about how social positioning and the status seeking associated with it works in and around international society. Most simply this is to ask: what are the 'closure games' that actors play with one another?

This book develops a theory of international social closure in order to yield an improved account of how the positional structure of international order hangs together and to generate new insights into its changing character. As Chapter 2 details, social closure is the means by which groups secure advantages for themselves at the exclusion of others. Such a theory helps us understand (i) how the closure game is played in terms of exclusion, entry, and incorporation so as to stratify the international domain; (ii) how the closure game is also played *within* status groups to produce further stratification; (iii) how the closure game played in Western European international society's globalisation is still being played today in contemporary international society; (iv) how the material and ideational dimensions of international order's reproduction can be accounted for in the game, regardless of what type of actor is involved; and (v) how the more assertive and more pacific dimensions of the closure game can be played at once. In short, the theory developed here offers us a new way to understand international structure and its reproduction.

This allows us to address key questions within the English School in IR: How is social order in the overall international domain (re)produced? How does inclusion in international society and other status groups within it work? How is order – as position and disposition – reproduced through the mechanisms governing (and contesting) inclusion? Has the way that international society reproduces itself by these means changed over time, and if so, how? And, what does this tell us about the relative justness of contemporary international society compared to its earlier iterations? From these general questions, three more specific ones follow, each of which are addressed in this book's empirical chapters: (i) how do group insiders exclude outsiders (Chapter 4)? (ii) how do outsiders try to overcome their exclusion and gain entry into groups (Chapter 5)? and (iii) how do insiders incorporate others into groups (Chapter 6)? It is necessary to stress that while much of the content of this book concerns how the closure game is played – how actors exclude others from groups, seek entry to groups, and incorporate others into groups – the primary interest here is to understand how clubs integrating multiple types of actors in (and outside of) international society hang together, rather than merely explaining the outcomes of closure strategies.[4]

This also allows us to look at international summits differently than we typically have in IR. Rationalist theories treat summits as being unworthy of theoretical attention. For realists, liberals, and their respective variants, summits are merely contexts in which IR takes place, but are nothing more. They do not affect outcomes, they do not condition actors or their interactions, and they have no ontological standing in their own right. Scholarship that does look at summits, however, tends to focus on policy and its negotiation, related either through institutional histories, as in the work of Nicholas Bayne, or through a neopositivist lens, as in the work of John Kirton.[5] Despite focusing on summitry, this body of work does not actually move the study of summits far from the rationalist position – summits are worthy of note only insofar as states' policies are influenced by interaction with others at them.

This sells summitry short. If we adopt a holist ontology, summits can yield valuable information about the international domain that rationalist theories miss. Summits, in and of themselves, become worthy of our gaze. Additionally, if we shake off the positivist straightjacket (or have the good sense to not put it on in the first place), we can examine broader dimensions of summitry through a richer assemblage of methods. The primary empirical contribution of this book is to do exactly this in two ways. First, it seeks to produce new insights based on ethnographic participant observation at summits between 2012 and 2018, elite interviews with summit organisers and participants, and archival research using previously unexploited documents.[6] Second, it seeks to fill two gaps in the literature. While extant scholarship focuses on how state members interact with one another and shape policy together, there is no detailed account of how membership and inclusion in G-summitry actually works, even in the institutional histories. There is likewise surprisingly few works in the literature that examine the roles of non-state actors in G-summitry.[7] The dominant literature on G-summitry is decidedly state-centric, containing little analysis of non-state actors' positions and roles in contemporary governance. Moreover, as Jönsson and Tallberg write,

> much of this literature remains engaged in the exercise of proving against a state-centred picture of world politics that transnational actors matter, and the literature is still weak in its analysis of how state and international institutions enable or constrain transnational participation.[8]

This book empirically examines the interaction between state and non-state actors and offers closure theory as a lens for understanding how actors enable and constrain one another's ability to participate in the management of international society.

The main points

I aim to make five main points: (i) closure barriers in the international domain are predominantly functional-individualist in nature; (ii) collectivism endures in international society; (iii) closure and stratification can be caused by factors other than exclusion strategies; (iv) social mobility has reduced over time; and (v) clubs survive in contemporary international society *because of* networks, not despite them. Taken together, I argue that international order is in part reproduced by a twin dynamic involving imposed, top-down collectivist exclusion and bottom-up, voluntary mimicry. The means of exclusion and marginalisation remain the same as in the past and the means by which outsiders attempt inclusion are likewise the same and likewise actually serve to in part reproduce the *status quo* order that they seek to challenge. While the actors may have changed, 'social closure' remains how the boundaries of international status groups are maintained. Social closure, in short, endures as the means by which international society distributes its principal good – not just membership within the society, but status within and around it.

I argue that the means of closure – exclusion barriers – in international society are predominantly open, being functional-individualist in nature (Chapter 4). The criteria that an actor needs to achieve to gain entry into a club are predominantly based on an assessment of the functional contributions that the actor can make and the ability to acquire the characteristic or competence to make this contribution largely are within that actors' ability to achieve. Most exclusion barriers are not crafted in such a way to prevent an actor from improving its own position, with there being relatively little in the way of collectivist barriers absolutely stalling an actor's social mobility. That is, there are relatively few barriers that necessarily exclude an actor based on attributes that are ascribed to it, which render it necessarily unsuitable for inclusion.[9] In short, looking solely at barriers erected by and for states, the status competition is actually a relatively meritocratic one with relatively fluid social mobility. As inductively we observe that this is not the case, this suggests something other than exclusion barriers must be in operation so as to produce the stratification and entrenchment of social positions in the international domain.

Collectivism endures. This is the second main claim I seek to advance. At the heart of international society is a deeply embedded legal-collectivism which serves as the primary closure rule of the system and renders the international domain one in which different types of actors face fundamentally different closure contests. The legal requirement of sovereignty divides the international domain into two, state and non-state actors. What is significant is not the existence of this division, but what it means for closure and the structure of the international domain. In short, legal-collectivism ensures that any incorporation of non-sovereign actors is necessarily as secondary and subordinate actors in the contemporary management of international society. This is the primary way that the entrenched club of sovereign states maintains its primacy in the contemporary context, by surrounding itself with networks of non-sovereign but functionally useful actors. Furthermore, collectivism endures in the 'cultural' ways that club insiders ascribe others as being unworthy or unsuitable for equal membership, primarily relying on collectivist stereotyping.

My third main claim is that stratification is also caused by means other than exclusion barriers, thus explaining how stratification is possible in a predominantly functional-individualist system (Chapters 3 and 5). I add Mobility Dampeners to the range of strategies available to insiders (and aspirant outsiders) which serve to prevent the rise of outsiders while concurrently preventing their own loss of position. Mobility dampeners are unlike closure barriers in that they are not rules or criteria governing membership but are means of preventing status changes that rely on the ideational underpinning of a club to achieve closure. They are thus more furtive means of exclusion. It is not enough to just describe status as being 'sticky,' as if it is naturally resilient against forces that warrant a loss in status.[10] Actors take deliberate measures to safeguard their positions, and these must be accounted for in order to have a comprehensive and accurate account of the way social competition works in international society. Mobility dampeners are one means by which status is guarded that make it appear 'sticky.'[11]

I also identify the inclusion strategies of outsiders themselves as being a cause of stratification in the system. Perhaps counter-intuitively, the very way that outsiders try to get into clubs actually serves to in part reproduce the *status quo* order. In addition, I expand the range of possible entry strategies beyond that offered by extant closure theory – solely that of Usurpation – to also include Banding, Differentiation, Legitimation, Normalisation, and Identity Adaptation. Significantly, deference and mimicry are embedded in these inclusion strategies which entrench the *status quo* order more through volition than through imposition. Moreover, intra-group closure by insiders against other insiders, and by outsiders against other outsiders, further accounts for stratification. As concerns insiders, Chapter 6 details that a particular kind of stratified incorporation makes this possible, while Chapter 5 details how outsiders engage in Differentiation and Abandonment to make this possible. Moreover, these chapters demonstrate that relations between insiders and outsiders are not necessarily antagonistic, prompting a further revision of extant closure theory.

My fourth claim is that there is less social mobility in the contemporary international domain than in the past. This is surprising given the shift to an apparently more open, less hierarchical networked global governance order. Mobility was actually more fluid for international actors facing the Standard of Civilisation than it is for actors today. This is so for a number of reasons developed throughout the book. First, G-summitry's functional-individualist closure barriers are predominantly only ostensibly achievable. While they seem like viable objectives for all actors, only a small subset of actors are structurally positioned and enabled to achieve them, whereas this was not the case with the Standard of Civilisation (making G-summitry more alike the Great Powers' club in this respect).[12]

Second, the legal-collectivism which stipulates that a necessary condition of membership in international society is the possession of sovereignty is now an absolute barrier, whereas previously the recognition of sovereignty was not always perfectly unachievable to actors who did not fit the mould of a Western European state (Chapter 4). Third, there is greater deference and mimicry required in contemporary inclusion strategies which further entrench the *status quo* and make an entry into G-summitry as equal members more difficult for outsiders (Chapter 5). There are also fewer opportunities for entry into G-summitry than was the case with other status groups. Finally, the shift to the ranking club managing international society being governed predominantly by the diplomatic institution further renders the club as relatively more closed, owing to the centrality of precedence and pragmatism in the group's governance (Chapter 3).

My final main claim, building upon the others, is that assertions that international politics have shifted to a more open and just governance order are overstated.[13] I demonstrate that clubs endure via social closure, that they do so by more hidden means than previously, and that social closure is more resolutely achieved in the contemporary context, thus reducing social mobility. This is not to say that there is not a networked governance order that manages international society, but rather to claim that at the heart of the networked international domain remain clubs. Networks have not supplanted clubs; rather, clubs endure being surrounded by networks. More than this, though, clubs in a large part survive *because of* the networks that they surround themselves with. Networks are the club's bulwarks, not their challengers.

In all, a theory of international social closure allows us to examine and analyse how positions in the management of international society are won, maintained, contested, and denied in a way that we were previously unable, and it allows us to capture dynamics that we had otherwise missed.

The status groups

I examine three international status groups: the Family of Civilised Nations, the Great Powers' club, and G-summitry. To be clear, these are not this study's cases, but rather are the contexts from which cases – instances of exclusion, inclusion, and incorporation – are drawn. Marginal cases of closure, those in which an actor nearly made it into a group but failed to do so and those in which an actor nearly was excluded but was not, are those which particularly feature as it is in these borderline cases that processes of closure may most readily be observed. This case selection is in line with that of Ayşe Zarakol who examines the 'most fortunate' of international society's outsiders.[14] As concerns the Family of Civilised Nations, the case of Japan's encounter is of prime importance, as are the cases of China's and Russia's encounters. In the Great Powers' club, closure as it applies to France and Russia is of particular concern, with the cases of Austria's, Italy's, and

Prussia's roles and positions in the club also being revelatory. Concerning state actors in G-summitry, closure strategies as they are related to Canada, Italy, Australia, Spain, the Netherlands, Switzerland, Indonesia, Malaysia, and Nigeria serve as key cases in this way.[15] Concerning non-state actors in the contemporary context, I am particularly interested in the closure game as it relies to international non-governmental organisations (INGOs). Larger civil society organisations (CSOs), including the Gates Foundation, ONE, and Oxfam serve as key cases, as does the game as it relates to international organisations (IOs) and international financial institutions (IFIs).

Why are these groups the most suitable contexts to use in developing a theory of international social closure? First, they are all clubs wherein membership in them is a means of obtaining, maintaining, and signalling a social position. As one of the aims of this study is to improve the understanding of status in IR, it is necessary to look at these groups as *status* groups, as it is through such social associations that actors achieve, deny, claim, confer, and signal relative standing. Their borders are sites of contestation, with outsiders wanting in and insiders guarding their membership rolls. This serves as a corrective to leading work on this topic in IR that focuses on how groups achieve position rather than how individual actors use groups to achieve a position for themselves.[16] That is, the ontological focus is on individual actors using group membership in the status game. This also implies an important limit to this theory's applicability: I am only interested in cases in which actors want to be included. Exclusion is not necessarily undesirable, and seeking entry is not necessarily an objective of outsiders.[17]

Second, in periods when the clubs coexist, a status move related to one club can be related to a status move concerning another. A defeat signalling unsuitability for the Great Powers' club, for example, could serve as a motivation for inclusion in the Family of Civilised Nations.[18] These clubs are each part of a general status game in the international domain and so should be studied together as such.

Moreover, these are all governance groups – the means by which ranking actors collectively manage international society. These clubs set standards for actors' conduct, both domestically and internationally – be it through the Family of Civilised Nations' Standard of Civilisation or G-summitry's more implicit neo-liberal criteria for membership. Indeed, Andrew Cooper's identification of the liberal 'glue' that has held G-summitry together mirrors Gerret Gong's elucidation of the Standard almost exactly.[19] In short, these are the clubs that set and enforce the rules of conduct in international society, as well as work to ensure its stability and survival. When we speak of global governance, they are the governors of the globe.

Examining these particular clubs is also important because, as is argued in Chapter 3, they are each products of different configurations of primary institutions within international society. This allows us to say something about the relationship between changes in international society's institutional underpinning as it relates to the closure game at play. G-summitry is

8 *The closure games*

predominantly a product of the diplomatic institution, whereas the other status groups are considered in the School's canon themselves to be primary institutions. While these groups differ in their institutional character, they are nonetheless all status groups governed by social closure, and are thus well suited for comparative analysis.

The institutional histories of the Great Powers' club and G-summitry are also worthy of note, arising in response to international crises threatening the stability – and perhaps even survival – of international society itself. The Great Powers' club formed in response to the system-threatening Revolutionary and Napoleonic wars; while G-summitry formed in response to global economic crises, the oil crisis and derivative economic shocks in the case of the G7, and the Global Financial Crisis in the case of the G20. According to Andrew Cooper,

> Diplomacy cannot in turn be divorced from global governance… States gain or lose territory and access to the negotiation table and negotiated institutions, such as a permanent membership of the UN Security Council [in postwar settlements]. Diverging from this script, the G20 was formed as a response to an immediate economic crisis rather than after a war. *Yet the exclusionary practices used to create its membership ensures that there remain both winners and losers.*[20]

Such origins particularly allow us to observe marginal actors taking advantage of crises to try to improve their positions. As Ian Clark relates in reflecting upon the division between international and world society, '…it is exactly the opening created by the large-scale disturbance of war that can be thought to have presented this opportunity [to begin to search for the presence of world society].'[21] Such disturbances allow us to see divisions within international society too, be it the clamouring of less powerful states seeking entry into the Great Powers' club at the Congress of Vienna or those seeking entry into G-summitry at the club's foundation in the 1970s or its expansion in the wake of the Asian Financial Crises in the late 1990s and the Global Economic Crises a decade later. What renders G-summitry an appropriate context for elucidating this theory, as opposed to the World Economic Forum or the Bilderberg Group, is that it is explicitly recognised as an institution through which the stability and survival of international society is partly managed, rather than primarily as a conference of elites.[22] It is further appropriate as the G20 is designed to substantively include both state and non-state actors in driving the year-round summitry process, principally through its 'engagement groups.'[23] The G20 is meant to be a flatter, more open, more inclusive governance forum, distinct from the states-only multilateral forums that have otherwise constituted global governance. One advantage of the theoretical lens developed here is that it allows us to see that such a characterisation exaggerates the degree to which the G20 is a break from the past.

It is necessary to momentarily pause and clarify the status groups' relation to one another and their orientation with respect to international society. Following Keene, I take the 18th and 19th centuries' Family of Civilised Nations as being a status group within international society.[24] I am sympathetic, however, to the English School's conflation of the Family of Civilised Nations and international society. This is the predominant way that the expansion story is told that Keene aimed to reform, particularly as the notion of the Family of Civilised Nations and the club of civilised states seem to have been held as largely synonymous by statespersons during this period. Before this international society became global, the Family of Civilised Nations was the status group dividing those considered by dominant Western Europeans to be civilised states and those considered to be uncivilised entities, be they semi-civilised, barbarian, or savage. After the idea of a Family of Civilised Nations fell out of favour and international society globalised, this broad social division changed in terms of what it was dividing – no longer dividing civilised and uncivilised states, but dividing states and non-state actors. Thus, at different periods covered in this book, the idea of international society as a status group produced two different social divisions. For the sake of ease, when referring to the historical division between civilised states and non-civilised entities, I refer to the status group as the Family of Civilised Nations; when I refer to the contemporary divide between sovereign and non-sovereign actors, I refer to the status group as international society.

Theoretical foundations

The English School

There are other reasons for updating the English School beyond the need to produce a general theory of inclusion/exclusion. First, the School's traditional 'expansion' story largely comes to an end after international society's universalisation amongst state actors in the decolonisation era. Tim Dunne, Christian Reus-Smit, and their contributors' recent efforts to correct this traditional account, particularly in emphasising that this story has not ended, are thus a welcome development in the field. What follows seeks to help in this endeavour.[25] According to the traditional account, with decolonisation the doors to the international club of states were flung open and all states became members (legally, though not substantively, as equals). As such, the story of international society's expansion is the one that takes place predominantly in the 18th, 19th, and first half of the 20th centuries. What this misses is that international society still has a frontier to manage, though now it solely divides sovereign and non-sovereign actors. What later accounts there are tend to look at the dissatisfaction and frustration of newer entrants to the club who, despite gaining entry as nominal equals, remain subjected to marginalisation and subordination as substantive inferiors.[26]

Moreover, work that does examine contemporary international society's outer boundary, which separates it from the still relatively conceptually and theoretically nebulous 'world society,' tends to look at the ideational and normative interaction across this border, as opposed to the material dimensions of interaction in accounts of states' entries into international society.[27]

While there is widespread acknowledgement of stratification within international society, there is – as far as I can tell – no work that looks at how the international domain beyond international society is itself also stratified and how stratification results from competition to participate in international society's management. The School's order-centric focus gives priority to whichever actors are positioned centrally in an international order and hold central roles in its management. With the sovereign state having edged out potential rivals, this gives them analytic priority.[28] The consequence of this is that non-state actors remain marginalised in the School's theoretical accounts, at best only considering them as part of the 'world society' category.[29] This, however, forces us to miss salient dynamics of international order's reproduction and international society's management.

This relates to renewed engagement with accounts of international society's globalisation and with the Standard's role in it. This work has yielded valuable correctives to the traditional story and has articulated discussions about whether new Standards might be in operation today.[30] While this literature discusses order as disposition in similar ways to earlier scholarship, there is a subtle – though significant – conceptual shift concerning order as position. The positional ordering effects of the Standard(s) now broadly concern position *within* international society. While we gain valuable insight in so shifting our focus, we nonetheless lose sight of the fact that contemporary international society still manages a frontier. International society might now be a universally inclusive – albeit stratified – club of sovereign states, but excluded are the panoply of non-state actors that nonetheless play central roles in the management of global politics and the maintenance of international order. This causes us to too easily miss the fact that a significant social division between the inside and the outside of international society has been put in place even before we come to look at the Standard's effects on ordering states within international society. We end up missing the first – indeed, primary – closure move in the international domain, which is to render international society a states-only club in the first place.

Another limitation in the School's more recent accounts of international society's story is that they tend to focus on the darker side of international society's 'Janus face.'[31] While this work rightly corrects the account we predominantly find in Bull and Watson's work, which tends to downplay the centrality of violence in international society's 'expansion' and in the revolts against it, we must not allow ourselves to entirely lose sight of the more pacific dimensions of international society's globalisation. We should not oversteer as we address the literature's earlier, problematic accounts. What follows is one effort to put this aspect of how international society works back in view alongside the brutal, violent, and racist dimensions of the story.

Additionally, the School also lacks a general theory that is capable of dealing with the 'micro-story' of the reproduction of international order so as to bring these empirical accounts together within a single framework. While a macro-account that tells the story of the reproduction of – and changes in – order over the course of decades or centuries is useful, it can be strengthened by one that details how the structure of international society is reproduced through the specific interactions and practices of the individuals (statespersons and their interlocutors) who give international society its physical expression.[32]

While there are shortcomings in the School's approach, there are nonetheless firm foundations upon which to ground a theory of international social closure. The School's earlier accounts of international society's expansion come close to expressing membership in terms of social closure. Bull states that the traditional view of the expansion of international society was that non-Europeans joined a formerly exclusive club once they met certain entry conditions, with the Europeans maintaining a superior position within this club.[33] While this is an outdated and inaccurate account – of which Bull, Wight, and others were themselves critical – it is nonetheless a straightforward description of system governed by closure.[34] It is the assumed superiority of the Europeans that Bull questions, arguing that it is the European *conception* of what international society is, which developed concurrently with its expansion, and what is dominant, and therefore advantageous, to the original club members.[35] Bull's revision is still describing a system governed by closure, the difference being that his account shifts the emphasis on order expressed in terms of rank towards an emphasis on order expressed in terms of disposition. For Bull, it is the underlying norms, values, beliefs, rules, and institutions which define what an international society is that are important – the variables that shape what an international society looks like, rather than those things that result from it. Furthermore, Bull's account contains a dynamic element which recognizes that the very conception of international society is itself fluid, and therefore open to contestation. Thus, it is not just the membership that is mutable and contested but, more importantly for Bull, the very rules that govern membership that are in flux. Expressed in terms of social closure, what Bull is describing here is the contestation over closure rules.

It was the dominant, 'directorate of European states' that set the rules of membership and who alone enjoyed membership in the society.[36] As Bull wrote in a paper presented to the British Committee, the predominant position of the Western powers 'was protected by the rules and institutions of international society, in which... European or western states alone enjoyed full membership of international society.'[37] In other words, their superior position was guarded by the rules of order (in both its expressions) that they set. Closure was how they maintained their own superior status and the inferior statuses of others. Bull and Wight thus also portrayed international society as being stratified. Bull relates that in the late 19th and early 20th centuries,

> [i]n the gradations of independence recognized by the European powers in the extra-European world, the spectrum of positions intermediate between full sovereignty and the status of colony... there could be seen the survival, alongside the concept of a society of equal sovereign states, of the older and historically much more ubiquitous concept of international relations as the relations between suzerains and vassals.[38]

The setting of membership criteria was, in part, directed by European assumptions about their superiority of religion and civilisation.[39] It is these 'standards' to which non-members were made to adhere, and it was against these standards that non-Western states 'laboured under the stigma of inferior status: unequal treaties, extraterritorial jurisdiction, denial of racial equality.'[40] Bull writes, 'nor should it be doubted that [the Europeans] sometimes used these criteria to deny others their rights and to acquire special privileges for themselves, or that that they required standards of behaviour they failed to observe themselves.'[41] Bull's observation here is an almost exact restatement of one of the most important tenets of sociologist Frank Parkin's theory of social closure, wherein the rules are used to confer unequal advantages to those in the club.[42]

Recognition of the centrality of deference to the prevailing order is also central to the traditional version of the expansion story. Bull placed an emphasis on the adoption of procedural values in the society's expansion, those that define how IR is conducted – diplomatic protocol being a prime example.[43] While agreement on substantive values such as human rights is unlikely – perhaps even impossible-the expansion of international society involved the increasing adoption of the institutions through which questions of substantive values were negotiated.[44] It is these procedural values of Western Europe that remain dominant, despite changes in the membership of international society and the relative power-political rank of those included. Actors who wish to be included in this society must adopt its values to at least some degree and in so doing necessarily consent to its rules and institutions.[45] They may or may not, however, adopt its substantive values, but it is only by being in the club that they may contest and seek to reform them once included so as to 'reflect their own special interests.'[46] It is because of this that there is an institutionalisation of *deference*, in which ascendant actors submit to the order which they may not be entirely content with, but do so in order to at least be included. It is only by being included in the club, even if only in a marginalised position, that an actor has an ability to reap at least some of the benefits afforded to club members – be they material, such as an increase in trade, or ideational, such as the recognition of status. Thus, even though substantive values may not be in alignment, ascendant outsiders nonetheless seek entry because it is the only way to improve their position. In so doing, they necessarily reproduce and perpetuate the prevailing order despite objecting to substantive elements of it and even their own position within it.

Current scholars' updated accounts of international society's globalisation are likewise interested in the sorts of things that closure theory is. Most notably, Edward Keene and Ayşe Zarakol draw links between social closure theory and international society, though they do so with little in the way of reform of extant closure theory.[47] It should also be noted that more sociologically oriented theorists similarly examine IR in ways that closure theory does and focus on the same kinds of questions, the recent work on hierarchy and stratification being of greatest import.[48] While not about the globalisation of international society *per se*, they are nonetheless about its social structure and status hierarchy.

Wider theoretical implications

Two other IR literatures are also concerned with broadly similar questions about order, though articulated through different vocabularies: the literature concerned with status in IR and the global governance and diplomacy literature focused on the shift from a club to a networked form of governance.

The status literature is particularly concerned with order expressed in terms of rank, while English School scholarship is more concerned with order expressed in terms of disposition. An added benefit of closure theory is that it allows us to discuss order in both ways at once. The status literature's concern with rank prompts scholars to investigate how order is changing, how and which actors are rising, and how the change in rank seems to be more peaceful than in the past.[49] Most notably, T.V. Paul, Deborah Welch Larson, and William Wohlforth's edited volume, *Status in World Politics*, incorporates a broad array of perspectives from across the field.[50] Conversely, though with less emphasis in the literature, the concern is also with the fall of powers and the implications of their loss of ranking status.[51] When we speak of rising powers or the decline of hegemony, it is the two dimensions of order – as position and disposition – that we speak about at once. We refer to the rise and fall of actors in terms of a social hierarchy while concurrently referring – and pondering the implications of – the possible replacement of a set of norms, ideas, values, beliefs, and practices by others.

Second is the literature concerned with a shift in global governance structure and diplomatic practice from a club to a networked form. Broadly, this literature argues that the principal agents of IR are no longer an exclusive group of states and their representatives working within strict and exclusive hierarchies according to defined set rules, and that there is now a heterogeneity of relevant state and non-state actors working at all levels of interaction simultaneously on governance issues beyond just the tradition issues of 'high politics.'[52] In short, the most salient elements of this shift is the entry of non-state actors into what was exclusively the preserve of states and the replacement of hierarchy with flatter forms of governance order. What is significant to note is that the concern with order as rank is concerned with the relative statuses and positions of state and non-state actors and the shift in the system's management.[53] The perspective is different, focusing more on the relative positions of state and non-state actors, as opposed to the relative positions of states alone; nevertheless, both literatures are fundamentally concerned with order.

While primarily focused on improving the English School's account of international society, what follows speaks to these two other literatures along the way. Articulated in terms of status, this book identifies the mechanisms of status accommodation and management. Of central concern to the present status literature is the question of whether or not admission to status groups works differently than it did in the past.[54] I argue that while status competition is still played out according to social closure, the present international context is defined by more entrenched status positions owing to a shift in the ways the closure game is played.

Paul, Larson, and Wohlforth's questions parallel those in the diplomacy literature concerned with the shift in governance order from a club to a networked form. While there is agreement in the literature that the composition and character of the diplomatic environment has changed – made more complex with new actors, new problems, and new levels of interaction, there is no agreement on the degree to which these novelties are included or on the means by which they are included.[55] On the one hand, the traditionalist diplomacy literature holds that diplomacy remains practised within and by a club of state actors, downplaying the inclusion of new types of non-state actors by characterizing them as either having peripheral and subordinate places in the diplomatic milieu or having no place at all.[56] On the other hand, the literature that characterizes diplomacy as shifting towards a more networked and apparently inclusive practice sidesteps answering the question of exactly *who* is included and *why*.[57] The seminal work of Paul Sharp serves as a noteworthy example. Sharp discusses at length the fact that membership in the diplomatic realm is always contested, that the identities of actors in that realm are shifting, and that so too are its boundaries.[58] He does not, however, discuss what the new rules of membership, identities, and boundaries might be, purposely leaving these as 'open questions.'[59] Indeed, as Sharp writes, '[i]t is much easier to imagine, however, a world in which such questions do not get resolved, and yet in which different types of actors enjoy some sort of diplomatic standing and representation.'[60] Just because these are 'difficult questions to which there are no settled answers,' it does not follow that it is not possible – and indeed not desirable – to explore these questions so as to find a way to answer them and so as to clarify what sorts of statuses might be said to exist.[61] Deliberately leaving them unanswered leaves us with a vague and limited picture of what the contemporary international landscape looks like.

In sum, both literatures are thus fundamentally asking questions about inclusion, motivated by a concern about the structure and management of contemporary order. What follows does so too.

Notes

1 Following Dunne and Reus-Smit, 'globalisation' better captures the story that has traditionally been described as international society's 'expansion'. See: Dunne and Reus-Smit (2017a).
2 What Bull referred to as the 'world political system'. Bull (1977, pp. 276–278). See also: Dunne and Reus-Smit (2017a, pp. 33–34).
3 Bull, H., & Watson, A. (1984). Introduction. In H. Bull & A. Watson (Eds.), *The Expansion of International Society* (pp. 1–12). Oxford: OUP; Gong, G. (1984). *The Standard of Civilization in International Society*. Oxford: OUP. More recent contributions include the following: Fabry, M. (2010). *Recognizing States: International Society and the Establishment of New States since 1776*. Oxford: OUP; Keal, P. (2000). An 'International Society'? In G. Fry & J. O'Hagan (Eds.), *Contending Images of World Politics*. Basingstoke: Macmillan; Keal, P. (2003). *European Conquest and the Rights of Indigenous Peoples: The Moral Backwardness of International Society*. Cambridge: Cambridge University Press; Johnston, A. I. (2008). *Social States: China in International Institutions, 1980–2000*. Princeton, NJ: Princeton University Press; Keene, E. (2002). *Beyond the Anarchical Society: Grotius, Colonialism, and World Order*. Cambridge: Cambridge University Press. Keene, E. (2012). The Treaty-Making Revolution of the Nineteenth Century. *The International History Review*, *34* (3), 475–500; Neumann, I. B. (2011). Entry into International Society Reconceptualised: The Case of Russia. *Review of International Studies*, *37* (2), 463–484. Neumann, I. B., & Welsh, J. (1991). The Other in European Self-Definition: An Addendum to the Literature on International Society. *Review of International Studies*, *17* (4), 327–348; Okagaki, T. T. (2013). *The Logic of Conformity: Japan's Entry into International Society*. Toronto: University Press of Toronto; Stivachtis, Y. (1998). *The Enlargement of International Society: Culture versus Anarchy and Greece's Entry into International Society*. Basingstoke; Hampshire: Palgrave Macmillan; Suzuki, S. (2014). Journey to the West: China Debates Its 'Great Power' Identity. *Millennium*, *42* (3), 632–650; Towns, A. E. (2010). *Women and States: Norms and Hierarchies in International Society*. New York: Cambridge University Press; Watson, A. (1992). *The Evolution of International Society: A Comparative Historical Analysis*. London; New York: Routledge; Zarakol, A. (2010). *After Defeat: How the East Learned to Live with the West*. Cambridge; New York: Cambridge University Press; Zhang, Y. (1998). *China in International Society: Alienation and Beyond*. New York: Palgrave Macmillan, Print (Dunne and Reus-Smit, 2017b).
4 I use 'group' and 'club' interchangeably to refer to social configurations in which actors arrange themselves to signal and affirm alikeness to one another and, conversely, dissimilarity with others.
5 Bayne, N. (2000). *Hanging in There: The G7 and G8 Summit in Maturity and Renewal*. Aldershot: Ashgate; Bayne, N. (2005). *Staying Together: The G8 Summit Confronts the 21st Century* (1st edition). Aldershot; Burlington, VT: Ashgate; Kirton, J. (2012, September 23). Contemporary Concert Diplomacy. Retrieved 23 September 2012, from www.g8.utoronto.ca/scholar/kirton198901/index.

16 *The closure games*

html; Putnam, R. D., & Bayne, N. (1984). *Hanging Together: The Seven-Power Summits*. London: Heinemann for the Royal Institute of International Affairs; Putnam, R. D., & Bayne, N. (1987). *Hanging Together: Cooperation and Conflict in the Seven-power Summits*. Cambridge, MA: Harvard University Press; Smith, G. (2011). G7 to G8 to G20: Evolution in Global Governance. *CIGI G20 Papers*, No. 6 (see: www.cigionline.org/sites/default/files/g20no6-2.pdf). Other notable works include the following: Daniels, J. P., Kaiser, K., & Kirton, J. J. (Eds.). (2000). *Shaping a New International Financial System: Challenges of Governance in a Globalizing World*. Aldershot: Ashgate; Fratianni, M., Savona, P., & Kirton, J. J. (Eds.). (2003). *Sustaining Global Growth and Development: G7 and IMF Governance*. Aldershot; Burlington, VT: Ashgate; Fratianni, M., Savona, P., & Kirton, J. J. (2007). *Corporate, Public and Global Governance: The G8 Contribution*. Aldershot: Ashgate; Hajnal, P. I. (1999). *The G7/G8 System: Evolution, Role and Documentation*. Aldershot: Ashgate; Hajnal, P. I. (2007). *Summitry from G5 to L20: A Review of Reform Initiatives*; Hodges, M. R., Kirton, J. J., & Daniels, J. P. (1999). *The G8's Role in the New Millennium*. Aldershot: Ashgate; Kirton, Contemporary Concert Diplomacy, 2012; Kirton, J. J., Daniels, J. P., & Freytag, A. (Eds.). (2001). *Guiding Global Order: G8 Governance in the Twenty-first Century*. Ashgate; Kirton, J. J., Fratianni, M., & Savona, P. (Eds.). (2002). *Governing Global Finance: New Challenges, G7 and IMF Contributions*. Aldershot; Burlington, VT: Ashgate Publishing Limited; Larionova, M. (2010). Is it G8 or G20? For Russia, Of Course, It's Both. *Studia Diplomatica*, 63 (2), 81–90; Martinez-Diaz, L., & Woods, N. (2009). *Networks of Influence?: Developing Countries in a Networked Global Order*. Oxford; New York: OUP; Renard, T. (2010). G20: Towards a New World Order. *Studia Diplomatica*, 33 (2), 7–22.
6 See Appendix for methodological discussion.
7 C.f. Hajnal, P. I. (2007). Can Civil Society Influence G8 Accountability? CSGR Working Paper Series 7.
8 Jonsson and Tallberg (2010, p. 9); Risse (2007, p. 259).
9 See Chapter 2 for a detailed explanation and development of these concepts.
10 Contra Welch Larson, D., Paul, T. V., & Wohlforth, W. C. (2014). Status and World Order. In T. V. Paul, D. Welch Larson, & W. C. Wohlforth (Eds.), *Status in World Politics* (pp. 3–32). New York: Cambridge University Press.
11 In addition to exclusion strategies.
12 At least, as concerns the liberal, explicitly articulated dimensions of the Standard. This obviously does not hold for the implicit racism embedded in it.
13 Contra Slaughter, A.-M. (2005). *A New World Order*. Princeton, NJ: Princeton University Press; Thakur, R. (2008). Conclusion: National Diplomacy and Global Governance. In A. F. Cooper, B. Hocking, & W. Maley (Eds.), *Global Governance and Diplomacy: Worlds Apart?* (pp. 288–299). Basingstoke: Palgrave Macmillan.
14 Zarakol (2010, p. 253).
15 By "relate," I mean inclusion strategies exercised by the actors in vying for inclusion, exclusion strategies exercised by actors trying to deny their inclusion, or incorporative strategies exercised by club members bringing them into the club.
16 Larson, D. W., & Shevchenko, A. (2010). Status Seekers: Chinese and Russian Responses to U.S. Primacy. *International Security*, 34 (4), 63–95. Welch Larson, Paul, & Wohlforth, Status and World Order, 2014.
17 On what motivates status moves, see Towns, A. E., & Rumelili, B. (2017). Taking the Pressure: Unpacking the Relation between Norms, Social Hierarchies, and Social Pressures on States. *European Journal of International Relations*, 23, 756–779; Towns, *Women and States*; Larson & Shevchenko, Status Seekers, 2010.

18 Neumann and Welsh, The Other in European Self-Definition: An Addendum to the Literature on International Society, 1991, 344.
19 Cooper, A. F., & Thakur, R. (2013). *The Group of Twenty*. New York: Routledge, 25.
20 Ibid., 75. *Emphasis mine.*
21 Clark, I. (2007). *International Legitimacy and World Society*. Oxford: OUP, 9.
22 In English School parlance, G-summitry is a 'secondary institution'.
23 Government of Argentina (How does the G20 work? 2017). Retrieved from: https://www.g20.org/en/g20-argentina/engagement-groups 19 July 2018.
24 Keene, *The Treaty-Making Revolution of the Nineteenth Century*, 2012.
25 Dunne and Reus-Smit (2017b).
26 See especially: Adler-Nissen, R. (2014). Stigma Management in International Relations: Transgressive Identities, Norms, and Order in International Society. *International Organization, 68* (1), 143–176. Okagaki, *The Logic of Conformity: Japan's Entry into International Society*, 2013; Suzuki, *Seeking 'Legitimate' Great Power Status in Post-Cold War International Society: China's and Japan's Participation in UNPKO*, 2008; Zarakol, *After Defeat*, 2010.
27 See especially: Buzan, B. (2004). *From International to World Society?: English School Theory and the Social Structure of Globalisation*. Cambridge: Cambridge University Press; Clark, *International Legitimacy and World Society*, 2007; Stivachtis, Yannis A., & McKeil, A. (2018, January 1). Conceptualizing World Society. *International Politics, 55* (1), 1–10.
28 Spruyt, H. (1994). *The Sovereign State and Its Competitors: An Analysis of Systems Change*. Princeton, NJ: Princeton University Press.
29 C.f. The *International Politics* special issue on Conceptualizing World Society, *55* (1), (2018); Buzan (2004); Clark (2007).
30 Most significantly, see the *Millennium* special issue on Rethinking The Standard(s) of Civilisation(s) in International Relations, *42* (3), (2014). Following Dunne and Reus-Smit, it is more accurate to characterise the history of the development of the current, global international society as being one of 'globalisation' than of 'expansion'. See: Dunne and Reus-Smit (2017a).
31 Suzuki (2009). C.f. Okagaki (2013); Zarakol (2010).
32 C.f. Jackson, R. (2000). *The Global Covenant: Human Conduct in a World of States*. New York: OUP, 29–43; 112–113; Neumann, I. B. (2002). Returning Practice to the Linguistic Turn: The Case of Diplomacy. *Millennium, 31* (3), 627–651; Peterson, M. J. (1997). *Recognition of Governments: Legal Doctrine and State Practice, 1815–1995*. Macmillan, 1; Manning (1962); Pouliot (2016).
33 Bull, H. (1984). The Emergence of a Universal International Society. In H. Bull & A. Watson (Eds.), *The Expansion of International Society* (pp. 117–126). Oxford: OUP, 123.
34 Bull and Watson, *The Expansion of International Society*, 1984, 6; Bull, *The Expansion of International Society*, 1984, 123.
35 Ibid., 123–124.
36 Bull and Watson, *The Expansion of International Society*, 1984, 438.
37 Bull, H. (1977). *The Anarchical Society: A Study of Order in World Politics* (4th edition). Basingstoke: Palgrave Macmillan, 175.
38 Bull, *The Expansion of International Society*, 1984, 125–126.
39 Ibid., 125.
40 Ibid.
41 Ibid.
42 Parkin, F. (1979). *Marxism and Class Theory: A Bourgeois Critique*. Taylor & Francis, 44.

18 *The closure games*

43 Alderson, K., & Hurrell, A. (2000). The Continuing Relevance of International Society. In K. Alderson & A. Hurrell (Eds.), *Hedley Bull on International Society* (pp. 54–76, 6). Basingstoke: Macmillan.
44 C.f. Hopgood (2006); Vincent (1986).
45 Bull, *The Expansion of International Society,* 1984, 124.
46 Bull (1984, p. 124).
47 Keene (2012b, 2014); Zarakol (2010).
48 Albert et al. (2013); Buzan and Albert (2010); Cooley (2008); Keene (2007a, 2007b, 2007c); Lake (1996, 2011); Mattern and Zarakol (2016); Pouliot (2008, 2016); Towns (2010); Towns and Rumelili (2017).
49 See especially: Paul and Shankar (2014).
50 Paul et al., Status and World Order, 2014.
51 C.f. Ringmar (2002).
52 See especially: Cooper et al. (2013, 2008); Slaughter (2005).
53 Cooper et al. (2013); Slaughter (2005).
54 See especially: Neumann, I. B. (2014). Status is Cultural: Durkheimian Poles and Weberian Russians Seek Great-Power Status. In T. V. Paul, D. Welch Larson, & W. C. Wohlforth (Eds.), *Status in World Politics* (pp. 85–114). New York: Cambridge University Press.
55 For example, more traditionalist understandings of diplomacy, such as *Satow*, characterise non-state actors as having peripheral and subordinate places in the diplomatic milieu, while others that give greater focus to the changing nature of global governance do not give such a preferential place to state actors (Cooper, Hocking, & Maley, *Global Governance and Diplomacy: Worlds Apart?* 2008); see especially: Heine, J. (2008). *On the Manner of Practicing the New Diplomacy.* In Cooper, B. Hocking, & W. Maley (Eds.), *Global Governance and Diplomacy: Worlds Apart?* (pp. 271–287). Basingstoke; New York: Palgrave Macmillan, Print; Thakur, *Conclusion: National Diplomacy and Global Governance,* 2008.
56 Berridge, G. (2005). *Diplomacy: Theory and Practice* (Vol. 3). Basingstoke: Palgrave Macmillan; Barston, R. (2006). *Modern Diplomacy*. Pearson; Kleiner, J. (2009). *Diplomatic Practice: Between Tradition and Innovation.* Singapore; Hackensack, NJ: World Scientific Publishing; Roberts, I. (Ed.). (2009). *Satow's Diplomatic Practice* (6th edition). Oxford: OUP.
57 Cooper et al. (2008); Sharp (2009).
58 Sharp, P. (2009). *Diplomatic Theory of International Relations*. Cambridge; New York: Cambridge University Press, 2009.
59 Ibid., 291.
60 Ibid.
61 Ibid., 266.

2 International social closure

Introduction

As ⌊status is fundamentally a social phenomenon, theorising it necessarily requires a social theory.⌋ In terms of group membership and the status that is derived from it, what is required in international relations (IR) is an approach that is able to (i) identify the mechanisms through which membership is claimed, denied, maintained, and granted, and (ii) compare how this works today with how it might have worked differently in the past. In terms of order, what is required is an approach that is able to (iii) account for stratification and exclusion in the system and at the same time (iv) account for the apparent inclusiveness in contemporary order. Finally, in line with the English School's concern with ⌊order and justice,⌋ the kind of approach that is required is the one that can (v) assist us in making judgments about the relative fairness of a status system, particularly in terms of the relative fluidity of social mobility.

This chapter develops a theory of international social closure to achieve these tasks. I proceed with an outline of extant social closure theory, drawing from the work of neo-Weberian sociologists Frank Parkin and Raymond Murphy. As ⌊closure theory⌋ as it stands is not suitable for IR, I revise it to make it so. My reformed theory of international social closure (i) develops a means of classifying how ⌊relatively open or closed an exclusion barrier is⌋; (ii) provides a means of explaining how exclusion can be achieved in what seems to be an open closure system; (iii) demonstrates how closure can be achieved by group insiders through more than just exclusion strategies; (iv) shows how closure and stratification can also be caused by the strategies adopted by outsiders seeking inclusion; (v) reconceptualises the range of strategies available to outsiders seeking inclusion; (vi) demonstrates how the closure game can be relatively peaceful; and (vii) accounts for closure games played within groups, not just between them.

Closure theory

Actors and groups

The ontology of extant closure theory is groups and its principal concern is the political struggle between them – how superiorly positioned insiders attempt to exclude others and monopolise advantages for themselves, and how inferiorly positioned outsiders try to overcome their exclusion.[1] As is expanded upon below, closure theory's emphasis on the strategies groups use to participate in this struggle, either to maintain or change their position, is particularly useful for addressing the questions that guide this book.

The ontology of closure theory warrants reform in order for it to be a useful tool in IR. The focus needs to be on individual actors – state and non-state alike – working to improve their position rather than actors collectively organising themselves in groups to improve their position (though, remaining open to the possibility of such organisation). There is actually very little in the way of collective organisation to improve status in international society. While political struggle for status is rife in international society, it rarely manifests as collective class struggle as it does in domestic societies. This is not to say that there is no collective organisation to improve social position in international society, the G77 and the Brazil, Russia, India, China, and South Africa (BRICS) being examples, but that the preponderance of status moves are individualist in character. Within this study, even those cases that do involve group coordination, such as the Banding strategy, are more accurately seen as a means for particularly status conscious actors in a group – not necessarily the most powerful – to improve their own position, sometimes at the eventual cost of others in the banded group. Status competition in international society is predominantly an individualist game.

Divisions

There are three concepts that form the basis of this theoretical framework: social division, social stratification, and social closure. These are closely related concepts that need to be disentangled. In short, division is about identity, stratification is about position, and closure is about conflict and control. Social division refers to society-wide distinctions that divide groups composed of individual actors.[2] Social stratification, a theoretical subset of social division, refers to a social hierarchy being organised according to these groups (rather than individuals) and that this ordering persists over time.[3] Social closure refers to the process by which actors seek to maximize rewards by restricting access to resources and opportunities to a limited circle of eligibles. This entails the singling out of certain social or physical attributes as the justifactory basis of exclusion."[4] These advantages may be material or ideational, such as the accumulation of capital or the accumulation of social prestige. Generally, I use social division to refer to differentiation between groups (i.e. the production and identification of groups in a system), stratification to refer to the structure of differentiation between groups (i.e. the relative position of groups in a system), and closure to refer the processes by which stratified groups – or, more precisely, the individual actors who make up the group operating collectively – contest resources, set or meet rules for inclusion, and maintain or overcome the system of differentiation (i.e. the political struggle between groups in a system).

There are three principal constitutive features involved in social division: (i) the (re)creation of group identities, (ii) the (re)creation of group subject positions, and (iii) the perpetuation of the logic which gives the rationale for the groups and their relative positions. The construction of subject identities and subject positions is thoroughly developed in post-positivist literature, and it is not the aim of this chapter to rehearse it here, but it is necessary to acknowledge its importance in underpinning this theoretical framework.[5] In the closure game an advantaged group co-constitutes itself and the disadvantaged group(s) by ascribing itself as being superior in relation to others who are ascribed as being inferior and excluded. Group identities and group positions are thus linked with one another, though they are conceptually distinct aspects of a single productive process of differentiation. Additionally, not only are the disadvantaged groups cast in inferior subject positions, but they are also defined as being ineligible for the opportunities that are closed off to them.[6] There is a logic, which may or may not be just or rational, underpinning their exclusion – it is not arbitrary.

What defines this ineligibility is the third constitutive dimension: that of the logic of division. This is given emphasis throughout this book, as examining the changing rationales and justifications for division and the membership rules which make these divisions are of central concern. Changes in the underlying logics are what we are looking for in our aim to investigate whether the closure game has changed over time in international society.

Group identities are formed around a trait, which may be ideational or material, common to all members of the group. Each group is a social construct that is made "real" or "natural" through the exercise of productive power.[7] The identities of groups are thus inherently political. To refer to domestic analogies, groups may be defined by physical characteristics – tall/short, male/female – or by ascribed characteristics – bourgeois/proletarian, uneducated/educated. Groups are not necessarily dyads. Systems in which groups are defined by nationality or ethnicity, for example, have multiple categories within them. In Weber's formulation, collectivism justifies the exclusion of actors on the basis of their shared attributes with a particular group.[8] I am critical of Weber in this respect, however, as he misses the importance of the underlying logic of the system that justifies the selection of a particular attribute in the first place. The selected attribute must be supported by a rationale for its choice. An attribute cannot be chosen arbitrarily in a system of closure. For example, in a patriarchal system defined according to gender, males may be superiorly positioned to females. Males are not superiorly positioned just because they are males, but because the masculine identity is produced so as to ascribe to it qualities that are constructed as being superior within a system governed by particular values.

To import this into IR, in the international domain states are superiorly positioned and advantaged actors because the possession of sovereignty is held as being exceptional. This is so because the underlying normative underpinning of the system prioritises values including representative legitimacy, non-intervention, self-determination, and the monopoly control of the legitimate exercise of violence domestically. Sovereignty's exceptionality is an expression of these values and is thus neither arbitrarily the attribute that organises the system nor the full extent of the justification for exclusion. For example, when actors justify the prohibition of non-state entities as being full members in multilateral forums, they often do so claiming that they lack representative legitimacy.[9] The argument does not stop at stating that they do not possess sovereignty but goes one step further to appeal to a commonly held value.

The (re)production of identity and subject positions is always co/multi-constitutive. Defining one's own group according to a particular attribute or attributes necessarily defines and positions others. Indeed, the power to name and define is itself a privilege of the superiorly positioned. As closure theorists tend to focus on material resources, opportunities, and advantages secured by closure processes, in doing so they tend to underplay the significant advantage of having such productive power.[10] This ability allows the superiorly positioned to continually (re)enforce the system's structure, which is articulated so as to serve their own interests, usually at the expense of the inferiorly positioned. Closure is thus a result not only of the monopolisation of material advantages, but also of the ideational advantage to successfully exercise productive power. Accounting for both the material and ideational dimensions is thus necessary for a comprehensive account of how closure works. Extant social closure theory overemphasises the material dimension, for which this reformed theory of international social closure corrects.

I am equally critical, however, of post-structuralist IR scholarship for overemphasising the ideational dimension, a position I share with Rebecca Adler-Nissen.[11] I thus take an approach that accounts for both the ideational and the material, a particular advantage of approaching this topic from an English School perspective.[12] Social division, stratification, and closure is not just about the (re)production of identities. While the construction and co-constitution of the Self/Other dyad is critically important, a comprehensive account of the international domain does not just take stock of group identities, but must also look at how the borders between them are traversed in thoroughly material ways.[13] As the empirical chapters that follow detail, this is largely a material undertaking. Mark B. Salter points to Gong's explanation of how the Standard of Civilisation "was mobilized to distinguish those states that could expect sovereignty and those that could expect domination. This boundary between Western and non-Western states was patrolled earnestly."[14] I, however, suggest we go one step further. The Standard was not just about identifying a stratified social division, and the boundary divide was not just something that was patrolled to keep outsiders out. The Standard was not just a border guard, but also an immigration tribunal, judging the suitability of an actor to cross the border (in either direction). Closure theory allows us to see that what is also involved in processes that produce Others is the management of the border between the Self and Other; that is, providing a means, one that is often material, to judge when an Other is no longer belonging to the out-group, but has become self-same (and conversely, when an actor ascribed as being self-same is no longer so).

Logics, rules, and criteria

Closure logics are the criteria according to which inclusion in (and exclusion from) groups is governed.[15] Sociologist Frank Parkin identifies two logics of closure that broadly categorise the types of membership criteria: collectivist closure and individualist closure. Collectivist closure criteria refer to group traits, such as gender or race, and collectivist systems of closure thus include patriarchy and apartheid. Individualist closure criteria refer to individual traits, such as academic credentials or wealth, and individualist closure systems thus include meritocracy and capitalism. Collectivist traits tend to be impossible for an individual actor to achieve, whereas individualist traits – at least ostensibly – are achievable. The significance of this is that if an actor is excluded on collectivist grounds, there is nothing that he/she can do to overcome his/her exclusion other than to overturn the entire logic of the closure system. In contrast, individualist exclusion can be overcome by the achievement of whatever is necessary for inclusion without the need to challenge the prevailing order. No system is purely collectivist or purely individualist; they are ideal types. However, a system can generally be characterised according to the dominant mode of closure.

There are two other ways in which we can categorise types of closure rules: ascribed versus achieved criteria; and legitimist versus functionalist criteria.[16] To categorise rules along collectivist versus individualist lines is to emphasise the *type of attribute* that is being selected to judge the suitability of an actor for membership. In analysing closure in this way the chief concern is identifying whether exclusion is being based on the characteristics of the group to which an actor belongs (collectivism) or a characteristic of the individual actor (individualism). Categorising closure along ascribed versus achieved lines delineates closure rules in almost the same way. What is different is that this emphasises the possibility (or lack thereof) of an actor changing those characteristics. Ascribed characteristics cannot be acquired, whereas achieved ones can. Race-based exclusion provides a clear example: if a club has a rule banning non-white people from entry, an individual excluded by this rule can himself/herself do nothing to make himself/ herself suitable for entry. The only way to overcome this unjust exclusion is to challenge the logic of the closure system itself. If a club, on the other hand, has a rule preventing entry to anyone below a certain income level, an individual seeking entry has the ability – at least ostensibly – to increase his/her earnings. Ascribed versus achieved characteristics thus map closely onto the collectivist versus individualist delineation, but in this analytical frame the emphasis is on the *mutability* of attributes.

The third way to categorise closure rules is along legitimist versus functionalist lines, wherein the analytical focus is on the *justification* for an actor's suitability for membership. Legitimist closure holds than an actor should be included because of who/what it is, whereas functionalist closure justifies inclusion based on what the actor can do or contribute. Legitimism includes (and excludes) based on *who the actor is* of the actor, whereas functionalism does so based on *what the actor can do*. Again, this delineation follows the other two closely – legitimist, collectivist, and ascribed closure focus on the group identity of an actor, whereas functionalist, individualist, and achieved closure focus on individual identity.[17]

We thus have three different axes along which we can classify types of closure rules. It is tempting to opt for parsimony and use only one schema, but doing so would come at the cost of missing important dimensions of closure. We need to hold on to all three axes to achieve a thorough analysis of closure that accounts for attribute type (collectivist versus individualist), attribute achievability (ascribed versus achieved), and membership justification (legitimist versus functionalist). To focus only on achievability is to miss how actors try to change their attributes in order to improve their chances of gaining inclusion or the importance of underlying justifications for exclusion. Actors can improve their achieved characteristics, but if they face a legitimist mode of closure, their efforts will be of no effect in overcoming exclusion. This is the situation faced by non-sovereign actors – they can never overcome the legal-collectivism that demands the possession of sovereignty by its membership. States are included by legitimist right as sovereign actors at the exclusion of all others, regardless of their functional import to the management of international society.

A collective-legitimist closure system that excludes (or includes) based on ascribed characteristics is a more closed system than a functionalist-individualist system that excludes (or includes) based on achieved characteristics. Social mobility is greater in the latter as actors have the ability to achieve whatever is necessary for them to gain entry into status groups. Conversely, actors in groups who fail to no longer have whatever achieved characteristic(s) is required for membership can lose their position in the group. Social mobility works in both directions. In a collectivist system, the position of in-group members is far more secure. As outsiders cannot gain the ascribed characteristic(s) necessary for inclusion and as insiders cannot lose those characteristics, positions are entrenched so long as the logic of the system holds.

This theory's treatment of mobility is useful as it comprehensively captures social mobility in all directions, whether it be an actor's rise or fall in status. This overcomes bias in Social Identity Theory which tends to focus only on positive status moves and on IR more generally which tends to approach status by only looking at the movement of a single actor in a single direction. Scholarship tends either to look at rising powers or at falling powers, but rarely at both rising and falling movements at once, while also failing to look at how the strategies of rising and falling actors relate to one another.[18] Onea, and DiCicco and Levy make the same point, the strategic interaction between the superior/falling and inferior/rising actors needs to be accounted for.[19]

Social stratification is more easily perpetuated over time in a collective-legitimist system. Collectivist modes of closure allow dominant groups to better guarantee the transfer of their privileges to their successors than individualist modes of closure. An aristocratic system is a case in point – hereditary titles and property are passed down generationally, almost guaranteeing that the continued dominance of the superior status group and the continued exclusion of the 'lower orders.' In contrast, the inheritance of privilege and the consequent perpetuation of a particular stratified order are not so assured in systems of individualist closure. In a meritocracy, for example, a superior position is the result of individual characteristics that are 'achieved,' such as a professional qualification, rather than 'ascribed,' such as a hereditary title. Again, these are ideal-typical situations. As Keene notes, many meritocratic societies allow for the inheritance of properties or use elite education as a means for ensuring structural advantages for privileged groups to gain sought after credentials.[20] Equally, as Raymond Murphy contends, '[t]here was always a certain degree of upward mobility for a few individual members of the dominated collectivity, especially when the dominant collectivity saw those individuals as useful means for the accomplishment of specific ends.'[21] Upward mobility, though rare and difficult in highly differentiated societies marked by collectivist rules of closure, can be achieved if the attributes of an individual are judged by the dominant group to be functionally useful.[22] Murphy raises this point as part of his discussion of Weberian rationalisation, claiming that in the shift from 19th-century collectivist closure to 20th-century individualist closure, the dominant class could secure its position "by a more rational use of the talents of those under its domination."[23]

This rationalisation of exclusion resulted in a shift in the closure logic such that 'the capacity to convince others that one had the means to accomplish valued goals' became the criterion for inclusion in the dominant group.[24] As a result of this shift, membership in the dominant group was no longer generationally transferred strictly according to *who* an individual was, but according to *what* an individual could do, which, in this example, is the ability to accomplish a goal valued and desired by those in the dominant position. What is significant about this for our purposes is that the power to decide who is included in the dominant group (and who is excluded from that group) remains with those already superiorly positioned. However, the membership criteria for inclusion in that group change and so too does the group's composition, but the status positions of actors largely do not.

This is key for understanding how incumbents' status positions in international society endure despite a shifting normative context and shifts in power-political capabilities. The ability to set a system's closure rules is itself a privilege of the superiorly positioned, affording them the ability to structure the closure game in ways the inferiorly positioned cannot. The closure game is rigged in favour of superiorly positioned. Not only does the in-group have the ability to decide what outsiders – if any – could be included in the club, but it has the ability to define on what terms it could be included. For example, the ability to decide who gets included and on what terms has had a significant effect on maintaining the status of G-summitry's incumbents. In short, despite the shift to an apparently more open, inclusive, less-Western G20, the decision of whom to include and on what terms was firmly that of the incumbent G7 members and was ultimately decided by two men: then-Canadian Finance Minister Paul Martin and then-US Treasury Secretary Lawrence Summers. Excluding any incumbents was "out of the question" in crafting the new group, and the inclusion of new members was decided based on whom they perceived to be the regionally "systematically significant" countries who subscribed to a largely neo-liberal economic agenda and upheld a standard of good governance domestically.[25]

As I argue, international society is predominantly a functional-individualist closure system, but one with a deeply imbedded collectivism at its heart. This collectivism is a legal-collectivism that sets the possession of sovereignty as being the primary closure rule of the system, creating the broad social division in international society between state and non-state actors. Moreover, collectivist stereotyping further entrenches the positions of actors. Functional-individualist rules serve as the system's secondary barriers which are what mark international society as appearing to be a relatively meritocratic society, wherein full membership in status groups is theoretically possible so long as an actor overcomes the primary closure rule.[26] Should an actor not satisfy the primary, collectivist rule – however, regardless of whatever functional contributions it might make – it can never achieve full membership.

Closure strategies

Closure strategies are the means by which actors exercise power in the status game in order to achieve or maintain status for themselves, or deny or grant it to others. It is fundamentally about power; indeed, power is an 'attribute of closure.'[27] Parkin outlines two basic types of closure strategies: exclusion and usurpation.[28] He defines exclusion as

> the attempt by one group to secure for itself a privileged position at the expense of some other group through a process of subordination... it is a form of collective social action which, intentionally or otherwise, gives rise to a social category of ineligibles or outsiders.[29]

He characterises this as "the use of power in a 'downward' direction because it necessarily entails the creation of a group, class, or stratum of legally defined inferiors."[30] While strategies of exclusion are the most prevalent in stratified systems, the second type of strategy outlined by Parkin is that of usurpation which is a consequence of, and a response to, exclusion.[31] Whereas exclusion is the strategy adopted by the superiorly positioned group, usurpation is the strategy adopted by inferiorly positioned groups "to win a greater share of resources" by "bit[ing] into the privileges of legally defined superiors."[32] Usurpation always contains "a potential challenge to the prevailing system of allocation and to the authorized version of distributive justice,"[33] and it tends to manifest as activities like mass mobilizations, such as demonstrations or marches.[34] Parkin also identifies a third type of closure strategy, that of dual closure. In dual closure, a subordinate group exercises a strategy of exclusion against other subordinate groups while, at the same time, exercising a strategy of usurpation against the dominant group. Dual closure is thus the exercise of the two basic forms of closure strategies at once. Dual closure can thus account for how divisions and struggles amongst subordinate groups form further substrata in a system.

Exclusion and mobility strategies

Extant closure theory's conceptualisation of closure strategies most heavily require reform to develop a suitable theory of *international* social closure. First, as concerns the exclusion of actors, it is necessary to adopt greater sophistication in understanding how exclusion barriers work. I reform closure theory's treatment of rules adding an additional dimension to their categorisation as the existing framework does not adequately capture how rules govern closure in the international domain. While the closure rules are predominantly functional-individualist in nature, this does not give an accurate picture of how the rules structure the closure game. Chapter 4 thus categorises closure rules as Achievable, Unachievable, and Ostensibly Achievable. Achievable rules and unachievable rules graft onto the individualist and collectivist distinction, respectively. Ostensibly achievable rules are those that are functional-individualist in character but are structurally impossible (or, nearly so) for most actors in the system to actually achieve. Exclusion based on wealth serves as a useful domestic example. A club may set conditions for entry such that a member must be a millionaire. This is an individualist criterion and so on the face of it, according to closure theory's framework, the club is relatively more open than one levying a collectivist criterion. However, this is a highly set barrier to entry that is extraordinarily difficult – if not outright impossible for most actors in the system – to overcome, thus rending it as only ostensibly achievable. Chapter 4 focuses on this as concerns powers seeking inclusion into the Great Powers' club and G-summitry. It is not enough just to characterise the rules of the system as being open or closed based on the *types* of attributes the criteria demand,

		Mode of Exclusion	
		Collectivist	**Individualist**
Criteria of Exclusion	Achievable	-----	Functionalist criteria
	Ostensibly Achievable	Legal-Collectivism (in early expansion of international society)	Functionalist criteria (highly set barrier)
	Unachievable	Legal-Collectivism (in universal international society)	-----

Figure 2.1 Exclusion Strategies.

we must also evaluate them based on how structure might constrain the achievement of any particular criterion (Figure 2.1).

Second, closure and stratification are achieved by more than just exclusion strategies. This is how it is possible to have a relatively open international society in terms of its exclusion barriers, but one that is nonetheless marked by stratification and entrenched status positions. The maintenance and denial of status is far more complex than extant closure theory suggests it could be.

We also need to develop the concept of Mobility Dampeners as a means of both maintaining and denying status that extant closure theory fails to capture. As Chapter 3 details, they are a furtive means of closure as they rely upon the norms, values, beliefs, ideas, and practices of a club in their operation. Mobility dampeners are not exclusion barriers, they are another means of preventing the loss of status while concurrently preventing the rise of others, thus preventing or stalling both upward and downward mobility. For example, the diplomatic norm of precedence is an influential force that perpetuates the *status quo*. Social closure is thus not just about rules, but is also about less explicit conventions and practices. Further, mobility dampeners, like exclusion barriers, are concerned with the status of outsiders and are 'exercised' against them, in what Parkin characterises as "the use of power in a 'downward' direction."[35] However, mobility dampeners are also applied to insiders to safeguard their own status. Achieving closure and maintaining status is not just about exerting a force externally, but also about the ideational underpinning of a status group.

Inclusion strategies

Extant closure theory's treatment of the strategies available to inferiorly positioned outsiders is also too simplistic. As Chapter 5 demonstrates,

	Assertive	Deferential
Relational	Usurpation	Banding / Differentiation	Legitimation / Normalisation
Identity Adaptation	Geopolitical Mimicry	Cooperative Mimicry	Grovelling (Absent)

Figure 2.2 Inclusion Strategies.

I broaden the list of strategies available to outsiders beyond just usurpation to improve the analytical ability of closure theory. I divide inclusion strategies into two general categories: Relational Strategies and Identity Adaptation Strategies. Both general types of strategy range from being more assertive, involving geopolitical competition, to more deferential, involving diplomatic, institutional cooperation. This way of conceptualising strategies helps us identify what type of game is being played in what sort of normative context. Relational strategies are predominantly aimed at challenging order in terms of position, while identity adaptation strategies predominantly aim to challenge it in terms of disposition. Relational strategies range from being more assertive, as with usurpation strategies, to being more deferential, as with what I have called Legitimation and Normalisation strategies. Identity adaptation strategies range from being more assertive, which I have categorised as Geopolitical mimicry, to being more deferential, which I have labelled as Cooperative mimicry. Absent as an identity adaptation strategy, but theoretically possible, is an entirely deferential form of mimicry which we can refer to as Grovelling. Its absence is unsurprising given that grovelling is not an effective way to acquire status (Figure 2.2).

Relational strategies

Banding involves actors organising themselves as a group in order to attempt to achieve inclusion collectively. If an individual actor cannot achieve inclusion on its own, banding serves as a useful fallback strategy as the group may have a greater ability to achieve inclusion than an actor on its own (as is the case in domestic societies). What is noteworthy about banding is that actors seek inclusion collectively, which marks it out as distinct from other types of strategies wherein seeking inclusion is an individualist undertaking. Banding may thus be a collective enterprise wherein an absolute gain of inclusion is sought for a group of outsiders rather than an individualist activity seeking the relative gain of inclusion for a single outsider. However, it does not have to be so. As the analysis in Chapter 5 details, banding can be an interim means for an outsider to seek inclusion with the help of other outsiders, but then that actor can be quick to abandon its group once its own inclusion has been achieved.

Whereas banding may be characterised as individual actors organising themselves collectively to gain a greater absolute degree of inclusion for them all, Differentiation, in contrast, may be understood as its inverse, wherein an actor socially differentiates itself from alike actors in order to gain its own inclusion while denying it to similar others. While banding is cooperative, differentiation is competitive. Parkin's 'dual closure' is a strategy wherein an actor at once tries to usurp those positioned superiorly while concurrently excluding those positioned inferiorly.[36] Closure is not just exercised by a dominant group against a lower one but may be exercised by actors within a group against others in that same class/stratum.[37] Conceptually, the problem with dual closure is that it is not one closure strategy exercised by an actor but two different closure strategies (usurpation and exclusion) exercised by an actor against two different actors (or groups of actors). The exclusionary move against other inferiorly positioned outsiders need not have any relation to the usurpatory move against superiorly positioned insiders. Differentiation, however, is a single strategy wherein an outsider acts against other outsiders in order to make a claim for inclusion to insiders. The actor differentiates itself from others whom are ascribed as being similar in order to signal its suitability for inclusion into the club and, by implication, others as being unsuitable. The differentiation strategy is truly a dual movement in that the force exerted on other outsiders is designed to have an effect of improving the position of the actor exerting the force by means of an appeal to insiders. It is not just about keeping other outsiders in marginal positions and/or relatively inferior positions as it is in Parkin's formulation, but about an actor keeping others in those positions in order to improve its own position.

Material contributions are not the only type of functional benefit that an actor can bring to a group, as is predominantly the case concerning the benefits that actors bring via cooperative mimicry. A legitimation strategy is the same quality of strategy in that outsiders seek inclusion by offering a club an ideational 'good' that it is deficient in legitimacy.[38] Broadly, there are two moves involved in a legitimation strategy: First, a claim made by an outsider (or group of outsiders) that the club is unrepresentative and therefore illegitimate; second, a claim is made that inclusion would increase the legitimacy of the club. Who or what the actor is/represents is what confers or boosts legitimacy. The focus with these types of strategy is on the legitimacy of the group to be an exclusive club whose members, by virtue of inclusion, are superiorly positioned to outsiders. In order to have authority in contemporary international society, clubs must be seen to be legitimate, to at least some degree. If a club lacks legitimacy, it means that it may lose its dominant position in the governance of the international domain. Therefore, any legitimacy deficit is an entry opportunity for outsiders if their inclusion would bolster the club's legitimacy and in so doing maintain its superior position.

The final Relational Inclusion Strategy is that of normalisation. Normalisation is based on a diplomatic norm of precedence. A normalisation strategy can be seen as the inverse of insiders' Mobility Dampeners, as both use the force of precedence to improve (or maintain) an actor's position in the closure game. What must be noted is that normalisation does not just rely on precedence but involves its establishment in the first place. This sets normalisation apart from Mobility Dampeners, as dampeners do not set precedence, but only rely upon it for its operation.[39] Normalisation is the routinisation of an actor's inclusion, or, more colloquially, it is the strategy of getting one's foot in the door. Normalisation is used here rather than simply 'precedence' because while the strategy relies upon precedence as a norm, the term does not capture all the relevant dynamics of the strategy. The strategy does not involve an actor simply pointing to past occurrence and justifying inclusion based on that antecedent. Rather, the strategy necessarily involves the actor setting up that antecedent in the first place. The strategy begins before the claim for precedence can be made.

Identity adaptation

The second general category of inclusion strategy is that of identity adaptation (or, mimicry, for short). Outsiders mimic insiders to make themselves seem like club members, thus signalling their suitability for inclusion by virtue of appearing like insiders. Those seeking inclusion not only *do* particular things to get into the club, they also generally *act* like they are suitable for inclusion. More than this, though, in mimicking insiders they are concurrently signalling dissimilarity with other outsiders. Differentiation is thus a central attribute of such a move. In all, outsiders mimic insiders to appear suitable for inclusion and may use those mimicked attributes to try overcome their exclusion, such as in using Western international law to overturn unequal treaties. What is significant about mimicry is that it is another way in which those seeking inclusion in part reproduce the *status quo* order, as adopting the practices of the club means perpetuating the values and institutions in which they are embedded. Even if the same actors do not remain superiorly positioned in the club, their values, beliefs, ideas, norms, and practices do. Mimicry is thus another significant way that a particular kind of international society may be perpetuated by means other than coercion or imposition.[40]

It is important to distinguish mimicry from just rational moves to reduce transaction costs. An outsider may act like an insider in relations with insiders because it has chosen to carry out that interaction within the same institution for reasons of efficiency. Or, they may do so because that practice has been imposed upon the outsider.[41] What allows us to be more sure that we are observing mimicry is when outsiders carry out such mimetic practices in relations with other outsiders, wherein there is no direct transactional advantage to be had in acting like the in-group and when outsiders use practices of the in-group.

Incorporation strategies

I am critical of extant closure theory's emphasis on conflict between groups and its lack of an account of how the superiorly positioned may bring inferiorly positioned actors into higher strata. It further lacks an ability to accept that inferiorly positioned actors may accept their subordinate positions and not contest them. These are problematic omissions because they miss prevalent dynamics in the closure game. With interaction being limited to exclusionary or usurpatory strategies, there is no accounting for the possibility of incorporative action on the part of superiorly positioned insiders where they bring the excluded in – or, at least closer – to their group; nor is there space in extant closure theory for cooperative action on the part of the inferior actors to accept their position and try not to change it, but to nonetheless work cooperatively with the superiorly positioned club members. There is a hint of this in a few brief lines in Murphy's work, but it is excused as "an unusual exception" rather than as a primary feature of how practices of closure stratify a society.[42] Again, with the theoretical focus being so directed at conflict between groups it is not hard to understand why the prospect of cooperation or an acceptance of subordination is disregarded as an exception. Such a dynamic, however, is anything but an exception in international politics. As Chapter 6 details, owing to the predominant functionalism governing the closure system, group insiders often bring outsiders into the club according to its functionalist needs to manage international society. Outsiders are incorporated so as to make use of their capabilities to maintain the club's overall aims and thus perpetuate its position. The relationship between superiors and inferiors can thus be cooperative.[43]

The significance of the identification of incorporation strategies is not just that it reveals how the status game can be played with relative pacificity. It also demonstrates that status may be maintained through means other than exclusion, as it is through a particular mode of incorporation that outsiders are included: *stratified* incorporation. Outsiders are brought into the club in marginal and subordinate ways so as to protect the relatively higher status positions of the club's incumbent members. Incorporation is cooperative, but it is also stratifying. Insiders tend to justify stratification according to *functionalist* necessity. More than this, though, when functionalist necessity fails to keep others in a relatively lower position, insiders will stratify according to a more *collectivist* logic. Insiders guard their status positions against emerging/rising others by pointing to collectivist traits as justification for a continued inequality of status.

While there has been a normative shift in international society which requires representative legitimacy, a group may stratify newly included members according to collectivist ascriptions. Thus, while the contemporary closure game seems more just and open, owing to this persisting collectivism, it is not. Chapter 4 details how legal-collectivism endures as the primary means of closure, and Chapter 6 makes the case for adding a 'Logic of Culture' as enduring as a collectivist means of secondary closure, though a collectivist Logic of Culture stratifies rather than outright excludes.[44] In short, there are two important dimensions to highlight here: international closure theory must be able to account for instances of cooperative incorporation between superiorly positioned insiders and inferiorly positioned outsiders, and it must add incorporation strategies to the list of ways that status can be maintained (by insiders) and gained (by outsiders).

While this more pacific dimension of the closure game that played *between* groups must be accounted for, there is conversely a more conflictual dimension that extant theory largely misses: that of the closure games being played *within* groups. Group members engage in closure strategies against one another in a further game of status differentiation. Thus, to get a full account of the closure game being played in the international domain, intra-group closure must also be accounted for. Stratification is not only the structure of the relationship between groups, it is also the structure of the relationship between actors *within* those groups.

Conclusion

A theory of international social closure allows us to examine how actors contest inclusion in clubs and how clubs themselves endure as the means of governing the international domain and as the means of managing international society. This chapter has developed a theoretical framework through which we can identify how this happens by looking at the *contexts* in which closure games are played and by looking at the *strategies* through they are played. While social closure operates differently in the international domain than the domestic context for which the theory was originally developed, the aim here has been to reform it so as to produce a theory suitable for use in IR. The remainder of the book puts this theoretical lens to use.

Notes

1 Murphy, R. (1988). *Social Closure: The Theory of Monopolization and Exclusion*. Oxford: Clarendon Press; Parkin, F. (Ed.). (1974). *The Social Analysis of Class Structure*. Tavistock Press; Parkin, F. (1979). *Marxism and Class Theory: A Bourgeois Critique*. Taylor & Francis.

2 Payne, G. (2000). Social Divisions and Social Cohesion. In *Social Divisions* (pp. 242–253). Basingstoke: Macmillan.
3 Bottero, W. (2005). *Stratification: Social Division and Inequality*. London: Routledge.
4 Parkin (1979, p. 44).
5 Doty (1996, 1993); Hall (2003); Medina (2004); Neumann and Welsh (1991); Weldes and Saco (1996).
6 Murphy, *Social Closure: The Theory of Monopolization and Exclusion*, 1988; Weber, M. (1922). *Economy and Society: An Outline of Interpretive Sociology* (G. Roth & C. Wittich, Eds.). Berkeley: University of California Press, 34–36, 302–307, 339–348, 635–640, 926–966.
7 Barnett, M., & Duvall, R. (2005). Power in International Politics. *International Organization*, *59* (1), 39–75.
8 Weber (1922, pp. 34–36, 302–307, 339–348, 635–640, 926–966).
9 C.f. Collingwood, V. (2006). Non-Governmental Organisations, Power and Legitimacy in International Society. *Review of International Studies*, *32* (3), 439–454.
10 Inayatullah, N., & Blaney, D. L. (2004). *International Relations and the Problem of Difference*. New York: Routledge.
11 Adler-Nissen, R. (2014). Stigma Management in International Relations: Transgressive Identities, Norms, and Order in International Society. *International Organization*, *68* (1), 143–176, 146; Okagaki, T. T. (2013). *The Logic of Conformity: Japan's Entry into International Society*. Toronto: University Press of Toronto, 30.
12 Black and Hwang (2012, p. 432); Buzan (2004, p. 61); Black, L., & Hwang, Y. J. (2012). China and Japan's Quest for Great Power Status: Norm Entrepreneurship in Anti-Piracy Responses. *International Relations*, *26* (4), 431–451, 432; Buzan, B. (2004). *The United States and the Great Powers: World Politics in the Twenty-First Century* (1st edition). Cambridge; Malden, MA: Polity, 61.
13 Campbell (1992); Lebow (2008); Neumann (1999); Said (1978).
14 Gong (1984, p. 10); Salter (2002, p. 17; see also 10–11).
15 Parkin (1979).
16 Hurd, I. (1999). Legitimacy and Authority in International Politics. *International Organization*, *53* (2), 379–408.
17 Cf. Qin, Y. (2010). Why Is There No Chinese International Relations Theory? In A. Acharya & B. Buzan (Eds.), *Non-Western International Relations Theory Perspectives on and beyond Asia* (pp. 26–50). New York: Routledge.
18 For a recent exception, see Shifrinson (2018).
19 DiCicco, J. M., & Levy, J. (2003). The Power Transition Research Program. In C. Elman & M. Fendius (Eds.), *Progress in International Relations Theory: Appraising the Field* (pp. 109–158). MIT Press, 138; Onea, T. A. (2014). Between Dominance and Decline: Status Anxiety and Great Power Rivalry. *Review of International Studies*, *40* (1), 125–152, 125–126. Others who hint at this but do not pick up on it include the following: Doran, C. F. (1991). *Systems in Crisis: New Imperatives of High Politics at Century's End*. Cambridge University Press; Lebow, R. N. (2008). *A Cultural Theory of International Relations* (1st edition). Cambridge; New York: Cambridge University Press.
20 Keene (2007a, 2007b); Keene, E. (2007a). Hierarchy and Stratification in International Society: A Comparison of the Old and New Diplomacies. Presented at the *International Studies Association*, Chicago, IL; (2007b). Stratification, Hierarchy and Closure in International Relations. Presented at the International Studies Association, Chicago, IL.
21 Murphy (1988a, p. 220).
22 Payne (2000, pp. 242–243).

23 Murphy (1988a, p. 220).
24 Ibid.
25 Martin (2012, August 23). [In-person]; Summers, L. (2012, October 23). [Telephone and Skype].
26 Having primary and secondary rules marks international society out as having a 'tandem' closure structure (Murphy 1988b, pp. 73–74).
27 Parkin (1979, p. 46).
28 For more comprehensive overview and critique of Parkin's treatment of closure, see Murphy (1988b, pp. 10–14; 65–81).
29 Parkin (1979, p. 45).
30 Ibid.
31 Ibid.
32 Ibid.
33 Ibid.
34 Ibid., 74.
35 Ibid., 45.
36 Parkin (1979, pp. 89–116; see especially 91–92).
37 Parkin (1979, p. 89).
38 Contra (Yonding, 2004, p. 20). Yonding argues that G-summitry does not require legitimacy.
39 The other difference, of course, is that mobility dampeners are a tool of insiders, not outsiders.
40 For more on the more pacific ways that closure perpetuates order, see below.
41 The two scenarios are not mutually exclusive.
42 Murphy (1988b, p. 220).
43 C.f. Lake, D. (2011). Hierarchy in International Relation. In M. Larionova (Ed.), *The European Union in the G8: Promoting Consensus and Concerted Actions for Global Public Goods* (1st edition). Farnham: Ashgate.
44 C.f. Neumann and Welsh (1991); Stivachtis Y. A. (1998). *The Enlargement of International Society: Culture versus Anarchy and Greece's Entry into International Society*. Basingstoke; Hampshire; New York: Palgrave Macmillan.

3 Institutions and mobility

Primary institutions

What follows is a discussion of the English School's conception of primary institutions in terms of their relevance to the status groups under consideration and the closure games through which they are formed and maintained. I demonstrate how the institutional context within which the closure game takes place matters- with different contexts come different means by which the game can be played. Closure is not just achieved exclusion strategies, but also by relying upon the norms, values, ideas, beliefs, and practices embedded within the institutional underpinning of a status group.

Despite the centrality of institutions to the English School's theoretical apparatus and their role in international society's globalisation story, with few noteworthy exceptions, there is surprisingly little direct engagement with them.[1] Christian Reus-Smit's work is one such exception, problematising the constitution of actors and regimes in the 'hierarchy of modern international institutions,' as is Buzan's focusing on the distinction between primary and secondary institutions.[2] While their conceptual frameworks and terminologies differ, they are not incongruous, and what follows here fits within both schemas. While I primarily use Buzan's terminology, I am interested in what Reus-Smit refers to as the effect of 'Fundamental Institutions' on 'Issue Specific Regimes' – the top two levels of his institutional hierarchy.[3] Focusing on institutions is critical given that, as Buzan relays (in building upon Charles Manning), 'the institutions of international society define in the game of states, 'what the pieces are and how the game is played'.[4] More than this, though, institutions not only constitute actors but also the social categories through which they arrange themselves. What is critical for my purposes here is not just that institutions play these roles, but that different primary institutions are dominant in an international society at different periods. It's not just that 'societies of states tend to privilege certain institutions over others', but that any particular international society can have a different mix of privileged institutions over the course of its history.[5] This matters because it means that secondary institutions and regimes are then conditioned by (and themselves give priority to) different norms, values, beliefs, ideas, and practices depending on the mix of primary institutions that are dominant/privileged during their genesis and operation. The significance of this to international social closure is that it means that particular configurations of primary institutions condition how the closure game is played in each club.[6]

G-summitry is set apart from the other clubs because it is primarily a product of the fundamental/primary institution of diplomacy. As what follows argues, this renders G-summitry a relatively more closed system. While G-summitry appears to be more open on the face of it, substantively it is less so owing to how diplomatic norms and values entrench the *status quo* order more than is the case with other clubs. Social mobility is actually more restricted on the whole.

Primary institutions condition order in both its expressions. Order as rank is conditioned by what types of actors are permitted to have any sort of standing in international society, and on what terms. Order as disposition is conditioned by defining how those who are included relate to one another, particularly as concerns how those actors maintain and manage international society. To use Bull's schema of primary institutions as an example, the Balance of Power's function has been to prevent the emergence of empire and domination, as well as provide the conditions through which other institutions can operate.[7] International law solidifies sovereignty as the means of organising the system, instils the rules of coexistence for sovereign states, and mobilises compliance with those rules.[8] Diplomacy facilitates communication, negotiation, information gathering, friction reduction, and the symbolic reproduction of international society itself.[9] War has determined the overall shape of the international domain, provided the impetus for maintaining the system, and provided a means of enforcing rules and norms.[10] Finally, great powers have provided a means of resolving conflict, containing conflict, and promoting the survival of international society itself.[11] Later generations of English School scholars have added to the list of institutions and their functions, including the market, nationalism, human rights, and environmentalism.[12] Keene argues that the Standard of Civilisation also needs to be added to the list of primary institutions given its function in determining the membership of international society. It is 'the key institution for differentiating political communities in the global international system and mediating their "entry" into international society.'[13] Each primary institution thus makes a different contribution to maintaining the same international society, though in varying degrees depending on the type of society and the particularly historical context, while reinforcing one another.[14]

As above, whatever institution – or institutions – is privileged/dominant in an international society at a given moment in time particularly conditions that society, its members, and their interactions. For example, an international society in which the primary institution of war is dominant is likely a relatively violence-prone, pluralist society; while one in which the institutions of international law, diplomacy, and the market are dominant is likely relatively pacific and solidarist (at least procedurally) in character. There is likewise an effect on the status groups within international society, conditioning what they do, how they operate, and – critically – how membership within them works. This is the relationship between the top two levels of Reus-Smit's hierarchy. If we can identify the institutional underpinning of a group, we can then tease out how the norms, values, ideals, beliefs, and practices instilled in them by the dominant primary institutions affect the politics of membership in it.

Comparatively analysing multiple status groups across time allows us to infer how the status game might have changed as a result of changes in international societies' institutional mix. We can thus infer how the ideational fabric (and changes in it) might condition the closure game. This is significant because it allows us to explore the possibility that the ideational structure of international society affects the closure game, in addition to more agential closure strategies. It is also significant because it means that actors can rely on resources beyond closure strategies to maintain, deny, achieve, or grant inclusion and the status that comes with it.

As concerns the Family of Civilised Nations, the criteria primarily governing membership derive from two primary institutions: the Standard of Civilisation and, implicitly a part of it, the institution of sovereignty. Great powers are distinct in this framework as they themselves are identified as a primary institutions while also being a status group within international society, within which membership is predominantly a function of material power and the recognition of that status by others. These two status groups thus graft relatively easily onto the established English School framework. G-summitry is more difficult, being more of a secondary institution (or issue-specific regime, in Reus-Smit's terms). In terms of membership, it shares commonalities with the Great Powers' club, replying on the material power of its membership to manage international order. Members need to be systematically significant to belong, just as with the great powers. However, such a reading misses the extent to which membership is not derived in such a straightforward manner. Indeed, membership in G-summitry is more a function of diplomatic manoeuvring than it is a reading of the gross domestic product (GDP) league tables. The market could likewise be seen as serving as the dominant underpinning of the club. While G-summitry is obviously focused on the management of the global economic system, as what follows in this book details, the primary institution of diplomacy is a far better candidate for serving as the foundation of the club, particularly in terms of determining its membership. The implications of this are significant.

G-summitry displays critical hallmarks of the diplomatic institution. First, one of the defining characteristics of the group is the emphasis on personal contact and frank, informal exchange. The public face of diplomacy is characterised by much formality, most often articulated as protocol. The private face of diplomacy, in sharp contrast, is very much the opposite. Informality was at the very heart of what French President Valéry Giscard d'Estaing had envisaged for the group, given its centrality in the club's immediate antecedent, The Library Group. Indeed, Giscard vehemently objected to the entry of any new members on the grounds that it would reduce the ability of the group to conduct itself informally.[15] In objecting to the inclusion of the European Commission (EC) he argued, "that further additions were likely to destroy the informality of these meetings."[16] So important is informal exchange to the operation of the club that when the G20 was established at the ministerial level, then-Canadian Finance Minister Paul Martin ensured that the practice of interacting in frank, informal exchanges would be adopted by all the new entrants to the club. Observing that 'certain members had some difficulty adjusting to the G7's tradition of informal, unscripted exchanges with all members at equal footing,' Martin started the first G20 meeting by inviting the South African Finance Minister Trevor Manuel and Lawrence Summers to 'have at it on the issue of agricultural subsidies.'[17] Martin's intent was to show new participants how they ought to conduct themselves in the meetings – to demonstrate that frank, informal exchange was not just allowed, but was the rule. This is so for Sherpas as much as it is for leaders. Sherpas always stress the importance of informality in their contact with one another. As British Sherpa Lord Armstrong related, Sherpas 'meet often enough to develop a camaraderie and a network of personal friendships which persists even when they cease to be Sherpas.'[18] Indeed, G-summitry was created through personal diplomacy, relying on the efforts of George Shultz to meet with Wilson, Giscard, and Schmidt to get the idea off the ground. Thereafter, it was the diplomats in the invited countries that shepherded the idea to fruition, and, conversely, it was through diplomatic channels that the excluded states protested their status as outsiders.[19]

Second, G-summitry is not a single, annual meeting of leaders; it is a continuous diplomatic process. G-summitry is not limited to one (or two) summit(s) per year as they are popularly portrayed. Rather, G-summitry is a year-round process that involves constant interaction between leaders, their Sherpas, ministers, and civil servants in a number of ministries, though chiefly the foreign and finance ministries. Third, the symbolic emphasis of the summit is placed on a textual output, just as it is in diplomacy. The summit communiqués are the pinnacle of the process. The communiqué is the outcome that all stakeholders are trying to influence, the dimension of the summit that involves the most intense negotiation by the Sherpas, and the primary textual artefact that is used by outsiders as a means to gain inclusion. Indeed, the focus of the entire summitry process is a negotiation over the communiqué further emphasises the extent to which G-summitry is a diplomatic institution – the process itself is an exercise of one of the essential elements of diplomacy.[20]

40 *Institutions and mobility*

Mobility dampeners

G-summitry is thus an institutional context different from the other status groups under examination here. The contemporary international domain is a highly institutionalised one within which actors' interdependence is mediated primarily via diplomacy and international law.[21] As is detailed in the following chapter, this removes more assertive, geopolitical status claiming moves from the closure game as they are rendered both more difficult to carry out and less legitimate even if they were to be. Russia's annexation of Crimea is a case in point. The second consequence of this is that diplomatic norms and practices have a greater role to play in contemporary status competition, thus effecting how the closure game is played.

As G-summitry is predominantly conditioned by the diplomatic institution, the norms, values, beliefs, ideas, and practices that are central to diplomacy serve as the foundation of the club's operation and it is these norms that inject *Mobility Dampeners* into the club. Specifically, it is the diplomatic principles of *pragmatism* and *precedence* that change the closure game. Pragmatism privileges concerns for expediency over principles of fairness or justice, while precedence gives privileged standing to incumbents (to the detriment of newcomers). In the case of the G20, the principle of representative governance is also central to its construction. The G20 is not just a club of systematically significant economies, but also is a club whose membership was crafted to ensure just geographic and cultural representation so that the club could claim the representative legitimacy that the G7 lacks. As is detailed in the following chapters, in attempting to have greater representative legitimacy, however, the G20 ends up actually being a more closed system because of the twin effects of precedence and pragmatism. Thus, despite more just principles guiding its composition, the institutions which shape its identity and operation as a club actually render G-summitry more closed than other groups.

Pragmatism

Pragmatism guided the G-summitry's membership composition from the beginning. The purpose of the brief history below is to demonstrate how the diplomatic norm of pragmatism is central to G-summitry's constitution and character, and how pragmatism affects the operation of the closure game in and around the club.

The G7 was envisaged as being small and exclusive so as to help ensure that the group's meetings were intimate and informal. The rationale guiding this was that the fewer the number of people in the room, the more likely that frank, informal exchanges could be used to break political deadlocks. This was what prompted US Treasury Secretary George Shultz to bring together the individuals whom would later be key in founding the club. The standard account of the G7's development puts its roots in "The Library Group," describing the G7 as the elevation of this group to the leaders' level.[22] The Library Group was composed of the UK, US, French, West German, and Japanese finance ministers who first came together in 1972 as a result of an effort lead by Shultz to fix the international monetary system (and, soon thereafter, held together to respond to the oil crisis). The Smithsonian Agreement, which was signed in December 1971 and amended the Bretton Woods system of fixed exchange rates, had failed to work as the signatories had hoped, with further devaluation of the US dollar against European currencies and readjustment of the value of the US dollar against the gold standard. Prior to an IMF G20 meeting (not to be confused with the current G20), Shultz invited the finance ministers of West Germany, France, the UK, and Japan to come to his office, one at a time, to read a speech that he had prepared about the problems with the current system in an effort to forge a common position before meeting with the larger, 'unwieldy' IMF G20.[23] This group continued to meet on the margins of IMF meetings, as well as at other times.[24] They met often enough and was small enough that the members became friends who, in the words of Shultz, 'could call on one another... we could trust each other, we were honest and candid.'[25]

In July 1975 Giscard mused about the idea of a summit to discuss economic and monetary policy.[26] Giscard suggested a summit in Paris in the autumn amongst France, the UK, the US, West Germany, Italy, and 'other industrialised nations' which would not reach any formal agreements, but would focus on informal exchanges over the course of a week of private talks.[27] From the moment the possibility of a summit was raised, those who thought they ought to be included began lobbying for an invitation, most notably Canada and Italy.[28] Outsiders continued to request inclusion for a number of years as the summit became an annual event, with appeals made by smaller European states including Luxembourg, Belgium, Ireland, and Denmark, as well as Australia.[29] Notably, those seeking inclusion did so by mobilising their diplomatic corps (as is detailed further in the following chapters). Outsiders did not appeal to international law or threaten to wage war; rather, they mobilised their diplomats.[30]

The club also repeatedly denied entry to outsiders on the grounds that doing so would jeopardise the informality and intimacy of the summit. The club excluded outsiders in order to keep the group small (and therefore effective). Giscard was particularly adamant on not letting anyone but the original G5 countries into the group on these grounds. This was most clearly articulated in objecting to Canada's inclusion, wherein he stated that increased membership would reduce the informality and flexibility and would increase the difficulty in 'declining the claims to participation from still additional countries; especially in Europe, and from international organisations like the OECD.'[31] In objecting to the participation of the European Community, Giscard likewise argued 'that further additions were likely to destroy the informality of these meetings.'[32] It is worthwhile to note here that Giscard not only objected on the grounds that the inclusion of more actors in this particular case would threaten the efficacy of the meetings, but also objected to the possibility of a non-state actor having the same standing as a sovereign state, threatening that '[i]f the view was taken that the Commission had to attend, by right, he would not himself go.'[33]

The pragmatic imperative to keep summits small has endured throughout G-summitry's history. Sherpas continue to lament the extent to which summits have expanded far beyond the small gatherings they were envisaged to be.[34] The 2009 L'Aquila G8 summit was popularly regarded as being the most extreme example of this, being described as 'an absolute circus' with the G8, the Outreach 5 (O5), thirteen other guest countries, ten international organisations, and civil society invited.[35] The Canadian government, who hosted the following summit, purposely designed their Muskoka G8 summit to halt this trend and 'strip the summit back to what it was.'[36] For this reason the Canadian government invited only the G8 heads of government and the EU, much angering those actors whom had become accustomed to inclusion, including representatives of the UN, international financial institutions (IFIs), and civil society. The continued imperative to keep the club small remains as it was in 1975 – to ensure that the club is effective. This is particularly important for the G7 who lack representative legitimacy. It is only by being effective that they can maintain some – however marginal – claim to their special status.[37] Sherpas often state that the biggest threat to the G20's survival is that it will be unable to reach meaningful consensus decisions because the club has become too large.[38] Scholarship on the G20 also focuses on this trade-off between the size of the membership and the legitimacy that it confers and the efficacy of the group.

The point to emphasise here is that pragmatism is a – if not *the* – guiding principle for determining the composition of G-summitry. Outsiders, despite a potential ability to functionally contribute to the club and/or be potentially worthy of inclusion by virtue of achieved characteristics, were excluded on these grounds (as is detailed in the following chapter). This has the twin effect of maintaining the status of insiders as (i) no additional members mean that the prestige derived from inclusion in the group is not diluted and (ii) the continuance of a smaller group may increase the likelihood of the club being effective, and thereby maintains its claim to the right of special status. Conversely, this pragmatic exclusion prevents the upward mobility of outsiders whom otherwise might be expected to be in the club.

This is distinctly different from the Family of Civilised Nations and the great powers, as in neither of these groups was the exclusion of an actor whom otherwise was judged to be suitable for inclusion denied entry for reasons of pragmatic expediency (though they were excluded for other reasons, including abject racism). With the great powers, excluding a power of sufficient heft and systematic import could actually threaten the survivability of the club and the society as a whole. As a primarily diplomatic institution, however, G-summitry does close off opportunities for rising (or risen) outsiders as, in the case of this club, the larger its composition, the potentially less effective it is at achieving its function.

Precedence

The second mobility dampener in G-summitry that renders it more closed is the diplomatic norm of precedence. Much of the composition of the club can be explained as a result of the nature of diplomacy, in which precedence is central for ensuring continuity and order. This is a function of diplomacy's inherently conservative nature, necessarily concerned with maintaining the *status quo*, unless ordered otherwise by political masters.[39]

Precedence is a shrewd means of exclusion because it depersonalises the decision to exclude, placing the responsibility on a norm rather than as a decision made by an actor (or group of actors). In G-summitry, questions of closure can be politically costly for a host leader, owing to the offence taken by the excluded. Giscard's decision to exclude Canada from Rambouillet in 1975 was damaging the relationship between France and Canada, and between Giscard and Trudeau personally.[40] As is detailed in Chapter 5, in 2010 Korea expelled the Netherlands from the G20 as an invited guest, which was convenient for Nicolas Sarkozy who would be the next summit host at the 2011 G20 Cannes summit. Sarkozy was under pressure to reduce the number of Europeans around the table in order to fend off critiques of European over-representation. He did not want to have to be the one to take the decision to exclude a fellow European owing to the difficulties this could yield within the EU.[41] Korea's decision to exclude the Netherlands from the Seoul summit provided Sarkozy with a precedence-based reason not to include the Netherlands.

The same holds true for contemplation of revisions to the club's membership. One of the G20's founders, Paul Martin, described it as a 'Pandora's box that no leader in their right mind would try to open.'[42] Revisiting membership subjects the club to bids for inclusion that it would likely have to turn down and so cause offence to the excluded, which comes with political costs. It is less costly to appeal to precedence. For this reason that the composition of the G20 did not change when it was elevated to the leaders' level in 2008.[43] This holds for the mass addition of invitees to the summit too. For example, in crafting the invitation list for the Kananaskis summit in 2002 the Canadian hosts had to decide which African countries to include as invitees. The Canadian Sherpa, Robert Fowler, decided to rely on precedence as the strategy to craft the invitation list so as to cause minimal offence to the excluded and provide a clear rationale with which to confront bids for inclusion, and so he decided to invite the New Economic Partnership for African Development (NEPAD) framers.[44] Despite "lobbying from all of Africa and the rest of the G7 to let others in," the Canadians held the line according to this rationale.[45]

More significantly, precedence allows for actors whose relative rank has fallen to remain in the club. There are more Europeans in the club than states from any other region. At first glance this seems to suggest collectivist closure, but it is not. Rather, the continued plurality of Europeans in the group is better explained as being a result of the club being governed by individualist closure and being one in which precedence is a central force. As Europeans had the advantage of having a head start industrialisation, they used that advantage to structure order (and the closure game that maintains it) to their benefit. The group is composed disproportionately by those who were first to industrialise during 'the global transformation' and so were able to grow and position their economies to be larger and more systematically significant than others.[46] They need not rely on collectivist exclusion to protect their position, as their structural advantage in the economic system gives them a seat at the table based on individualist criteria, and as the force of precedence keeps them there even as incumbents' relative rank might decline. Despite original club members no longer being undisputedly larger economies than others, they remain in the top-tier group. G7 members have not maintained the relative economic power that they enjoyed in 1975. Within only five years both China and Brazil had displaced Italy to make it ranked eighth in 1980. By the time the G20 was established at the ministerial level in 1999, India had achieved the rank of being the seventh largest economy.[47] Despite club members' declining rank, their status was unaffected. This was particularly so for Italy and Canada. Indeed, Canada has never ranked as a top-seven economy and Italy has not been worthy of the distinction since 1980. They were able to maintain their spots because of precedence. As a result, having gained inclusion they could not lose it.

The same could be said of actors whose continued presence in the club detracts from the legitimacy of the club, as is the case with the predominance of Western states in G-summitry. Whether the argument about the unsuitability of their membership is articulated in power-political terms of no longer meeting the economic power criterion, or in normative terms of unfairly over-representing the developed, industrialised West, the point remains the same that precedence prevents incumbents from easily being kicked out of the club. This is especially disadvantageous to outsiders who want into the club but are in the same geographic region as the plurality of insiders – namely, other Western states (and, more specifically, Western European states). The club is reluctant to include other Europeans as doing so detracts from the club's already shaky legitimacy. The club could fend off critiques of its illegitimacy by reducing the number of Europeans in the group, but it is unable to do so by virtue of precedence.[48] As such, the best it can do is not further increase the number of Europeans in the club, an imperative which drove closure in the early years of the G7 when smaller European states were clamouring for a seat at the table, and in the formation of G20 at the ministerial level and in its later elevation to the leaders' level.[49] States that otherwise meet individualist criteria for inclusion – whether it be economic size in the G7 or systematic significance in the G20 – are thus denied entry because of the twin effect of precedence and the need for representative legitimacy. The Czech Republic, Switzerland, Poland, Spain, and the Netherlands all sought inclusion in the club but were thus excluded. The latter three, in terms of economic rank, would be expected to be in the club if economic heft were the sole entry criterion. The norm requiring contemporary governance groups to have – at least nominally – fair(er) geographic and cultural representation thus actually serves to exclude actors who might otherwise be included in a purely individualist system which lacks a precedence as a mobility dampener.

Precedence is thus one significant way in which, in the absence of collectivist safeguards to potential losses of status, insiders protect their positions.[50] The system is thus not purely individualist and meritocratic. However, it is not purely so because of collectivist elements, but because diplomatic norms underpin its operation and are particularly critical given the absence of any formal membership rules.[51]

Credentialism

Social theorists, Collins chief among them, have pointed to credentialism as a significant way of ordering individualist societies.[52] Credentials are achieved characteristics which signal the competence of an actor, and testing them is – at least ostensibly – a meritocratic way of ascertaining the suitability of an actor for inclusion in a group. The most evident domestic analogy is the use of academic degrees to indicate the suitability of an individual for employment.

Credentialism features in each of the status groups under consideration here, signalling the suitability of an actor for admission. They are the entry criteria that insiders set and outsiders attempt to achieve, as is detailed in the following chapters. Credentialism does not work in the same way in all of the clubs, however. The way credentialism works in G-summitry renders it less fair to outsiders than it does in the Family of Civilised Nations or the Great Powers' clubs. In this dimension too, G-summitry is less open than the other clubs.

The Standard of Civilisation served as a relatively clear list of the credentials that an outsider needed to achieve to gain entry into Western international society as it globalised. What is significant about the Standard in the context of the current argument is that it was applied both to the club's insiders and outsiders.[53] While the notion of the Family of Civilised Nations ceased and its accompanying Standard of Civilisation was no longer in use by the 1920s, implicitly the key dimensions of the Standard still governed a division amongst states such that an actor could be kicked out of the club if it failed to uphold the membership criteria. Bolshevik Russia and Nazi Germany serve as prime examples. In an earlier period when the Standard was in use, the removal of smaller Germanic and Italian principalities from international society denotes their failure to meet the legal-collectivist criterion for inclusion.[54]

Likewise, states that no longer met the criteria for the status as a great power were kicked out of the club. 'A great power,' Wight remarks, 'does not die in its bed.'[55] Great powers have their membership credentials tested in war. This is not surprising given that the entry criteria for the Great Powers' club are so predominantly based on military might.[56] The loss of status, like its achievement, is often a gradual process such that pointing to a specific event or battle cannot denote the moment of an actor's exit from the club but does serve as a useful proxy.[57] Status may be lost by defeat – such as Sweden's loss to Russia in the Great Northern War in 1721 or Spain's loss to Napoleon in the Peninsula War in 1808 – or by Pyrrhic victory – such as Holland's defeat of Louis IX's France in 1672 or Britain's defeat of Nazi Germany in 1945 – after which the victor becomes dependent on other, greater powers.[58] Conversely, a successful display of a power's credentials in conflict either verifies its position as a great power or confirms a state's entry into the club. The relatively modest contribution of Austria-Hungary to fighting the Boxer Rebellion exemplifies two aspects of credentialism in the Great Powers' club. First, Austria-Hungary contributed military assets at all signifies the importance of contributing just to stay in the club. Austria-Hungary had no direct interest in China and comparatively few resources to send, but did so nonetheless because doing so signalled their status. Second, as a falling power, contributing to the club's cause preserved the state's membership, thus delaying its exit from the group. They were, in a sense, continuing to pay their membership dues.

In G-summitry, credentialism is exercised in a particular way that serves as a means of protecting the status positions of existing members. Only the credentials of aspirant members are tested, while existing members' credentials, as they relate to the club's functional purpose, are not. This uneven application of credentialism acts as a mobility dampener. Credentialism in G-summitry is thus distinctly different than it is in the other clubs. As above, the relative decline of the economic importance of G7 club members, particularly Canada and Italy, has not resulted in their dismissal. The force of precedence is here again evident and reveals how G-summitry, rooted in the diplomatic institution, is relatively closed by virtue of this norm. Uneven credentialism prevents incumbents' suitability from being retested and so the force of precedence keeps them included. From the beginnings of G-summitry, Italy had been regarded as not contributing much to the club.[59] Unlike in the Great Powers' club, a lack of contribution does not provide the grounds for the country's dismissal. In contrast, as the cases in the following chapters demonstrate, the credentials of aspirant, ascendant outsiders were scrutinised considerably and a failure to meet the entry criteria meant exclusion from the club. This uneven application of credentialism thus dampens mobility in both directions. It prevents the falling powers from loosing status because their credentials are not tested. It conversely limits or slows the rise of ascendant actors by scrutinising their credentials.

Even the apparently obvious counterexample of Russia's expulsion from the G8 in March 2014 actually lends evidence to the argument advanced here. Russia's economic credentials for admission had always been shaky at best. Indeed, the US Treasury was dead set against Russia's inclusion for this reason.[60] Even once admitted to the club, as their relative economic rank declined, they nonetheless remained (though, as is detailed in Chapter 6, as second-tier members excluded from finance discussions). It was only after the annexation of Crimea that Russia was ejected. There are two important dimensions that this highlights: first, to the extent that the membership is based on economic rank, Russia was not held to the standard. It was a violation of international society's core value of the inviolability of sovereign territory and the violation of international law that served as the impetus for Russia's expulsion, not the testing of Russia's economic suitability for the club. Second, this case points to the import of not examining status games in any particular club in isolation of one another. Russia's taking of Crimea is best as understood as an assertive geopolitical move as part of a bid to secure the status of a great power, a move that came at the cost of membership in G-summitry. Whether such a trade is worthwhile depends on the character of international society at a particular time. If it is one in which the great power institution is dominant, then this might be a wise status move; if it is one in which international law, sovereignty, diplomacy, and/or the market are dominant, it likely is not.

G7 members met in The Hague on the sidelines of the Third Nuclear Security Summit to discuss Russia's possible expulsion.[61] In advance of the meeting, Canada was most vocal about expelling Russia from the club, with Italy taking the opposing position.[62] The language in the sixth paragraph of the meeting's communiqué is noteworthy as it points to the ambiguity of how inclusion works in this club with no explicitly defined membership rules.[63] Technically, the G7 neither suspended nor expelled Russia from the G8, but rather suspended themselves from the G8, "[w]e will suspend our participation in the G-8 until Russia changes course and the environment comes back to where the G-8 is able to have a meaningful discussion…" Russian Foreign Minister Sergei Lavrov captured the essence of how membership in G-summitry effectively works in response to the suspension, alluding to the club's grounding in the diplomatic institution, its emphasis on informality and precedence, "[t]he G8 is an informal club. No one hands out membership cards and no one can be kicked out of it."[64]

The opportunities for the testing of credentials in G-summitry are also fewer than is the case with the other clubs. International conferences have typically served as proxies for identifying an actor's inclusion in the Family of Civilised Nations and wars have served the same purpose with respect to the Great Powers' club.[65] In the case of the Family of Civilised Nations, however, participation in international conferences is not the sole opportunity for an actor to demonstrate its suitability owing to the fact that there are more dimensions to the Standard than just diplomatic engagement. Japan's 'just' conduct and victory in the Sino-Japanese War and the Russo-Japanese War just as well signalled the state's suitability for entry, as did the Ottoman Empire's participation in the Treaty of Paris in 1856.[66] Different dimensions of an actor's adherence to the Standard could be tested by way of different primary institutions. There were thus multiple avenues and opportunities through which an actor could have had its credentials tested, owing to the multidimensional nature of the Standard.

This is less the case with other status groups. There are fewer opportunities for testing credentials in the Great Powers' club because the credentials required for inclusion are so predominantly focused on military power and its exercise. It is only in war that the recognition of great power status can be won, lost, or affirmed. A power may rise or decline in interim periods but it is only in war that its suitability could actually be tested. The composition of the Great Powers' club may then change depending on whether or not there is a change in the distribution of power as a result of conflict, with those included in the club being those powers of sufficient size that as a concert they can provide the club's functional role of providing a stable order. With economic power being the predominant criterion for inclusion in G-summitry, it is similarly the case that there are comparatively fewer opportunities for inclusion, as it is only at particular historical moments where the club is unable to accomplish its functional aim of ensuring international economic stability that the club is amenable to change.[67] Even at those moments in which club membership may be revisited, it is done so in a way that is less open than the Great Powers' club because incumbency is protected by the diplomatic norm of precedence. G-summitry has thus changed very little since its inception in 1975 – surprisingly little given the breath of changes in the global economy in the ensuing forty years.

Mobility dampeners are thus means other than exclusion barriers for maintaining a *status quo*. They are not overt means of closure; rather, like the ostensibly achievable closure barriers discussed in the following chapter, they are a means of achieving closure by stealth.

Notes

1 Beeson and Bell (2017); Buzan (2004a); Holsti (2004); Reus-Smit (1999); Schouenborg (2011).
2 Buzan (2014); Reus-Smit (1999).
3 Reus-Smit (1999, p. 15).
4 Buzan, *From International to World Society*, 2004, 162.
5 Reus-Smit (1999, p. 14).
6 C.f. Buzan, B. (2004). Primary Institutions in International Society. In *From International to World Society?: English School Theory and the Social Structure of Globalisation* (pp. 161–204). Cambridge University Press, 167.
7 Bull, H. (1977). *The Anarchical Society: A Study of Order in World Politics* (4th edition). Basingstoke: Palgrave Macmillan, 102.
8 Bull, *The Anarchical Society*, 1977, 134–136.
9 Ibid., 163–166.
10 Ibid., 180–181.
11 Ibid., 199–200. Of course, later generations of English School scholars have reformed Bull's formulation considerably. See especially: Buzan, Primary Institutions in International Society, 2004.

12 Buzan (2004b, p. 187). On human rights: Clark (2007); Donnelly (1998); Towns (2014); democracy: Clark (2009); Hobson (2014); Mayall (2000); Navari (2013); Stivachtis (2006); capitalism: Bowden (2009); Bowden and Seabrooke (2006); Fidler (2000); Gong (2002); environmentalism: Falkner (2012); Falkner and Buzan (2017); Palmujoki (2013); Reus-Smit (1996); liberalism: Fidler (2001); Mozaffari (2001); and economics and finance: Gong (2002).
13 Keene, E. (2014). The Standard of 'Civilisation' the Expansion Thesis and the 19th-Century International Social Space. *Millennium, 42* (3), 1–23.
14 Buzan, Primary Institutions in International Society, 2004. Buzan (2004b).
15 Kissinger and Sonnenfeldt to Porter, 8 November 1975, in *Presidential Letter to Prime Minister Trudeau*.
16 Callaghan and Giscard, 18 February 1977, in *Record of a Telephone Conversation between Chancellor Schmidt and the Prime Minister*; UK Government, 25 March 1977.
17 Martin, P. (2013). The G20: From Global Crisis Responder to Steering Committee. In A. F. Cooper, J. Heine, & R. Thakur (Eds.), *Oxford Handbook of Modern Diplomacy* (1st edition, pp. 729–744). Oxford: OUP.
18 Armstrong, R. (1991). *Summits: A Sherpa's Eye View*. Leeds: University of Leeds Review, 43.
19 Greenwald to Kissinger, 30 October 1975 in *Reluctance of the Member States to Assume Community Budgetary Obligations Signals Setbacks in EC Solidarity*; Hillebrand to Kissinger, 25 September 1975, in *Conservation with Chancellor Schmidt*; Wright (1976).
20 Jönsson, C., & Hall, M. (2005). *Essence of Diplomacy*. Basingstoke; Hampshire; New York: Palgrave Macmillan, Print; Nicolson, H. (1988). *Diplomacy*. Washington, DC: Institute for the Study of Diplomacy.
21 Ikenberry, G. J. (2009). *After Victory: Institutions, Strategic Restraint, and the Rebuilding of Order after Major Wars*. Princeton, NJ: Princeton University Press; Keohane, R. O., & Nye, J. (1977). *Power & Interdependence* (4th edition). Boston, MA: Pearson; Sharp, P. (2009). *Diplomatic Theory of International Relations*. Cambridge; New York: Cambridge University Press.
22 Putnam, R. D., & Bayne, N. (1984). *Hanging Together: The Seven-Power Summits*. London: Heinemann for the Royal Institute of International Affairs. Putnam and Bayne (1984).
23 Interview: Shultz, G. Interview by Telephone, 5 September 2012.
24 Ibid.
25 Ibid.
26 UK Foreign and Commonwealth Office, 12 February 1976, in *The Economic Summit Conference at Rambouillet: 15–17 November 1975*. It's unclear when exactly the interview occurred. Bayne refers to the idea having been reported in the press on the 8th and 9th of July, 1975 (Bayne 1975), later references to the interview state that it was on the 9th of July (UK Foreign and Commonwealth Office 1976). Unfortunately, the original transcript of the interview has been lost.
27 Ingersoll to US Embassy, 10 July 1975, in *Giscard Favors Summit of Industrialized Nations*.
28 Callaghan to Ford, 1 June 1976; Enders to Kissinger, 26 November 1976, in *Canada and Next Economic Summit*; Ford to Callaghan, 5 May 1976; Ford to Callaghan, 30 May 1976; Ford to Callaghan, 31 May 1976; Ford to Callaghan, 1 June 1976; Ford to Callaghan, 5 June 1976; Greenwald to Kissinger, 30 October 1975 in *Reluctance of the Member States to Assume Community Budgetary Obligations Signals Setbacks in EC Solidarit*; Hillebrand to Kissinger, 25 September 1975 and 18 November 1975, in *German Press Comment on Rambouillet Summit*; Hodgson, 21 October 1975, in *Economic Summit*; Kissinger to Volpe, 31 July

1975, in *Rumor's Complaint about Four Power Luncheon*; Kissinger to Volpe, 1 August 1975, in *Italian Complaints about Rumors of Economic Meeting*; Kissinger to Sonnenfeldt, 25 September 1975, in *Proposed Economic Summit*; Kissinger to Volpe, 30 September 1975, in *Secretary's Meeting with Italian Foreign Minister Rumour;* Kissinger to Sonnenfeldt, 2 October 1975, in *Economic Summit*; Kissinger, 9 October 1975, in *Economic Summit*, Kissinger, 10 October 1975, in *Economic Summit*; Kissinger and Sonnenfeldt to Porter, 8 November 1975, in *Presidential Letter to Prime Minister Trudeau*; Morris to Kissinger, 7 August 1975, in *Proposed Five Power Economic Conference*; Porter to Kissinger, 10 November 1975, in *Presidential Letter to PM Trudeau*; Porter, 14 November 1975, in *GOC Views on Rambouillet Exclusion and Future*; Rush to Kissinger, 18 December 1975, in *French-Canadian Relations: Ups and Downs*; Sonnenfeldt and Ingersoll to US Ambassadors in London, Bonn, Rome, and Tokyo, 28 September 1975, in *Possible Economic Summit*, Sonnenfeldt and Ingersoll to US Ambassadors in London, Bonn, Rome, Tokyo, and Paris, 1 October 1975, *Possible Economic Summit*; Volpe to Kissinger, 29 July 1975, in *Possible Big Five Monetary Summit*; Volpe to Kissinger, 30 July 1975, in *Big Five Economic Directorate*; Volpe to Kissinger, 13 September 1975; Volpe to Kissinger, 13 September 1975, in *Press Reports On Colombo-Giscard D'Estaing Talks*.
29 On exclusion of smaller Europeans: Wright to Callaghan, 4 June 1976; on exclusion of Australia: Percival to Kissinger, 21 July 1976, in *Economic Topics in Prime Minister's Discussion with President*; Hunt to Callaghan, 29 May 1978, in *Bonn Summit*; Rose, 12 January 1979, *Guadelope: Follow-up Action*; Government of Australia, 11 August 1976, *Tokyo Economic Summit possible Australian participation*; Government of Australia, 23 October 1975, *Cabinet Minute*.
30 Luxembourg went so far as to send a formal diplomatic *demarche* to the US to protest their exclusion. Wright to Callaghan, 4 June 1976.
31 Kissinger and Sonnenfeldt to Porter, 8 November 1975, in *Presidential Letter to Prime Minister Trudeau*.
32 Callaghan and Giscard, 18 February 1977, in *Record of a Telephone Conversation between Chancellor Schmidt and the Prime Minister*; UK Government, 25 March 1977.
33 UK Government, 25 March 1977.
34 Interviews: Allan (2012); Aranda Bezaury (2012); Bayne (2012); Carin (2012); Cunliffe (2013); Edwards (2012); Fowler (2012); Harder (2012); Khatchadourian (2012); Kitajima (2012); Ramos (2012); Smith (2011). It should be noted that this was not necessarily judged as being a negative development. Gabriella Ramos, for example, stressed that the relatively open G20 architecture allows for the inclusion of IOs which brings additional efficacy, legitimacy, and representation to the club without having to increase formal state membership as much as would otherwise be necessary.
35 Interviews: Burnley J., Interview in Person, 30 January 2012; Edwards L., Interview by Skype and Telephone, 15 March 2012; Khatchadourian, R., Interview in Person, 8 February 2012; Rea J., Interview in Person, 9 February 2012.
36 Interviews: Edwards L., Interview by Skype and Telephone, 15 March 2012; Khatchadourian, R., Interview in Person, 8 February 2012.
37 Interviews: Anonymous Interview Subject 1.1; Rea J., Interview in Person, 9 February 2012.
38 Interviews: Aranda Bezaury (2012); Cunliffe (2013); Edwards (2012); Harder (2012); Smith (2011) Scholarship on the G20 also focuses on this trade-off between the size of the membership and the legitimacy that it confers and the efficacy of the group. See especially: Cooper, A. F., & Bradford, C. (2010). The G20 and the Post-Crisis Economic Order. *CIGI G20 Papers*, (3). Retrieved from www.cigionline.org/publications/2010/6/g20-and-post-crisis-economic-order;

Cooper, A. F. (2012). The G20 as the Global Focus Group: Beyond the Crisis Committee/Steering Committee Framework. *G20 Research Group*. Retrieved from www.g20.utoronto.ca/analysis/120619-cooper-focusgroup.html; Martin, *The G20: From Global Crisis Responder to Steering Committee*, 2013.
39 Neumann, I. B. (2007). "A Speech That the Entire Ministry May Stand For," Or: Why Diplomats Never Produce Anything New. *International Political Sociology*, *1* (2), 183–200; (2012). *At Home with the Diplomats: Inside a European Foreign Ministry* (1st edition). Cornell University Press.
40 Interview: Bayne N., Interview in Person, 9 October 2012.
41 Interview: Anonymous subject 1.1.
42 Interview: (Martin, 2012).
43 Interviews: Anonymous Interview Subject 1.1; Martin (2012); Summers L., Interview by Telephone and Skype, 23 Octoer 2012.
44 Interview: Fowler (2012).
45 Ibid. Only Algeria "played a spoiler role".
46 Buzan and Lawson (2015).
47 When the G20 was elevated to the leaders' level in 2008 India was ranked 4th.
48 As an invitee, it was easier – though still difficult for The Netherlands to lose its invitation to the G20. Ejecting a member is near impossible.
49 Interviews: Anonymous subject 1.1; Reyes Leon 2018 Martin (2012); Summers (2012); Hillebrand to Kissinger, 25 September 1975, in *Conservation with Chancellor Schmidt*; Morris to Kissinger, 7 August 1975, in *Proposed Five Power Economic Conference*; Wright to Callaghan, 4 June 1976.
50 In addition to the other mobility dampeners discussed in this chapter.
51 That is, not as concerns state actors. It is not purely so for non-state actors because of collectivist elements.
52 See: Collins, R. (1979). *Credential Society: An Historical Sociology of Education and Stratification*. New York: Academic Press Inc; Parkin, F. (1979). *Marxism and Class Theory: A Bourgeois Critique*. Taylor & Francis, 54–60.
53 Though not necessarily equally insiders were held to a lesser standard than outsiders. The general point holds, however, as insiders were nonetheless still measured against a standard and failing to meet it meant the possibility of being kicked out of the club.
54 C.f. Fazal, T. M. (2007). *State Death: The Politics and Geography of Conquest, Occupation, and Annexation*. Princeton, NJ: Princeton University Press; Spruyt, H. (1994). *The Sovereign State and Its Competitors: An Analysis of Systems Change*. Princeton, NJ: Princeton University Press.
55 Wight, M. (1946). *Power Politics*. London: Leicester University Press, 47. See also Bridge, F. R., & Bullen, R. (2005). *The Great Powers and the European States System 1814–1914*. London: Pearson Education, 7; Levy, J. S. (1984). *War in the Modern Great Power System: 1495–1975*. Kentucky: The University Press of Kentucky; Scott, H. M. (2006). *The Birth of a Great Power System: 1740–1815*. Longman Publishing Group.
56 Levy, *War in the Modern Great Power System*, 1984, 24; Modelski, G. (1972). *Principles of World Politics*. Free Press, 150.
57 Levy, *War in the Modern Great Power System*, 1984, 24; see also: Volgy, T. J., Corbetta, R., Grant, K. A., & Baird, R. G. (Eds.). (2011). *Major Powers and the Quest for Status in International Politics: Global and Regional Perspectives*. New York: Palgrave Macmillan; see also: Volgy, T. J., Corbetta, R., Rhamey Jr., P., Baird, R. G., & Grant, K. A. (2014). Status Considerations in International Politics and the Rise of Regional Powers. In T. V. Paul, D. Welch Larson, & W. C. Wohlforth (Eds.), *Status in World Politics* (pp. 58–84). New York: Cambridge University Press.
58 Wight, *Power Politics*, 1946, 48. Wight notes that great powers may also temporarily loose status after war.

52 *Institutions and mobility*

59 Hunt to Callaghan, 16 June 1976, in *Puerto Rico*.
60 Interview: Fauver, R., Interview by Skype, 16 July 2013.
61 Russian annexation of territory has been relevant to discussions of its suitability for membership since inclusion was first discussed by the club. Japan originally opposed Russian inclusion because of its annexation of the Kuril Islands. Oxenstierna, R. F. (1993). *The 1992 Group of Seven Summit and Its Impact on the Middle East* (R. Carleton & I. Cleland, Eds.). London: Gulf Centre for Strategic Studies, Limited, 18.
62 Canadian and Associated Press (2014, March 23); Stephen Harper calls for Russia to be booted from G8 as U.S. warns Vladimir Putin likely prepping for invasion. *National Post*. Retrieved from http://news.nationalpost.com/2014/03/23/stephen-harper-calls-for-russia-to-be-booted-from-g8-as-u-s-warns-vladimir-putin-likely-prepping-for-invasion/; Goodman, L.-A. (2014, March 24). Harper ready to urge G7 to go tougher on Vladimir Putin. *Global News*. Retrieved from http://globalnews.ca/news/1226245/harper-to-urge-g7-to-go-tougher-on-putin/; ITAR-TASS News Agency. Italy Calls for Preserving Present G8 format. Retrieved 27 July 2014, from http://en.itar-tass.com/world/725097; Lunn, S. (2014, March 23). Ukraine crisis: G7 leaders to hold summit in Brussels without Russia. *CBC News*. Retrieved from www.cbc.ca/1.2583636; Parry, T. (2014, March 22). Stephen Harper says he'll push for Russia's expulsion from the G8. *CBC News*. Retrieved from www.cbc.ca/1.2583034.
63 See: President, European Council (2014, March 24). The Hague declaration. Retrieved from www.consilium.europa.eu/uedocs/cms_data/docs/pressdata/en/ec/141855.pdf.
64 De Clercq, G. (2014, March 24). Russia's Lavrov says no problem if G8 does not meet. *Reuters*. Retrieved from www.reuters.com/article/2014/03/24/us-ukraine-crisis-lavrov-g-idUSBREA2N1D820140324.
65 C.f. Levy, *War in the Modern Great Power System*, 1984, 24; Neumann, I. B. (2011). Entry into International Society Reconceptualised: The Case of Russia. *Review of International Studies, 37* (2), 466.
66 Clark, I. (1989). *The Hierarchy of States: Reform and Resistance in the International Order*. Cambridge; New York: Cambridge University Press, 95; Gong, G. (1984). *The Standard of Civilization in International Society*. Oxford: Oxford University Press, 32 and 107; Holbraad, C. (1970). *Concert of Europe: German and British International Theory, 1815–1914*. Harlow: Prentice Hall Press, 2; Okagaki, T. T. (2013). *The Logic of Conformity: Japan's Entry into International Society*. Toronto: University Press of Toronto, 2; Neumann, I. B., & Welsh, J. M. (1991). The Other in European Self-Definition: An Addendum to the Literature on International Society. *Review of International Studies, 17* (4), 327–348, 343.
67 Though, such a claim may be subject to observation error, the club may not have been around long enough to say with especially great confidence that this comparative claim is true.

4 Exclusion

Introduction

Insiders erect exclusionary closure barriers to secure material and ideational advantages for themselves. Moreover, as the previous chapter detailed, they may also rely upon mobility dampeners to try to safeguard their privileged position while maintaining the subordinate or marginalised positions of others. Employed together, closure barriers and Mobility Dampeners constitute an exclusive grouping's closure strategies to maintain a *status quo* in which they are the dominant and privileged actors. This chapter examines the strategies other than dampeners that insiders use to accomplish this, being principally concerned with (i) the implications of what it means for closure to be achieved according to a particular set of strategies rather than others and (ii) what this means for how relatively open or closed an international society is at a given point in time. This chapter also provides the empirical justification for reforming closure theory's typology of closure rules, presenting them here as follows: Unachievable, Achievable, and Ostensibly Achievable.

What follows draws four primary conclusions. First, looking primarily at the border between international society and the wider international domain, this chapter finds that international society's closure rules are predominantly functionalist and individualist in nature. This is significant because this mode of closure made Western European international society's globalisation possible and ensured that new entrants necessarily contributed to the society's management and perpetuation. As the rules are also predominantly individualist in nature, this further allows for the system to be characterised as being relatively open, as it means that outsiders, for the most part, are able to achieve the required entry criteria. This is not to say, though, that they enter as equals and that inequalities in status do not persist. Indeed, they do profoundly, and the remainder of this book explores this.

Collectivism, however, is present at the very heart of the closure system. Its role is central in giving the international domain its broad shape and character by making the possession of sovereignty the primary closure rule of the system. This legal-collectivism reproduces international society as a homogenous club of *states*. A second conclusion in this chapter is that international society's system of closure has a tandem structure.[1] Legal-collectivism serves as the international domain's primary closure rule while functional-individualist entry criteria serve as secondary closure rules. Secondary rules guide the positioning of an actor after the primary rule has broadly assigned that actor as being either inside or outside of international society. Additionally, because the system is structured in such a way that it has a collectivist primary closure rule and functionalist secondary rules, it ensures that any expansion or opening of the club involving non-state actors necessarily involves a subordinate and marginal inclusion of these outsiders. This is how networked expansion is achieved while the core of the international system remains a club. This is likewise further explored in the following chapters.

Third, this analysis finds the closure barriers erected in international society to be generally open. The means by which dominant insiders exclude others from groups do not provide a complete explanation of closure in the system. This suggests that the system is shaped by more than just exclusion strategies, prompting us to examine entry and incorporation strategies in the following two chapters (and mobility dampeners in the previous one).

Fourth, in terms of exclusion barriers, G-summitry is a more closed group than the great powers and the Family of Civilised Nations. This is counter-intuitive given the extent to which principles of representative legitimacy underpin G-summitry, particularly in the G20 with its membership in part being determined by a need for legitimacy derived from regional and cultural representation and, as it is for the G7, a domestic liberal political system being a criterion upon which an actor may be excluded.[2] Indeed, as is argued below, it is in fact partly because of the need for legitimacy derived from geographic and cultural representation that contemporary G-summitry is a relatively more closed club than its historical antecedents.

Closure

Unachievable criteria

Closure in international society is predominantly governed according to functionalist-individualist rules, rendering international society a relatively open system. However, collectivism forges the broad division in the international domain between the inside and outside of international society. Legal-collectivism, rooted in the principle of sovereignty, creates the division between state and non-state actors, the effect of which is that full membership in international society, and consequently all status groups within it, are restricted to one type of actor based on that actor's identity as a sovereign state. It does not matter how functionally useful another type of actor might be, its very identity renders its inclusion in the society of states impermissible.

The Standard of Civilisation set the criteria for entry into the Family of Civilised Nations. While, as is detailed in the following section, the Standard was predominantly comprised of individualist criteria, the major collectivist element, however, necessitated the possession of sovereignty and had the effect of ensuring the homogeneity of international society as being a club solely of states.[3] Paul Keal traces this criterion's roots to the shift from natural to positive international law, while others, notably Haldén and Keene, focus the increase in treaty-making capacities.[4] According to Keal, individuals could be included in international society according to natural law, but "the more that international society came to be defined as a body of rules to regulate relations between states, the more it excluded individuals, sub-state groups, and political communities that did not meet European criteria for statehood."[5] Gerry Simpson echoes this observation exactly in noting that

> "[t]he whole idea of statehood and sovereignty operates as a discourse of exclusion and hierarchy. Equality is possessed by sovereigns and states are universally subject to international law. The state has monopolised international legal life to the exclusion of other forms of political organisation."[6]

Jönsson and Hall take the argument a step further to argue that it is via diplomacy that this delegitimisation of all other forms of political entity from having standing in the international domain occurs.[7]

A key role of diplomacy as a primary institution within international society is to carry out the function of reproducing a particular kind of society (usually, but not always, the *status quo*).[8] For Bull, the first universal goal of international society is 'the preservation of the system and society of states itself.'[9] Diplomacy's symbolic function is to reify and give tangible expression to this international society. Indeed, in lamenting the decline of the solidarist international society Bull remarked that 'the symbolic role of the diplomatic mechanism may for this reason be more important [than the other primary institutions].'[10] This is not to say that diplomacy necessarily reproduces a states-only international society, but rather to emphasise that diplomacy is the institution through which the recognition of others as either belonging to the club or not is conducted. Moreover, diplomacy not only constitutes actors' subject positions, but it in part (re)produces their identities, interests, and dispositions via socialisation. Diplomacy is thus not a passive institution in the closure game. It does not just recognise an actor's belonging (or not), but it actively conditions their suitability.[11] The diplomatic institution thus plays a central role in the reproduction of order in terms of both position and disposition.

It has not always been the case that non-state actors were unable to traverse the border and join international society. It was only with the calcification of the Standard of Civilisation that the legal-collectivist criterion became unachievable, thus closing the door to other types of actors. During the early formation of the European international society and its expansion elsewhere, some non-state entities could gain recognition as states or as being sufficiently state-like that they could gain entry.[12] There was thus a window of opportunity for some actors to achieve this criterion, and thus, this legitimist closure rule was not always perfectly unachievable. It was, however, nearly so, as only a small subset of actors were sufficiently state-like to transform into states in the Western European image, such as dynastic monarchies such as Siam.[13] Okagaki describes such entities as 'functional equivalents' that 'could be remoulded and recreated.'[14] While the means by which actors achieved entry is discussed in the following chapter, what is necessary to stress here is not how they achieved this criterion, but that (i) it was necessary that they do so and (ii) during this period of time, it was *possible* to do so. Legal-collectivism has thus been central to the Standard for as long as it governed international society's border, and the sovereignty which it demands was not always an unachievable criterion, despite being so now.

Reshaping a polity to fit the Western European mould was necessary for overcoming this primary closure rule but insufficient for actually achieving sovereign status. Sovereignty must be recognised by others, not just unilaterally declared. As Western international society globalised, incumbent club members were in the position to grant or deny membership based on this recognition and, as such, could maintain their privilege by virtue of having the monopoly power of recognition.[15] Antony Anghie argues that the recognition of outsiders 'was about affirming the power of the European states to claim sovereignty, to reinforce their authority to make such determinations, and consequently, to make sovereignty a possession that they could then proceed to dispense, deny, create, or grant partially.'[16] Inclusion does not mean equality. Unequal relations of power persist and, even after a former outsider has been made an insider, the primary collectivist closure rule played a significant part in maintaining this unequal relationship. As such, collectivist closure reproduces hierarchy in both contexts of international closure: between the inside and outside of international society and within international society.

Legal-collectivist exclusion is not only achieved through diplomatic recognition (or a lack thereof). Power-political moves made by the club concurrently bolstered this type of closure, as is exemplified through the club's imposition of unequal treaties on outsiders, backed up either the threat or use of force. As with questions of recognition, insiders were not passive in merely setting the closure criterion but actively denied the achievement of full sovereignty. While the club required territorial sovereignty as the primary condition for entry, at the same time they denied its full achievement through the imposition of unequal treaties on potentially ascendant actors.[17] In the case of China, these were most strictly imposed after the cessation of conflict. The Treaty of Nanking, the first of the unequal treaties, was forced by the British on the Chinese after the Opium War. The treaty ceded Hong Kong to British and forced the opening of five treaty ports – Amoy, Canton, Foochow, Ningpo, and Shanghai – thus ending the Canton system through which China could control its trade with the West. Subsequent treaties signed with China, Japan, and other East Asian countries granted extraterritoriality to the club members' citizens, as well as opened further treaty ports. The articles of The Boxer Protocol, signed after China's defeat in the Boxer Rebellion, exemplifies well the degree to which unequal treaties undermined China's ability to claim itself as being fully sovereign.[18] Among other articles, the protocol granted the victors the right to occupation in twelve Chinese regions; exclusive control over the Legation Quarters in Beijing, which excluded Chinese nationals from residing in the area and gave the victors the right to defend the territory; and mandated the punishments for leaders of the rebellion including execution, exile, and life imprisonment. Actual conflict did not feature in forcing Japan and Siam to sign unequal treaties, but the threat of the use of force motivated their acquiescence to them, particularly as they had the example of China to learn from and know that it would be as costly, if not more so, for them to resist as China had.[19] Overturning unequal treaties were a priority for those vying for full membership in international society as their conditions so obviously – indeed, legally – marked the subordination of those upon whom they were imposed.

The following chapter explores how this was achieved as part of ascendant actors' mimicry strategies. What is important to note about unequal treaties in the context of the current discussion is that they are emblematic of how the club used its power-political advantage to make it more difficult for outsiders to overcome exclusion and to achieve any sort of equality even if they nominally made it into the club. International society thus not only set difficult closure barriers but defended them through military and diplomatic means, undermining the ability of outsiders to achieve entry. For outsiders in the closure games, the odds were never in their favour.

Whereas collectivism formerly excluded political entities that club insiders viewed as not possessing sovereignty, the same means now excludes the entire array of non-state actors. A constant refrain by state representatives about the position of non-state actors in G-summitry is to cite their lack of sovereignty, and the political consensus surrounding the legitimacy of representation that it implies, as the justification for their marginalisation.[20] This is particularly the case for civil society actors. While this is obvious and intuitive, it points to degree to which legal-collectivism has naturalised as the primary closure rule ordering the international domain. It is an unquestioned social fact that is so discursively successful that it is "virtually impossible to think outside it."[21] Indeed, this discursive construction is successfully – or hegemonically – dominant such that those who are marginalised and subordinated by it accept it as a *de facto* reality.[22] This was particularly evident in a response given by a European Union (EU) sous-Sherpa when asked about the EU presidents' privileged place alongside heads of state governments at the G7 and G20, 'there are nation-states sitting around the table and the EU. We have a high level of integration, but we're not yet a nation-state. So you have to behave accordingly at these meetings.'[23] The Organisation for Economic Cooperation and Development (OECD) Sherpa expressed much the same sentiment, stressing multiple times that international organisations (IOs) inform the policymaking process but 'unlike countries [they] have no say in political decision making.'[24] Despite the greater degree of inclusion afforded to the EU and, to a lesser extent, the OECD, their non-sovereign status informs the behaviours and perceptions of its representatives who accept and perform their subject positions.

International non-governmental organisations (INGOs) are doubly excluded by virtue of collectivism. As above, their legal status as non-sovereigns renders them impermissible as members. More significantly, collectivist stereotypes about civil society further justify their exclusion. They are often ascribed by state representatives as being disorganised and narrowly interested and, as such, as being unsuitable for inclusion. As Chapter 5 details, INGOs engage a banding strategy in a large part to overcome this stereotype. Despite many years of engagement with the G-summitry process, the idea that advocacy groups lack the capacity to contribute effectively endures. Civil society was granted a greater degree of inclusion at the 2012 Los Cabos G20 summit than they had ever before been granted. A Mexican sous-Sherpa relayed that one of the primary motivations for granting unprecedented inclusion to civil society at Los Cabos was to give civil society an opportunity to build "the technical capacity and lobbying expertise that comes from experience."[25] Particularly revealing was the sous-Sherpa's comparison of civil society with the B20, an entity created only two years prior at the 2010 Toronto summit, and the Think20, a new initiative in its first year,

> Who are the B20? This is a network that has met before, they're existing, having representation and legitimacy, having the capacity to organise themselves…They're entities that are already there. There is no core entity to civil society.… not one cupola, no unified body. If they were like this, we would have taken care of them,

he continued, "Mexico has opened spaces for them to build this body, build a single platform like with the B20 or Think20."[26] This echoes a comment relayed by the French sous-Sherpa responsible for civil society engagement to civil society representatives a year earlier at the Cannes summit stating that "[we] know what to do with business and the unions, but we don't know what to do with you guys."[27] Civil society was almost entirely cut out of the 2010 Toronto summitry process because "Canadian civil society wasn't big enough; they were non-players with no policy sophistication."[28]

As Chapter 5 details, INGOs, particularly the large advocacy organisations such as Oxfam, ActionAid, and ONE have no shortage of in-house capacity to engage in this policy environment; moreover, through organisations like Bond and InterAction, advocacy groups band together as a sector to engage in the summitry process. This ascription of civil society as a category of actor thus serves to marginalise these actors, regardless of the individual attributes of any particular advocacy group. That other non-state groups, like the B20 and Think20, are held as exemplars to emulate reveals the degree to which this collectivist stereotyping is particularly aimed at INGOs. That said, like any stereotype, the ascribed characteristic may have some degree of grounding in reality. InterAction's Director for International Advocacy conceded that 'global civil society is disorganised – advocacy groups don't get along with the protest groups and NGOs fight each other on who's more legitimate.'[29] The following chapter examines this in further detail.

Legal-collectivism is thus how the international society of states maintains its central position in global politics, keeping 'world society' at its margins.[30] This collectivist closure is near impossible to overcome in contemporary international society – only a revolutionary shift wherein sovereignty would no longer serve as a primary institution could conditions change such that more than one type of actor could be included, yielding a society could resemble that of pre-Modern Europe, prior to the sovereign state's edging out of all other types of polities from its international society. While this primary, collectivist closure rule is a blunt and sweeping means of exclusion that necessarily subordinates the plurality of types of actors in the international domain vis-à-vis sovereign states, it is above board. There is nothing hidden about this means of social division. Actors know where they stand in relative terms to one another. Non-state actors know that so long as this holds, they will never achieve equality of standing with state actors and so can plan and execute their strategies for engagement with these actors accordingly. As Chapter 5 details, operating within these conditions INGOs can adopt deferential strategies to improve their position and have greater influence in the management of international society. In contrast, moves made by non-state actors challenging this order, such as protestors met with heavy resistance. Furthermore, being an overt closure barrier marks it out differently from other means of closure discussed in the remainder of this chapter. While actors know where they stand within this social division and operate to achieve their interests accordingly, this is not the case with more covert means of exclusion.

Achievable criteria

While collectivist closure has the greatest effect in dividing the international domain, in terms of numbers, closure barriers within international society are predominantly functional-individualist in character. As such, for sovereign state actors who have overcome the primary closure rule, it is a relatively open system; though, it has become less so. Once the primary closure rule has broadly positioned an actor as being either inside or outside of international society, secondary closure rules serve to determine more precisely an actor's relative position to others in the social hierarchy. The significance of these rules is that by virtue of being individualist criteria their achievement is possible by any given actor. Whereas the claim of sovereignty requires the recognition of others and the ability to be recognised is limited to a narrow set of actors (or, after the calcification of international society, a single type of actor), this is not the case with individualist criteria. This is not to say that their achievement is easy, but that it is possible.

The Standard of Civilisation predominantly set functional-individualist closure criteria. Gong divides the Standard into five categories.[31] The first required basic, liberal rights including the freedom of movement, commerce, and religion; the second required an organised polity, including an efficient bureaucracy and an ability to muster defence; the third required an adherence to law, both in terms of international law and the laws of war as well as a liberal, domestic legal system involving courts, the principle of legal equality, and published codes; the fourth required participation in the international diplomatic system; and the fifth required conformity to liberal domestic norms, ranging from the banning of suttee, polygamy, and slavery to the acceptance of Western cultural more broadly, such as sartorial styles and musical tastes.[32]

What is important to note is that the explicitly articulated criteria are achievable. There is no collectivist barrier that limits that chances of any sovereign actor to achieve individual elements of the Standard. Once the Standard became explicitly articulated, sometime after Russia and the Ottoman Empire's marginal inclusion in international society, it served as a list that was relatively easy to follow, though not necessarily easy to achieve. Those bidding for inclusion were able to identify the key elements that constituted the Standard and take steps to achieve them. Japan's Iwakura Mission in the 19th century and the reforms put in place thereafter and Ataturk's modernisation of Turkey in the 20th century serve as good examples.[33] The secondary closure rules of international society are thus relatively open.

One obvious caveat that we cannot ignore is the racism that, while never explicitly articulated as part of the Standard, stratified the international domain during the 'expansion' period (profound legacies of which endure today). It was not until the principal of racial equality took hold in international society with the establishment of the UN Charter that this hidden collectivism was at least legally cast out of international society. A second caveat, as is further argued in Chapter 6, is the degree of elasticity to specific criteria within the Standard that afforded the superiorly positioned club members the ability to raise or lower particular closure barriers in particular cases. This is especially so in the case the cultural dimensions of the Standard, and as concerns racial equality. Furthermore, as Okagaki remarks, material power was the dominant measure of suitability for inclusion until the normative shift to positivist international law, which meant that at different periods different elements of the Standard were judged to be of different importance.[34] The club could shift the goal posts. If an ascendant actor were playing by the old rules after the shift to a greater emphasis on positive international law, and they were thus increasing their material power but not investing as much in institutions consistent with the legal dimension of the Standard, they would continue to find themselves excluded.[35] Japan's bid for great power status exemplifies this well as they set about their imperial expansion in the 1930s, at precisely the time that norms were shifting to render imperialism illegitimate.[36] Furthermore, the timing of an actor's bid for inclusion not only mattered because of changes in emphasis within the set of closure rules, but also in the explicit articulation of those rules in the first place. Russia and the Ottoman Empire likewise faced a different closure game than later entrants, as they sought inclusion before the Standard's criteria were explicitly articulated.[37]

The liberalism that runs throughout the Standard's criteria endures in contemporary international society. From its start the G5 was conceived as a group of like-minded Western democracies. It remained so until Russia's inclusion in the 1990s, which began with contact between Gorbachev and the group in 1991 and steadily developed until Russia was included as a member in 1997. Russia was included, however, not because the club changed its membership criteria but because Russia had signalled its intent to reform into a Western-style, liberal democracy. G7 membership was viewed by the Americans as one significant way to help with this transition. As Nixon less than eloquently relayed to Clinton's Ambassador-at-Large responsible for Russia's transition, Strobe Talbott, 'What Clinton will be remembered for is how he deals with Russia. And that means leading the rest of the world, especially those G-7 assholes, in support for what we're in favour of in Russia.'[38]

The limits of liberal criteria for governing inclusion in G-Summitry were tested with the advent of the G20. A distinction between a commitment to domestic and international liberal values and institutions here becomes evident. All members broadly subscribe to the neoliberal economic agenda. The same cannot be said of domestic, liberal governance – Saudi Arabia, Russia, Turkey, and China being obvious examples. With the G8, Russia may not have achieved the full set of domestic, liberal criteria at the time of their admission, but they at least committed to reform. While this is to say that the entry criteria have changed as G-Summitry broadens to include more state members, the story is actually more nuanced – it is not so straightforward as saying that domestic, liberal criteria have been altogether dropped. As the discussion of Nigeria, Malaysia, and Indonesia's inclusion below indicates, the adoption of domestic liberal principles is indeed not necessary for inclusion, but their absence is sufficient to justify exclusion. This particular set of criteria can be used to exclude but their achievement does not guarantee inclusion.

Nigeria and Malaysia were both originally identified by Paul Martin and Larry Summers as candidates for inclusion.[39] After being identified as potential members, however, their domestic political contexts changed such that they were subsequently deemed unsuitable for inclusion.[40] Malaysia's Deputy Prime Minister and Finance Minister, Anwar Ibrahim, was well known and respected amongst his finance minister colleagues around the world. When Summers and Martin first assembled, the list of potential G20 members in 1998 Malaysia was included in a large part due to their opinion of Ibrahim, having been 'incredibly, highly thought of by all of us.'[41] However, shortly after drafting their list of potential members, Anwar broke with Mahathir diverging on positions concerning the appropriate response to the Asian Financial Crisis and concerning civil liberties domestically. Perceiving Ibrahim as a political threat, Mahathir ejected him from government and his party.[42] Mahathir, subsequently having personally taken over the finance portfolio, adopted policies responding to the financial crisis that ran contrary to the Washington Consensus and the International Monetary Fund's advice.[43]

Eighteen days after his expulsion, following a mass rally against Mahathir in Kuala Lumpur, Anwar was arrested after a raid on his home and charged with corruption and police interference related to allegations of sexual misconduct levelled against him.[44] Two months later he was also charged with sodomy and was subsequently sentenced to fifteen years imprisonment. The international media saw the charges, arrest, and imprisonment of Ibrahim as a 'blatantly political fix-up.'[45] Amnesty International deemed him to be a prisoner of conscience, [46] and his fellow finance ministers were outraged.[47]

While they had neither set specific inclusion criteria nor explicitly defined a cohesive identity for the group, Martin and Summers agreed that Mahathir's defiance of the neoliberal economic agenda and his treatment of Ibrahim made Malaysia doubly unsuited for inclusion.[48] Other states on their list of members also did not subscribe to the Washington Consensus, notably Argentina and Brazil, and had spotty records on human rights and democratic governance, notably China and Saudi Arabia. Mahathir's actions were thus not necessarily barriers to Malaysia's inclusion in the club, but they did serve as sufficient reasons for exclusion.

Nigeria too nearly made it into the G20 but ultimately failed to do so. Nigeria was on Martin and Summers' initial membership list but in the lead-up to the first summit the poor governance situation in the country caused it to be excluded.[49] So wanting to include Nigeria in order to have greater representation for Africa in the group, a spot was held for the country in hopes that its domestic situation would improve in time for the first summit. As it did not, the twentieth – and to this day unfilled – spot in the G20 is Nigeria's.[50]

Indonesia was a third country that was initially identified as a potential member but then ran into domestic governance problems at the time that the G20 was being formed. After having become the country hardest hit by the Asian Financial Crisis, Suharto began to lose his grip on power as he faced having to deal with the effects of the economic crisis which included 'massive unemployment, food shortage, and a significant drop in living standards, as well as a rise in crime, looting, and other symptoms of social breakdown.'[51] At the same time, accusations of cronyism, corruption, and undue limitations on the freedom of speech and press were levelled against Suharto.[52] The political situation fast deteriorated with mass demonstrations, bombings, gang rapes, kidnapping, and ethnic violence. Local human rights monitors and the National Human Rights Commission identified the Indonesian military and policy as having participated and incited the violence against Sino-Indonesians.[53]

What sets Indonesia apart from Malaysia and Nigeria, however, is that after Suharto's resignation, the two successive governments, those of B.J. Habibie and Try Sutrisno, managed to reverse the situation. Indonesia embarked on a transformation programme which sought democratic reforms across all branches of government, a return of free speech, the prosecution of those responsible for violence, and greater regional autonomy. The transition governments were also able to see through the IMF reform programme, reluctantly signed in 1998 by Suharto. Indonesia thus returned to a position where its domestic situation was palatable to the club and its domestic and international policies were in line with those of the democratic, neoliberal West. As a result, 'we [Martin and Summers] put them in.'[54]

Malaysia, Nigeria, and Indonesia thus serve as three useful cases for analysing membership in the G20. Malaysia and Nigeria nearly made it into the club, having first been judged to be economies of systematic importance who provided greater geographic representation – and therefore legitimacy – and were sufficiently alike in terms of liberal, democratic values to the existing club. They were ultimately excluded, however, when circumstances changed such that this domestic liberal dimension was no longer satisfied. Indonesia was successful in gaining inclusion because the country was able to bring itself back in line with the club's values. It is also important to stress that in the cases of Malaysia and Indonesia, it was not their economic position that decided whether or not they were to be included or excluded. Both were hit hard by the Asian Financial Crisis and were faltering when the G20 membership list was first assembled. The economic situation of both improved between the creation of the list and the first meeting of the group. The critical difference was in their domestic governance.

In all, the predominant type of closure barriers faced by states in international society is functional-individualist in nature, thus marking international society as a relatively open system for this type of actor. The explicit domestic criteria in the Standard were liberal criteria which broadly continue to govern inclusion in the contemporary game. This has the effect of reproducing the same type of international society that the Standard sought to produce – namely, one within which the norms, values, beliefs, ideas, and practices of Western Europe are dominant. However, this particular type of order is reproduced not through coercive imposition by the club over others but by making adherence to it the condition for an actor to improve its position; because these criteria are functional-individualist, their achievement is possible. This is not to deny the more violent or imperial side of international society's Janus face, but to point out that much of the reproduction of order, particularly in contemporary international society, is achieved more with a carrot rather than a stick.[55]

Ostensibly achievable criteria

Other secondary closure rules governing inclusion are not as achievable as they at first glance appear to be. The majority of criteria governing inclusion to the Great Powers' club and G-summitry are merely *ostensibly* achievable. They are nominally achievable but structural constraints render them achievable to only a small proportion of actors in the system. Inclusion seems like an open and fair contest, but it actually is not as very few actors are in a position to play the game at all. In this respect, exclusion is achieved not by the setting of collectivist barriers, but by allowing structural factors to condition the contest.

Nearly all definitions of what counts towards achieving the status of a great power focus on war.[56] Taylor, Modelski, and Rake all define great power status as a power capable of fighting a major war.[57] Modelski in particular points to a positivist approach that was used to calculate great power status, wherein status was confirmed by counting the number of infantrymen in a state's army. Haas, Bull, Rothstein, Hoffman, and Treitschke define it as a power that can only be defeated in war by a coalition of others.[58] Howard defines it as a power that can 'control events beyond its own borders,' usually by military means.[59] Levy gives a composite definition as a state that plays a major role in international politics with respect to security-related issues. The great powers can be differentiated from other states by their military power, their interests, their behavior in general and interactions with other Powers, other Powers' perception of them, and some formal criteria.[60]

The formal criteria Levy points to are international conference participation, congresses, organisations, and treaties.[61] Simpson similarly points to the importance of these non-material dimensions of great power status, such as "diplomatic experience and cultural acceptability, which can compensate for a lack of raw power."[62] Simpson cites Austria in 1815 and Britain in 1945 as examples of falling powers that maintained their status because of these resources and, conversely, China in 1945 as a rising power that was denied great power status by virtue of lacking them.[63] To be included in the Great Powers' club a state thus had to act like a great power, not simply have the material resources of a great power. The notion of great power responsibility exemplifies this well. Scholars have a difficult time identifying when the US can be said to be a part of the club, placing its entry as early as the Civil War and as late as the end of the Second World War.[64] What makes identifying America's entry point difficult is that it had achieved the material criteria to warrant the status but its isolationist policies meant it was not engaging internationally in a manner consistent with that of a great power. Contemporary debates about China's great power status similarly focus on the question of whether the status is properly recognised if the country is not playing the role of a responsible great power, a charge which might be also be levelled at the US in the era of Donald Trump's 'America First' policy.[65] Membership in the Great Powers' club is about more than just material power.[66]

This highlights the relational dimension of achieving status. Exactly as membership in international society requires the recognition of sovereignty by others, so too is it not enough for a state to self-declare as a great power. They must be recognised as such. Scott likens the Great Powers' club to 'a British gentleman's club, with admission controlled by the existing members. If the established great powers began to treat another state as one of their number, that county *ipso facto* became a great power.'[67] Scott's analogy is only half right, however. What is different about intersubjective recognition in this club is that it is not just the insiders that must confer recognition, recognition also must be conferred by the lesser powers. Recognition from below signals the acceptance on the part of excluded lesser powers of the Great Powers' club because of its managerial role, and in so doing confers upon it legitimacy.[68] The Great Powers' club thus has a degree of exogenous legitimacy that the Family of Civilised Nations does not, as great power recognition comes from within *and* without.

These criteria are nominally achievable. What makes them different in quality from the liberal dimensions of the entry criteria for the Family of Civilised Nations and G-Summitry is that their achievement is only possible for a subset of the actors competing for status within international society. All states can join international society but not all states can become great powers. As concerns the material criteria for entry, only a relatively few states are structurally positioned to amass sufficient power or to take advantage of technological advancements to overcome structural shortcomings.[69] The Netherlands in the 18th century was able to make itself a commercial power, but it never was – nor would be – large enough to make itself a military power.[70] Smaller colonial powers were similarly excluded. Despite acquiring colonies – whether it be the Netherlands with the East Indies, Belgium with the Congo, or Portugal with its African colonies – this mimicry move did not overcome the fact that they were too small to achieve parity with the likes of technologically advantaged Great Britain or territorially advantaged France and Russia.[71]

The same can be said of small, rich Italian city states like Genoa, Naples, and Venice. While they were able to amass economic and diplomatic power, their limited territory and population rendered great power status unachievable. This definitively became the case with the advent of nationalism, making the mass mobilisation of populations possible.[72] As a result, the general rule became as follows: the larger the population, the larger the power; thus cutting small, but rich actors out of the game. The social transformation brought about by nationalism thus paved the way for a Great

Powers' club that excluded those entities who were unable to amass large armies through conscription and who were no longer able to rely on mercenaries, as they erstwhile had.[73] This at once made France the predominant power that it was in the late 18th and 19th centuries, while concurrently rendering smaller entities from ever being able to achieve membership in the club (and thus in part providing an impetus for the 19th-century unifications of Germany and Italy).[74]

Prussia was a marginal case of inclusion in the Great Powers' club that exemplifies how achievable criteria are only ostensibly so, such that some actors, despite efforts to gain and/or secure a position in the club, were structurally unable to completely overcome the closure barrier. As Scott relates, Prussia 'always lacked the demographic and economic strength to compete with the establish powers on anything approaching an equal footing.'[75] Moreover, 'very limited available resources, along with her strategic vulnerability, were always serious obstacles to Prussia ever securely establishing herself as a leading European power.'[76] To improve Prussia's marginal position, Frederick the Great tried to increase its population, largely by taking territory such that the population grew from 2.25 million in 1740 to 5.8 million in 1786.[77] With near-universal male conscription, Frederick was able to build a large army, but at an unsustainable cost of seventy percent of the crown's annual revenue.[78] These moves were complimented by the creation and maintenance of a 'widely admired administrative system, the centrepiece of which was the General Directory.'[79] Frederick made these moves knowing that Prussia, 'while a great power in name... was essentially a second-rank state in fact,' as Talleyrand would often remark.[80] It is for this reason that securing the legitimacy of territorial conquest within Europe was so important for Prussia at the Congress of Vienna. Without it, they could never gain equality with the other powers.[81] As a result, Prussia allied with Russia at the Congress. They alone supported this Prussian goal, as Russia too needed to expand its territorial holdings in Europe to secure its own position in the club.[82] Prussia remained, however, at best a junior member, due to its structural limitations. It achieved status as a European great power, but could not achieve status as a World great power.

G-summitry's closure criteria are also predominantly ostensibly achievable. As the following chapter details, gaining entry involves a mix of material and ideational resources. However, as with the Great Powers' club, only a relatively few number of states are able to do so – not every state is structurally fortunate enough to be a systematically significant economy. The point need not be explored further as it is fairly intuitive, but what is important to highlight is how different these clubs' treatment of achievable criteria are from those governing entry into the Family of Civilised Nations. There were no structural reasons barring outsider states from entering international society as it 'expanded.' A sovereign state did not need to be a powerful state to enter the Family of Civilised Nations (though, prior to the decolonisation period, it helped). As such, while the three status groups' closure rules are predominantly achievable as functional-individualist criteria, the great powers and G-summitry clubs are actually more closed in this respect than the Family of Civilised Nations because most actors are, *ab initio*, not contenders for membership.

In all, while entry criteria are primarily functional-individualist in nature, making the groups seem apparently open, because the barriers to entry are set so high, only a few actors are structurally capable of overcoming them. The *status quo* can thus be largely maintained, even in a system with apparently open closure rules. In contrast to overt collectivism, ostensibly achievable barriers are like mobility dampeners as they achieve closure by stealth.

Conclusion

If one looks at only the barriers faced by sovereign states in international society, the closure system appears to be mostly open, with the predominance of rules being functional-individualist in nature. In terms of closure rules, there seems to be little that restricts social mobility. Inductively we can observe, however, that this is not the case, and so phenomena other than exclusionary strategies are likely in operation so as to stratify the international domain. Indeed, the previous chapter argued that mobility dampers are one such phenomena. The following two chapters analyse further the dynamics responsible for the reproduction of the stratified international order.

Nonetheless, exclusion strategies employed by insiders do have an effect on order, mostly owing to the deeply embedded collectivism in international society. Collectivist closure plays a big role in social division in the international domain, dividing state and non-state actors into two broad categories and entrenching this division legally. Legal-collectivism gives international society a tandem closure structure wherein sovereign states are positioned superiorly.

Moreover, functional-individualist barriers can be set in such a way that overcoming them is structurally impossible for many or most actors in the system. This is one significant way that even in an ostensibly open system, the position of insiders is nonetheless protected. There are two significant implications to draw from this: first, status groups with more ostensibly achievable criteria are more closed than those wherein the same type of functional-individualist criteria are genuinely achievable. This marks the Great Powers' club and G-summitry as being more closed than the Family of Civilised Nations. Second, this offers a significant revision of extant closure theory, offering one explanation for how a *status quo* can be maintained in an ostensibly open system.

Notes

1 C.f. Murphy, R. (1988). *Social Closure: The Theory of Monopolization and Exclusion*. Oxford: Clarendon Press, 73.
2 Note that a liberal political system is not a required condition for entry into the G20. Its absence is a sufficient condition to justify exclusion, but it does not necessarily warrant exclusion.

68 Exclusion

3 C.f. Keal, P. (2003). *European Conquest and the Rights of Indigenous Peoples: The Moral Backwardness of International Society*. Cambridge University Press.
4 Haldén, P. (2013). Republican Continuities in the Vienna Order and the German Confederation (1815–1866). *European Journal of International Relations, 19* (2), 281–304; Keene, E. (2012). Social Status, Social Closure and the Idea of Europe as a 'Normative Power'. *European Journal of International Relations, 19* (4), 1–18.
5 Keal, *European Conquest*, 2003, 86. See also: Clark, I. (2005). *Legitimacy in International Society*. Oxford: Oxford University Press, 9; Lake, D. A. (2003). The New Sovereignty in International Relations. *International Studies Review, 5* (3), 303–323. Neumann, I. B. (2011). Entry into International Society Reconceptualised: The Case of Russia. *Review of International Studies, 37* (2), 463–484, 465; Okagaki, T. T. (2013). *The Logic of Conformity: Japan's Entry into International Society*. Toronto: University of Toronto Press, 7, 37–41, 104–107; Vincent, R. J. (1987). *Human Rights and International Relations*. Cambridge; New York: Cambridge University Press, 106.
6 Simpson, G. (2004). *Great Powers and Outlaw States: Unequal Sovereigns in the International Legal Order*. Cambridge; New York: Cambridge University Press, 84.
7 Jönsson, C., & Hall, M. (2005). *Essence of Diplomacy*. Basingstoke; Hampshire; New York: Palgrave Macmillan, Print, 125.
8 Ibid., 119–135.
9 Bull, H. (1977). *The Anarchical Society: A Study of Order in World Politics* (4th edition). Basingstoke: Palgrave Macmillan, 16.
10 Bull, *The Anarchical Society*, 1977, 176, 286–306.
11 Jönsson and Hall, *Essence of Diplomacy*, 2005, 119–121.
12 Keene argues that prior to the Standard, many non-European entities were regarded as states. With the setting of the Standard, this status was no longer recognized by the European club and it had to be earned back. [Keene, E. (2002). *Beyond the Anarchical Society: Grotius, Colonialism, and World Order*. Cambridge University Press, 26–28; see also: Alexandrowicz, C. H. (1967). *An Introduction to the History of the Law of Nations in the East Indies: (16th, 17th and 18th centuries)*. Clarendon Press.].
13 Gong, G. (1984). *The Standard of Civilization in International Society*. Oxford: Oxford University Press; Spruyt, H. (1994). *The Sovereign State and Its Competitors: An Analysis of Systems Change*. Princeton, NJ: Princeton University Press.
14 Okagaki, *The Logic of Conformity*, 2013, 97–101, 106.
15 Which points to further a question of who within those states determined membership: was it statespeople, lawyers, journalists? A combination?
16 Anghie, A. (1999). Finding the Peripheries: Sovereignty and Colonialism in Nineteenth-Century International Law. *Harvard International Law Journal, 40* (1), 1–80, 36. Though, I would go one step further than Anghie to suggest that it was not broadly European states, but a particular ranking set of Western European states.
17 C.f. Gong, *The Standard of Civilization*, 1984, 67; Marks, S. (2002). *The Ebbing of European Ascendancy: An International History of the World 1914–1945*. London: New York: Hodder Arnold, 213–215. See also: Resolution of Unequal Treaties of the *Conference des Juristes Afro-Asiatique, Damas*, 7–10 November 1957, 198, cited in Sinha 1965, 123–124 (cited in Gong, *The Standard of Civilization*, 1984, 67).
18 The Boxer Protocol is also significant in terms of Japan's entry into international society. Japan is a signatory of the protocol alongside the seven victorious European powers.
19 C.f. Gong, *The Standard of Civilization*, 1984, 212–213; Okagaki, *The Logic of Conformity*, 2013, 49–53.
20 Anonymous Interview Subject 1.1; Bezaury, A., Interview by Skype, 21 August 2012; Edwards, L., Interview by Telephone and Skype, 15 March 2012; Gomez, A., Interview in Person, 19 June 2012; Grey, J., Interview in Person, 23 January

2012; Khatchadourian, R., Interview in Person, 8 February 2012; Kobele, F., Interview by Telephone and Skype, 13 February 2012; Martinez, R., Interview by Telephone, 16 March 2012; Ramirez, L., Written Correspondence, 19 June 2012; Reynoso M., Interview in Person, 19 June 2012.
21 Doty, R. L. (1993). Foreign Policy as Social Construction: A Post-Positivist Analysis of U.S. Counterinsurgency Policy in the Philippines. *International Studies Quarterly, 37* (3), 297; Searle, J. R. (1995). *The Construction of Social Reality*. Simon & Schuster.
22 Naylor, T. (2011). Deconstructing Development: The Use of Power and Pity in the International Development Discourse. *International Studies Quarterly, 55* (1), 177–197, 181. See also: Doty, *Foreign Policy as Social Construction*, 1993; Doty, R. L. (1996). *Imperial Encounters: The Politics of Representation in North-South Relations*. Minneapolis: University of Minnesota Press; Hall, R. B. (2003). The Discursive Demolition of the Asian Development Model. *International Studies Quarterly, 47* (1), 71–99; Medina, L. K. (2004). *Negotiating Economic Development: Identity Formation and Collective Action in Belize*. University of Arizona Press; Weldes, J., & Saco, D. (1996). Making State Action Possible: The United States and the Discursive Construction of 'The Cuban Problem', 1960–1994. *Millennium, 25* (2), 361–395.
23 Kobele, F., Interview by Telephone and Skype, 13 February 2012.
24 Interview: Ramos, G., Written Correspondence, 20 April–22 June 2012. "The G20 is a member driven process. Countries are the only actors to have a political say in the G20 process. IOs contribute to the negotiation with our substance but don't provide political point of views" (Ramos, G., Written Correspondence, 20 April–22 June 2012).
25 Reynoso, M., Interview in Person, 19 June 2012.
26 Ibid.
27 Rea, J., Interview in Person, 9 February 2012.
28 Interview: Anonymous subject 3.3.
29 Ruthrauff, J., Interview by Telephone 2 August 2012.
30 C.f. Jackson, R. (2000). *The Global Covenant: Human Conduct in a World of States*. Oxford: Oxford University Press, 106–113.
31 Gong, *The Standard of Civilization*, 1984, 14–23. See also: Watson, A. (1992). *The Evolution of International Society: A Comparative Historical Analysis*. London: Routledge, 273–274.
32 Ibid., 14–15.
33 See Chapter 6; see also: Zarakol, A. (2010). *After Defeat: How the East Learned to Live with the West*. Cambridge; New York: Cambridge University Press, 143–148.
34 Okagaki, *The Logic of Conformity*, 2013. Timing also matters in that later aspirant members have the benefit of observing other outsiders' bids for inclusion which provides exemplars to emulate or mistakes to avoid. One of Okagaki's main arguments is that Japan benefited greatly from observing China's troubled earlier encounter with the West (Okagaki, *The Logic of Conformity*, 2013, 9–11, 49; see also: Zarakol, *After Defeat*, 2010, 162). Zarakol also argues that Japan's relative success with entry as compared to Turkey's is that its encounter with the West came after that of the Ottoman Empire, Zarakol, *After Defeat*, 2010, 196–197.
35 Gong, *The Standard of Civilization*, 1984, 42–44; Okagaki, *The Logic of Conformity*, 2013, 41; Zarakol, *After Defeat*, 2010, 248.
36 Marks, *The Ebbing of European Ascendancy*, 2002, 208–213; Okagaki, *The Logic of Conformity*, 2013, 118–119; Zarakol, *After Defeat*, 2010, 192–193.
37 Gong, *The Standard of Civilization*, 1984, 238.
38 Talbott, S. (2007). *The Russia Hand: A Memoir of Presidential Diplomacy*. Random House Publishing Group, 51.
39 Martin, P., Interview in Person, 23 August 2012; Summers, L., Interview by Telephone and Skype, 13 October, 2012.

70 *Exclusion*

40 On the domestic dimension to status recognition, see Neumann, I. B. (2008). Russia as a Great Power, 1815–2007. *Journal of International Relations and Development*, *11* (2), 128–151.
41 Martin, P., Interview in Person, 23 August 2012.
42 BBC News. (1998, September 20). Anwar arrested amid Kuala Lumpur protests. *BBC*. Retrieved from http://news.bbc.co.uk/2/hi/asia-pacific/175896.stm.
43 Martin, P., Interview in Person, 23 August 2012.
44 BBC News. (1998a, September 2). Malaysia's Deputy Prime Minister Fired. *BBC*. Retrieved from http://news.bbc.co.uk/2/hi/asia-pacific/163200.stm; BBC News. (1998b, September 19). Sodomy charges turn up heat on Anwar. *BBC*. Retrieved from http://news.bbc.co.uk/2/hi/asia-pacific/175339.stm.
45 Hartcher, P. (2010, February 23). Outdated Political Thuggery Embarrasses Malaysia. Retrieved 27 July 2014, from www.smh.com.au/federal-politics/political-opinion/outdated-political-thuggery-embarrasses-malaysia-20100222-ornl.html.
46 Amnesty International. (2008, August 8). Anwar Ibrahim continues campaign despite questionable charges | Amnesty International. Retrieved 27 July 2014, from www.amnesty.org/en/news-and-updates/news/anwar-ibrahim-continues-campaign-despite-questionable-charges-20080808.
47 Martin, P., Interview in Person, 23 August 2012; Summers, L., Interview by Telephone and Skype, 13 October, 2012.
48 Martin, P., Interview in Person, 23 August 2012; Summers, L., Interview by Telephone and Skype, 13 October, 2012. Summers added to the list of reasons for which Malaysia was ultimately excluded that 'Mahathir was on the edge of anti-Semitism.'
49 Martin, P., Interview in Person, 23 August 2012; Summers, L., Interview by Telephone and Skype, 13 October, 2012.
50 Martin, P., Interview in Person, 23 August. The EU likes to claim that they are the twentieth member. They are not. Egypt was also considered for a seat at the table, though lacked support within the in-group for inclusion.
51 Bureau of Democracy, Human Rights, and Labor, US Department of State. (1999, February 26). Indonesia Country Report on Human Rights Practices for 1998. Retrieved 27 July 2014, from http://fas.org/irp/world/indonesia/indonesia-1998.htm.
52 Erlanger, S. (1998, May 22). The Fall of Suharto: The Legacy. *The New York Times*. Retrieved from www.nytimes.com/1998/05/22/world/fall-suharto-legacy-suharto-fostered-rapid-economic-growth-staggering-graft.html.
53 Bureau of Democracy, Human Rights, and Labor, US Department of State 1999.
54 Martin, P., Interview in Person, 23 August 2012.
55 C.f. Suzuki, S. (2013). *Civilization and Empire: China and Japan's Encounter with European International Society*. London: Routledge.
56 Levy, J. S. (1984). *War in the Modern Great Power System: 1495–1975*. The University Press of Kentucky, 11; Scott, H. M. (2006). *The Birth of a Great Power System: 1740–1815*. Longman Publishing Group, 117.
57 Modelski, G. (1972). *Principles of World Politics*. Free Press; Ranke, L. von. (1973). *The Theory and Practice of History* (G. G. Iggers & K. von Moltke, Eds.). Indianapolis: Bobbs-Merrill; Taylor, A. J. P. (1971). *The Struggle for Mastery in Europe, 1848–1918* (New edition). London; New York: Oxford Paperbacks (cited in Levy, *War in the Modern Great power System*, 1984, 11).
58 Bull, *The Anarchical Society*, 1977; Haas, M. (1975). *International Conflict*. Indianapolis, IN: Bobbs-Merrill Co Inc.; Hoffmann, S. (1965). *The State of War: Essays on the Theory and Practice of International Politics*. New York:

Praeger; Rothstein, R. L. (1968). *Alliances and small powers*. New York: Columbia University Press; von Treitschke, H. (1916). *Politics* (B. Dugdale & T. de Bille, Trans.). London: Constable, 607 (cited in Levy, *War in the Modern Great Power System*, 1984, 11).
59 Howard, M. E. (1971). *Studies in War and Peace*. Viking Press.
60 Levy, *War in the Modern Great Power System*, 1984, 16.
61 Ibid., 17.
62 Simpson, *Great Powers and Outlaw States*, 2004, 108.
63 Ibid. See Chapter 7 for a discussion on these types of cases as "Frustrated" or "Status inconsistent" powers.
64 Wight, M. (1946). *Power Politics*. London: Leicester University Press, 47.
65 Huang, X., Patman, R. G., & Zhao, S. (Eds.). (2013). Core Interests and Great Power Responsibilities: The Evolving Pattern of China's Foreign Policy. In *China and the International System: Becoming a World Power* (pp. 32–56). New York: Routledge; Xiao, R. (2011). The Moral Dimension of Chinese Foreign Policy. In R. Xiao & A. Carlson (Eds.), *New Frontiers in China's Foreign Relations: Zhongguo Waijiao de Xin Bianjiang* (pp. 3–24). Lexington Books; Hu, W. (2000). Escaping the Periphery. In *China's International Relations in the 21st Century: Dynamics of Paradigm Shifts* (pp. 40–70). University Press of America; Cheng, S. (2004). Gauging China's Capabilities and Intentions under Deng and Mao Cheng. In C. J. Nolan (Ed.), *Power and Responsibility in World Affairs: Reformation versus Transformation* (pp. 103–126). Westport, CT: Praeger; Buzan, B., & Foot, R. (Eds.). (2004). *Does China Matter?: A Reassessment: Essays in Memory of Gerald Segal* (New edition). London; New York: Routledge.
66 Though, of course, having material power is a necessary condition of membership.
67 Scott, *The Birth of a Great Power System*, 2006, 119.
68 Bull, *The Anarchical Society*, 1977, 196; Dunne, T. (2003). Society and Hierarchy in International Relations. *International Relations*, *17* (3), 303–320. 307; Gilpin, R. (1983). *War and Change in World Politics*. Cambridge University Press, 30.
69 Great Britain benefiting from its Industrial Revolution being a prime example.
70 C.f. Levy, *War in the Modern Great Power System*, 1984, 18.
71 Ross, G. (1983). *The Great Powers and the Decline of The European States System 1914–1945*. London; New York: Longman, 5.
72 Nationalism and a large population are necessary conditions but not sufficient for mobilisation. A state bureaucracy is also required. C.f. Scott, *The Birth of a Great Power System*, 2006, 5.
73 Osiander, A. (1994). *The States System of Europe, 1640–1990: Peacemaking and the Conditions of International Stability*. Clarendon Press, 236.
74 As is a theme running throughout this thesis, Italy's unification was not enough to secure for itself an unquestioned a ranking power.
75 Scott, *The Birth of a Great Power System*, 2006, 49.
76 Ibid.
77 Ibid.
78 Ibid., 50.
79 Ibid.
80 Ibid., 4.
81 Osiander, *The States System of Europe*, 1994, 182. See Chapters 4 and 5 for further discussion.
82 Ibid., 183. The terms of their bargain would give Saxony and the Rhineland to Prussia and Poland to Russia. Osiander, *The States System of Europe*, 1994, 180–181.

5 Inclusion

Introduction

How do actors attempt to gain inclusion into status groups? And what do their strategies, successes, and failures in doing so tell us about the international domain? Chapter 4 left us with only a partial explanation of closure. While inductively we observe that there is much stratification, the previous chapter found that exclusion strategies of superiorly positioned insiders do not entirely explain the total stratification in the system. Even in more closed clubs, the extent to which a *status quo* is reproduced cannot be explained by the exclusion strategies of insiders alone. We thus turn our attention to the flip side of the closure game: inclusion.

This chapter makes two general claims. First, as is suggested above, it claims that the strategies adopted by outsiders to attempt inclusion in the management of international society also explains stratification in a society with relatively open closure rules. Outsiders trying to achieve inclusion actually in part cause the very stratification in which they are subordinated. This is so because *deference* to the existing order is a key part of successful inclusion strategies. Outsiders largely seek to improve their position within the existing order rather than try to outright usurp insiders and overturn that order. In so doing the prevailing order is largely reproduced and perpetuated, even if the positional rank of particular actors within it changes. Even with changes in order as rank, order as disposition endures. A *status quo* is maintained not just – or perhaps even mostly – because of the exclusion strategies of insiders who seek to secure their own status positions, but through the Mimicry, Legitimation, and Normalisation strategies of outsiders seeking to get a seat at the table.

This chapter also concludes that social mobility is in part more constrained in the contemporary context, owing to the particular set of strategies available to outsiders seeking entry to status groups. It also provides the empirical basis for the reformation of closure theory's conceptualisation of entry strategies, rendering usurpation as being one of many strategies. It broadly categorises entry strategies as being one of two types: a Relational Strategy or an Identity Adaptation Strategy. In the case of the former, actors predominantly attempt to change their position in the order in terms of rank; in the case of the latter, actors predominantly attempt to change their position in the order in terms of disposition.

Relational inclusion strategies

Relational Inclusion Strategies involve an actor attempting to directly insert itself into a particular place in the status hierarchy via specific interactions with other actors. Relational inclusion strategies range from being more assertive to being more deferential. A more assertive strategy, if successful, has a greater likelihood of an actor entering the club as a relative equal to its incumbents. Conversely, more deferential strategies, if successful, are unlikely to achieve inclusion as an equal for an outsider. The trade-off involved is that an assertive strategy is costlier and less likely to succeed than a deferential strategy. There are two main, related claims advanced through the analysis that follows. First, there is no ability to gain entry into G-summitry via an assertive strategy, thus rending it relatively more closed. There are fewer ways and fewer opportunities to seek inclusion than is the case with other status groups, and the ways that are possible necessarily require deference. Second, because the act of deference helps perpetuate the *status quo*, superiorly positioned incumbents in G-summitry are even more secure in their status positions than incumbents in other clubs, thus further rendering G-summitry more closed. What is significant is that the *status quo* is perpetuated by those seeking entry through their deference, not through the coercive imposition of that order.

Usurpation

Usurpation is the most assertive inclusion strategy available to outsiders wherein they try to forcefully gain a position equal to others within the club (or by setting up a rival club to overtake it). It is by definition conflictual, particularly as the club members resist such moves in order to preserve their own status.[1] By virtue of this, usurpation does not feature in the strategies of outsiders seeking inclusion in the Family of Civilised Nations or G-summitry. In the case of the former, it is absent as a closure strategy because its membership is not limited in number and as one actor's inclusion is not dependent on another actor's exclusion. This is not to say that seeking entry into international society did not involve violence; indeed, it involved a great deal – both in its 'expansion' and in opposition and revolt against it – but that engaging in conflict with members of the in-group was not necessary for attempting entry.

As with the Great Powers' club, G-summitry is limited in the size of its membership. However, usurpation is absent as an inclusion strategy for a different reason. As a diplomatic institution, its identity as a group is premised on cooperation rather than conflict. Fighting one's way into a diplomatic club does not make much sense. G-summitry's function is to help manage the complex interdependence of the globalised world and so, as below, inclusion strategies seek to demonstrate an actor's suitability for contributing to this institutional governance function. This too contributes to G-summitry being a relatively more closed club because an assertive usurpation strategy is not a possible means of entry. The possible ways to seek inclusion are thus necessarily more deferential in nature, reproducing and perpetuating the *status quo* order. It is only by paying deference that an actor can hope to gain even a degree of inclusion. It is, however, possible to try to usurp the club altogether and set up a rival institution, such as the Brazil, Russia, India, China, and South Africa (BRICS) which was viewed as a threatening rival and so co-optive moves were accordingly taken.[2] As Paul Martin relayed about the 2005 Gleneagles G8 summit lunch to which the Outreach 5 (O5) (Brazil, India, China, South Africa, and Mexico) were invited, they were waiting outside the meeting room to be summoned in by the G8. Those inside the room were keeping the O5 waiting as they discussed strategy to deal with them in the luncheon.

> There we were talking while making the leaders of the emerging economies wait outside. The heads of China, India, and Brazil were just sitting there. Looking at Berlusconi I said 'We're talking about all this stuff, but the leader of the Chinese is outside.' There is something worse going on, Lula and Singh and Jintao are out there. We're in here preparing for them, you don't think they're out there preparing for us? The last thing we want to do is create a G5.[3]

As such, usurpation's *threat* prompts the club to at the very least reconsider its membership given changes in status and power internationally, but actually engaging in usurpation is not a means of entry into this diplomatically rooted club.

Usurpation is also absent as an inclusion strategy to the Family of Civilised Nations, but it is less an issue of closure in this context because the club is not limited in numbers. G-summitry is more like the Great Powers' club, with membership credentials primarily being based on material resources and having a membership but entering G-summitry as an equal and/or as a revolutionary of the *status quo* order is not possible. The absence of this entry strategy in this context is thus another way in which G-summitry is a relatively more closed club.

Aggression can get an actor into the Great Powers' club, however. Indeed, as conflict is where a power's credentials are tested, it is required. That a power must seek entry into the club via conflict is in itself neither surprising nor interesting, but the way it does so and with whom it does so is significant. A power cannot be great if it is a victor against just any actor – it must be a power that is (or hitherto was) recognised as a great power. Like a boxing title, a heavyweight champion must beat the current champion to gain the status.[4] Beating up on any country will not do. The claim of status in the Great Powers' club required that a power be able to show that it can deny that status to others. This is what was so significant about Japan's defeat of Russia in the Russo-Japanese War, it paved the way for Japan's entry into the club because it beat a European (or, at least, pseudo-European) great power.[5] Likewise, while Britain's entry point into the club is debated by scholars, it is undeniable as of its 1588 defeat of the Spanish Armada.[6] With Russia and Sweden we observe a direct swap in status wherein Russia's victory over Sweden at the Battle of Poltava marks Russia's entry into the club and Sweden's exit from it.[7]

Usurpation is a contextually limited inclusion strategy, featuring as an effective entry strategy in the Great Powers' club alone. Its absence, however, yields useful insight into those clubs within which it does not feature, marking them out as clubs wherein inclusion cannot be achieved as an equal. The analysis below of Geopolitical mimicry further explores how usurpation bears out in practice. What is significant to note is that while usurpation is possible in the Great Powers' club, because entry is governed according to the particular type of credentialism, the values embedded in these credentials and the way they are tested are perpetuated with each new entry (or exit) from the club. In the case of the Great Powers' club, these values include status being derived through territorial conquest and the ability and willingness to uphold the social order and its values through the projection of power.[8] As such, inclusion as a ranked equal is possible in ways that it is not in other clubs. Even still, the values of the system are maintained, even if the actors whom originally instilled them are not.

Banding

Banding is largely absent as a strategy to gain entry into the Family of Civilised Nations. The closure game to gain entry into international society during its expansion was largely individualist in nature. Notably, though, during international society's globalisation in the decolonisation era, the story is less clear-cut.[9] That said, what is important to point out is that the banding together of former colonies can be seen as a fallback strategy for gaining inclusion in international society as fully sovereign, independent states. After a long history of individualist attempts to gain recognition in and by the club, such banding served as the means to ultimately achieve entry (and was made possible by the changed normative context in the wake of the Second World War). As is detailed in the following chapter the Standard's collectivist elements made it such that even if an actor achieved the Standard's criteria, it could still be marginalised and subordinated in the club through collectivist (indeed, mostly racial) prejudice, Japan's frustrated entry being a clear example. Banding was a successful means of overcoming this collectivism. In domestic societies, collective action is almost necessarily required to overcome collectivist exclusion as exemplified by the

76 *Inclusion*

civil rights, women's suffrage, and anti-apartheid movements. As below, it is through such collective international non-governmental organisations (INGOs) in contemporary international society attempt to overcome the collectivist barriers levelled against their inclusion in international society's management.

What might appear to be banding can be observed as a means of entry into the Great Powers' club. Though, as is illustrated below, it was really a masking of an individualist bid for entry by post-Napoleonic France. Indeed, as the Great Powers' club is necessarily limited in size, a genuine banding strategy would make no sense. Initially at the Congress of Vienna, the 'real inner committee' was formed by Britain, Prussia, Austria, and Russia whom together self-selected themselves as being the controlling directorate of the Congress by virtue of having been the victorious combatants against Napoleon. Stratified below this club-within-the-club were Spain and Restoration France who, added to the Four, made up the Congress' formal directing Committee.[10] Spain and France were recognised as being great powers of the "first order" but were regarded as having relatively less status than the central Four.[11] Indeed, the Four did everything they could to maintain exclusive control of the Congress. Despite the Congress formally including all of Europe and the Treaty of Paris having eight signatories, the Four had signed a secret article to keep control and important decisions to themselves.[12] France managed, however, to gain entry into the exclusive top-tier club, achieving full recognition as having standing equal to the Four, thus enlarging the "real inner committee" from Four to Five.[13]

France, through the diplomatic efforts of Talleyrand, achieved entry through this pseudo-banding strategy. The Four initially excluded France to prevent Talleyrand from taking advantage of cleavages within the group in order to further France's own interests.[14] Upon learning of France's exclusion from the inner committee, Talleyrand at first protested and argued for inclusion on the grounds that France was an equal to the other powers, thus arguing for France's inclusion owing to its rank based in terms of material power.[15] As Webster relates, "Talleyrand... used all his diplomatic arts of persuasion, insinuation, and intimidation to claim from the first a position of full equality with the four Powers..."[16] He failed.

In response to his failure, Talleyrand switched to a more deferential (and apparent) banding strategy, positioning himself as a lesser who had a right to inclusion based on a principle of legitimate representation for the excluded parties. An analysis for legitimation entry strategies follows below, but it is necessary to momentarily pause and explain why Talleyrand's actions at Vienna are properly understood as a seeming like a banding strategy rather than a legitimation strategy. While Talleyrand argued for inclusion using the rhetoric of legitimacy, his words were empty of substance. Talleyrand had no genuine intention of representing the smaller, excluded powers and thereby increasing the legitimacy of the group, as is evidenced by his abandonment of the other excluded powers once he had won France's inclusion.[17]

Seeing that the Four would not recognise France as a top-tier power, Talleyrand chose to embrace this ascription and base his entry bid on having this lesser status rather than try to continue to achieve entry by asserting that France was an equal to the Four. This is important as it is the crux of what distinguishes a more deferential banding strategy from a more usurpatory one: Talleyrand deferentially accepted France's position within the existing order and used the identity conferred by this position to claim a right of entry. As below, Switzerland made the same sort of strategic switch in trying to gain entry into the G20. The brilliance of the move was that once France was included, despite winning entry as a relatively lesser power, France would gain the status of a ranking equal. Deference could eventually achieve equality.

Talleyrand ostensibly banded together with excluded, lesser powers, claiming a position as the leader amongst them.[18] The decision of the Four to exclude all others from the inner committee meant that Saxony, Bavaria, Denmark, Sweden, Hanover, Holland, Spain, Portugal, and the Pope were all marginalised, and all were frustrated by this position.[19] Independently of one another they could not force their way in, but they could improve their common position by organising themselves together a group whose shared common identity was that of powers who felt unjustly excluded. While they had different and often opposing interests, by banding together and at least temporarily putting their differences to the side, they could potentially improve their position.[20] As Talleyrand assumed leadership of this group, he could then appeal to principles of legitimacy to bolster France's position, arguing that the Four lacked any legal foundation for their power and exclusivity and so required at the very least political legitimacy – what he called "political morality" – to affirm their position.[21] The absence of any legal treaty legitimating the exclusivity of the Four was a particular vulnerability for the group which they acknowledged in private amongst themselves.[22] The inclusion of France, Talleyrand argued, gave the Four this legitimacy.[23]

It was over the Polish-Saxony question that Talleyrand's strategy yielded success. Russia wanted to take Poland making Tsar Alexander the King of Poland, and Prussia sought Saxony in order to increase its own power.[24] Russia's and Prussia's interests were aligned as both sought to increase their territorial holdings in Europe, while Britain and Austria were allied in opposition, fearing that territorial increases would destabilise the balance of power, particularly by making Russia too powerful. It is worth noting that Russia's bid for Poland was itself an entry strategy to improve its position in the club.[25] Russia saw Poland as its "foot in the European door,"[26] with the Tsar and his ministers believing that only by controlling Eastern Europe would Russia be taken seriously by the dominant West, particularly as Russia perceived itself to be seen by the club as being semi-barbarous outsiders.[27] The Four were evenly spilt on the issue without any scope for resolution; indeed, they came to the brink of war over it.[28] War, however, was desirable to none of the group, not least of all Russia who sought to avoid war with the other powers for fear of being pushed back to the European periphery.[29] The solution was to include France in the group. Britain and Austria supported France's inclusion as they had assurances that Talleyrand would support their position of halting (or at least limiting) Prussia and Russia's territorial expansion; Prussia and Russia acquiesced to France's inclusion as a means of avoiding war and the breakdown of the Congress process.[30] France thus gained entry into the top-tier of the Great Powers' club having banded together with the smaller Europeans as their representative and exploiting the major cleavage between the Four at the opportune moment.

Banding may also be observed in G-summitry. In 2005, the G8 began an outreach process with five "O5" partners: Brazil, China, South Africa, India, and Mexico. The stratification dimension of the G8 and O5 relationship is discussed in detail in the following chapter; for now, the important observations to note are (i) the way that the group banded together in order to be a more powerful bloc vis-à-vis the G8 and (ii) the way that Mexico assumed a leadership role within the group to help ensure its own inclusion. The O5 were not a cohesive group, sharing little in the way of common policy positions. The O5, like the BRICS, share an upward economic trajectory as emerging economies, but little else. With less policy coherence, there was a greater opportunity for the G8 to play those differences off against one another as a way to divide and rule.[31]

The closest thing to a common position within the group that could be found was a collective distrust of Mexico who were seen by the others as being too close to the US.[32] As the only Organisation for Economic Cooperation and Development (OECD) member in the O5, they were the odd one out. Furthermore, recognising its relatively smaller size and less significant systematic importance compared to the other O5 states, Mexico felt that it had a need to guard against the possibility of being marginalised by the others, particularly as the BRICS began formally organising themselves in 2006.[33] As such, to mitigate the risk, Mexico assumed the role of the leader of the group in order to secure their position. By assuming a role as the central organiser of the O5, Mexico at once could try to bring a degree of coherence to the group so as to strengthen the O5 vis-à-vis the G8, while at the same time securing its own position.[34] Mexico continued to assume a leadership role after the elevation of the G20 to the leaders' level. Wanting to 'play a role' in the formation and solidification of the club, the Mexican government hosted (and co-chaired with the US) a critical meeting in January 2010 whose purpose was to resolve once and for all membership in the G20 at the leaders' level.[35] This not only guaranteed beyond doubt that Mexico would remain a member, but also helped to pave the way for Mexico to be given the honour of being the first non-OECD member to host the summit.

Non-state actors also engage in banding to gain inclusion in G-summitry. In the US, an organisation called InterAction serves as the coordinating body for American NGOs; in the UK, it is an organisation called Bond. Both are large umbrella groups, with InterAction having 190 organisations in its membership and Bond having 358.[36] Just as organisation as a group was critically important for the O5, so too is it the case for INGOs, as organising in this way has the objective of overcoming the collectivist stereotype ascribed to civil society as being too disorganised and as having too many divergent policy positions to be manageable to work with.[37]

Not all INGOs, however, band together in this way. ONE, as a noteworthy example, chose not to be part of the InterAction Alliance prior to 2010.[38] The reason for this was because they were powerful enough on their own to be influential and powerful enough that they could avoid having to compromise their positions in order to band with the others.[39] As InterAction's Director of International Advocacy assesses, "When you have Bono you don't need anybody else, you don't need alliances, you don't need to make compromises."[40] The absence of the Gates Foundation from InterAction's membership roll further supports this point. By virtue of their power, they do not need to join coalitions to achieve their goals, whereas less well-resourced actors do.

However, just as the banding together of the O5 could only gloss over major policy differences, the same is true for INGOs. As an example, InterAction's position papers relevant to the G7/8 and G20 lack references to abortion or contraception.[41] This is curious given the G7/8's focus on child and maternal health since 2010, but the inclusion of especially large and influential NGOs such as World Vision and Catholic Relief Services in InterAction's membership means that such topics cannot be included as part of a unified civil society position.

There are two significant implications to be drawn from this. First, banding has the effect of marginalising some policy options and this occurs even before engagement with the club begins. The benefit of organising in this way is that it presents a united front to the state actors as a means of gaining inclusion and having influence. However, it comes at the cost of narrowing the range of acceptable policy positions. Second, by virtue of their size and power, larger and well-resourced INGOs in these umbrella groups have the ability to set the conditions for their participation with their partners, thus revealing gradations of power within the advocacy community. This is in line with the point made above about the Gates Foundation and other more powerful NGOs. By virtue of their size and strength, they are able to have considerably more influence than smaller NGOs who are resigned to following their lead. These implications are indicative of how this strategy can gain greater inclusion in the summitry process, but at the cost of limiting an actor's freedom of its policy positions.

The B20 and the L20 are two further examples of groups that have also engaged in banding in order to achieve inclusion in G-summitry. The B20 was officially formed at the 2010 G20 summit in Toronto; however, there is a long history of business leaders being included in parallel summit events dating back to the G7 summits of the late 1970s.[42] The L20 was formed a year later at the Cannes G20 summit, after union representatives argued to Sarkozy that it was unfair in the governance process to have business represented and not labour.[43] What is noteworthy is the greater degree of inclusion in the earlier G20 summits than was afforded to INGOs. To take the 2012 B20 summit as an example, the process received strategic, institutional direction from the World Economic Forum, McKinsey and Company, and the International Chamber of Commerce. Its eight task forces covered the same themes being discussed by the Sherpas and included over 150 business leaders from 25 countries. The B20 prepared detailed recommendations for the G20 two months in advance of the summit liaised with Sherpas throughout the process. At the summit itself, the B20 met for the first time with the G20, an unprecedented degree of inclusion. The L20 was equally active with a parallel planning. As noted in the previous chapter, the collectivist stereotype of civil society as being disorganised was a primary justification of state representatives to deny INGOs a greater degree of inclusion, and thus, the entry strategies discussed in this chapter are predominantly aimed at overcoming this ascription. As is explored below, what is most important for INGOs in gaining (and keeping) a seat at the table is for them to differentiate themselves from more radical elements of civil society. While the business and labour sectors are not so ascribed, they nevertheless banded together in the same way so as to present themselves to the club as a cohesive group, which the club rewarded with a greater degree of inclusion.[44]

Finally, it must be noted that ascendant actors who have newly achieved entry may exclude similar others with whom they might otherwise be expected to band, or with whom they previously did band but then subsequently abandoned. As the below section on Differentiation details, social competition is fierce amongst actors whom are ascribed by others as being alike. As in domestic societies, intra-class competition is as competitive – if not arguably more so – as inter-class competition. As such, an actor within a group will differentiate itself from alike others in order to claim or protect a superior status. In the case of actors who have recently gained entry, they tend to stall the upward mobility of alike others in order to guard the exclusivity of their new status position. The significance of this is that it is one way that outsiders (or newly introduced insiders) cause stratification in the system. France banded together with the smaller European powers to gain entry into the inner committee at Vienna, arguing on their behalf for inclusion. Once France had achieved entry, Webster writes, "Talleyrand, now that he was admitted to the inner Committee, abandoned all ideas of constituting a general Congress; and no more was heard of the rights of the small Powers."[45] Nicholson relays Duff Cooper's characterisation of Talleyrand's abandonment of his former partners,

> [h]e had succeeded in getting his foot into the door of the European Council Chamber... very soon those who were already ensconced there

were glued enough that he should come in and shut the door behind him, leaving his former partners in the passage.⁴⁶

Likewise, Canada was happy to slam the door shut behind it after gaining entry into the G7, most notably shutting out its Commonwealth partner, Australia, who was bidding for inclusion.⁴⁷ As below, Australia attempted to do the same to Spain after having won entry into the G20. Miles Kahler makes note of this move broadly in international relations,

> [a]s [rising powers] enter the upper echelons of the international hierarchies, whether as traders, investors or nuclear-capable powers, their embrace of equality with other non-incumbents also become more ambiguous, exemplified by China's resistance to permanent UNSC membership for India and Brazil.⁴⁸

Differentiation

Social differentiation was useful for getting into the Family of Civilised Nations, as those seeking entry could contrast themselves with other outsiders whom they pointed to as being barbaric or savage. Neumann and Welsh highlight the centrality of differentiation in the construction of international society and the maintenance of stability within it.⁴⁹ The construction of a civilised identity necessarily requires a barbarian or savage 'Other' against whom this identity is given definition.⁵⁰ Differentiation, however, is significant not just for constructing and maintaining identities, but also for understanding how an actor may cross the social divide and gain entry into a status group – outsiders differentiate against one another as an entry strategy. For example, Neumann and Welsh remark that

> [i]n the case of Russia we have an outstanding example of how the idea of 'the Turk' as the Other is used to bolster the case for Russia's own Europeanness, which was in doubt in quarters at home as well as in Western Europe.⁵¹

This type of argument is not just about claiming an identity, but about seeking an improved social position.

Japan likewise engaged in differentiation as part of its entry bid. Japan's subordination of Korea and its military campaigns against China exemplify this well. Japan pointed to Korea as a barbaric country so as to socially differentiate itself and to justify its actions on the peninsula. Japan cast itself in a paternalist role in South East Asia, as a civilised leader whom could bring the others towards civilisation.⁵² The 'foremost intellectual leader of the era,' Fukuzawa Yukichi's "'Theory of Leaving Asia' argued that, if Japan did not wish to be mixed with other underdeveloped countries,

Japan must forget Asia."[53] The same was the case for Russia, as Neumann points out in quoting the Russian Foreign Minister Aleksandr P. Izvol'sky, "decline to the level of a second class power [...and] become an Asiatic state [...] would be a major catastrophe for Russia" (Lievan 1983:6).[54]

Japan made the case that it could save Korea from being an uncivilised vassal of China, whom they also claimed to be barbaric.[55] The Sino-Japanese War, in which the question of Korea's allegiance to China or Japan was brought to a head, provided the opportunity for the Japanese to differentiate themselves from the Chinese, particularly in the conduct of warfare.[56] The Japanese similarly did so against the Russians in the Russo-Japanese War, "denounc[ing] Russia as an 'uncivilised country still sunk in barbarism'."[57] Differentiation was especially important in the context of war for Japan as the West was not convinced that Japan would honour the Treaty of Geneva, despite signing it in 1886 as a signal of their adoption of Western civilisation.[58] Deliberate steps were taken to ensure compliance, "[i]n their victorious war against China, Japanese soldiers were instructed to observe international law faithfully and to avoid any conduct that might invite accusations of violating these codes."[59] Just conduct both won the approval of the West and signalled differentiation from other outsiders.[60] Okagaki relates,

Not only did [international lawyer] Ariga [Nagao] appeal to the West by displaying the lawfulness of the conduct of the Japanese army, but he also contrasted Japan's behaviour with that of China as 'unlawful' behaviour. Ariga mentioned that the critical feature of the war between China and Japan was that one party (Japan) strictly followed international law, while another (China) never observed any legal practice of war. Moreover, Ariga stated that Japan's unilateral observance in a case where mutual observance of international law was impossible showed the obligation to humankind that Japan was demonstrating. He insistently emphasised that Japan never sacrificed its faithful observance of law in pursuing its strategic gains and that the war between Japan and China set a precedent for wars between the 'civilised' and the 'uncivilised.'[61]

Takahashi Sakue, another leading international lawyer, made the same sort of claim, characterising the fault lines in the Sino-Japanese War as being between civilised Japan and uncivilised China and "[h]e criticised China's not joining the Treaty of Geneva or the Paris Declaration and its 'barbarian' conduct of the war."[62]

Japan did not just assume a role to lead the others towards Western civilisation. At the same time, Japan saw itself as a leader whom could defend the others against the West. For Japan, elements of the West thus at once served as a desirable 'Other' to emulate and as an enemy 'Other' against whom to defend.[63] That international society was 'Janus' faced allowed for this apparent contradiction, the 'good' side could be sought after while the 'bad' side could be secured against.[64] Either way, there is a dual 'Othering' in operation. Ascribed positively, the West served as an actor whom

Japan was more alike in contrast to its geographic and cultural neighbours; ascribed negatively, the West served as an Other against whom the superior Japan could protect its relative inferiors. Despite the enemy Other being the Europeans, this paternal role for Japan made it seem more alike those in the club, being the type of role assumed by the European great powers. Regardless of the frame, Japan could claim to be worthy of membership in the Western club in contrast to the rest of South East Asia.

Differentiation amongst outsiders likewise features in G-summitry. There is no agreement in civil society over what the role of civil society ought to have in the summitry process. Indeed, different elements within civil society have fundamentally different – and often incompatible – objectives. This cleavage is most apparent in the divide between protest and advocacy groups.[65] As previously, state representatives tend to lump civil society actors together into a single category, regardless of differences between particular actors.[66] This is especially problematic for advocacy organisations who seek cooperative inclusion in the summit process, but can be marginalised because they are yoked together with protest groups who seek to disrupt the process.[67] Broadly speaking, advocacy groups seek to influence the discussions, whereas protest groups seek to disrupt them.[68] Protestors' right to protest is recognised and respected but they are afforded little more in terms of inclusion. Indeed, when protests are allowed, they are almost always well removed from the summit site and always closely controlled and monitored by the host government. That media coverage of protests tends to focus on the negative dimensions of them – be it the death of Ian Tomlinson at the London G20 or the riots and heavy-handed tactics of police at the Toronto G20 – does not help to paint protest groups, in particular, and civil society, in general, in a good light.

Advocacy organisations engage in social differentiation against protest groups in order to achieve and maintain a seat at the table. The primary way in which they do this is through mimicry of state actors' engagement in the summit process in order to demonstrate that they are 'functional equivalents' worthy of being included in the management of international society. While the popular conception of civil society at international summits is as protestors, such an image captures a very narrow band of activity and almost entirely misses the substantive interaction between governments and INGOs.

Successfully drawing a line of demarcation between advocacy organisations and protest groups can be difficult, given that collectivist ascriptions made by state actors tying them together is such an entrenched, dominant narrative. It is even more difficult for advocacy organisations who engage in protests as part of their campaigns, as they straddle the social division that differentiation attempts to create. These are actors that play both the "insider" and "outsider" games in the summitry process – seeking to be insiders influencing the policy process while at the same time being outsiders using public campaigns to pressure governments and communicate their

84 *Inclusion*

message.[69] Oxfam and Make Poverty History are two well-known examples of such organisations. Oxfam, for example, has become renowned for its "giant heads" protests at summits. This media stunt earns them coverage which gives them an ability to get their message out publicly, which is a key task for civil society representatives to achieve at the summits themselves, but sits somewhat uncomfortably with their more substantive need to be seen as an integral and productive part of the summitry process. For those organisations who seek to engage both in advocacy and protest it is thus difficult – if not ultimately impossible – for them to differentiate themselves from entirely non-collaborative protest groups.

Cooper argues that the ability of some civil society actors to be flexible in their approach, at times acting like outsiders and at other times acting like insiders, can be advantageous in negotiations with state actors.[70] This was a particular strength of the Bono and Bob Geldof double act at the 2005 Gleneagles G8 summit – Bono assumed the role of the insiders, whereas Geldof assumed that of the outsider.[71] Tactically this may be true, but from a strategic perspective it only serves to reinforce the marginalising collectivist stereotype of civil society as a whole, thus ultimately undercutting their own efforts to maintain inclusion.

Legitimation

Legitimation is absent as a strategy for entering the Family of Civilised Nations because the club's legitimacy did not rest on the composition of its membership being fair or representative.[72] Rather, the supposed legitimacy of the Family of Civilised Nations was premised on the idea that its members have achieved a level of civilisational achievement and should be 'naturally' dominant by right. The entry of Japan did not make the club any more legitimate because it is an Asian country. Japan's entry, however, did make it appear that the Standard was a legitimate means of governing closure, serving as a 'proof of concept' for the 'expansion' of international society outside of Europe.[73] Moreover, Japan did not enter as an Asian country *per se*, it entered as a 'civilised' state. In this respect the club is a homogenous one. Legitimation strategies do not work in homogenous clubs because all its members (and potential members) necessarily represent the same thing – in this case, a civilisational standard.

The composition of the Great Powers' club is partly tied to its legitimacy but not in a way that a legitimation strategy would be useful. For the club to achieve its function as a steward of international stability, all the relevant powers must be included. What matters in terms of composition is that the actors who can contribute to achieving the group's function are included. Great power legitimacy is in part conferred by excluded, lesser powers who give consent to great power superiority in exchange for the order and stability provided by the club.[74] The conferral of legitimacy has nothing to do, however, with the possible inclusion of any states who are otherwise excluded from the club.

G-summitry began with the same premise. Its exclusivity was justified on the premise that its members provided the function of international financial and economic stability.[75] Two changes in international norms, however, made the club subject to legitimacy critiques, opening the door for entry on those grounds. The first involved its static composition and the second involved the adoption of principles of representative global governance. As concerns the former, and as is detailed in the previous chapter, the club's composition did not change in step with shifts in economic rank. The Asian Financial Crisis in 1997 and the Global Financial Crisis in 2008 demonstrated that the exclusive club did not have the capacity to provide order and stability and lacked the ability to demand the compliance of outsiders (particularly during the Asian Financial Crisis). The club lacked authority and could not achieve its function without the inclusion of outsiders, thus opening the possibility for entry. In order to keep the club as the top-tier club of economic governance, it had to revisit membership.

The history of how the club incorporated others is laid out in the following chapter. What is important to note now, though, is how these crises caused legitimacy deficits which made incorporation a necessary response in order to erase (or, at least reduce) its shortcomings. The Asian Financial Crisis tested the club's ability to achieve its function as the international economic steward. The crisis demonstrated the limitations of the club in the late 1990s where the group did not include the largest or fastest growing economies and the club no longer had the ability to dictate terms, principally via the IMF, to those worst affected. In recognition of the club's inability to address crises of globalisation with its current composition, there was a movement within the club to expand. As the following chapter details, incorporation first happened via the establishment of the G20 at the finance minister's level, owing to some of the incumbent G8 members not wanting an expanded club at the leaders' level over fears of a loss of status.[76]

The 2008 Global Financial Crisis forced the club to revisit its composition for the same reasons as it was forced to do so during the Asian crisis. Different in this instance was the fact that the G8 were those worst hit by the crisis. The premier club could not rescue itself. Recognising its impotence, the G8 had to look to the G20 states for help. The G20 was then crowned as the premier economic forum shortly after its elevation to the leaders' level. The G8 members surrendered their identity as curators of the international economy in exchange for regaining efficacy (and therefore legitimacy) in that role, though now having to share the position with a larger group of former outsiders. The financial crises of 1997 and 2008 thus challenged the efficacy of club and thereby reduced its legitimacy, as the crises revealed that the G8 lacked the capability to achieve the managerial function it was responsible for. The entry of others into the group could help the club regain its footing.

The second change that rendered G-summitry subject to inclusion bids based on a legitimation strategy was the change in ideas about what constitutes just global governance. Functional efficacy became no longer

86 *Inclusion*

sufficient for legitimating exclusivity. The consequences of this shift is twofold. First, it opened up the space for the inclusion of INGOs in the summitry process; second, it made regional and cultural representation criteria for inclusion in the G20, thus constituting this club in a fundamentally different way than the G7/8. Membership in G-summitry is not purely functionalist, thus distinguishing it from the Great Powers' club and making legitimation inclusion strategies possible.

The first actor to seek entry to G-summitry according to a legitimation strategy were the smaller European states who felt they had a right to inclusion in 1975. The excluded Europeans protested that the club formed by self-selected *fiat* without any consultation, the implication being that such a move was illegitimate. Those excluded sought entry by critiquing this move, arguing that their inclusion would correct this legitimacy deficit.

After word about the G5/6 Sherpa group's first meeting in 1975 leaked, smaller, industrialised European Commission (EC) states were particularly upset about their exclusion.[77] "The Benelux Ambassadors formally protested about the lack of prior consultation."[78] Brussels' position was that there should be a discussion within the EC for how France, Germany, and the UK could represent the EC.[79] Belgium's Deputy Permanent Representative, Hervé Robinet, relayed to the US that what particularly upset smaller European states was the way in which their exclusion was decided – by *fiat* by the five.[80] It is thus to the very way that the dynamics of closure work that Robinet claimed the smaller Europeans states objected. In the days leading up to first G6 summit at Rambouillet, Commission officials took the line that the EC's exclusion from the summit would "have a negative impact on EC solidarity... exacerbating the small member states' concerns about being dominated by the large ones."[81] They also objected on grounds that their exclusion was unjustified as the issue of trade fell within the competency of the EC rather than the member states.[82] The EC finally won inclusion at the third G7 summit in London, though was incorporated as a second-tier member (owing to the primary, collectivist closure rule).[83] What is important to note here is that the EC sought entry based on an argument that the G5/6 club members failed to live up to procedural norms and rules that they were bound to by virtue of their membership in the EC (with the exception of the US), that as result the new club lacked legitimacy, and that the legitimacy deficit could thus be corrected with the inclusion of formal EC representation.

The literature on civil society as international legitimators is extensive so less treatment will be given here.[84] What is necessary to note, though, is that ideas and norms of what constitutes just global governance have evolved since the founding of G-summitry. The club's purview extends well beyond the interests of only those included in the club, as was the case with the Great Powers' club. As the decisions that are taken by the club have an effect on excluded actors, its foundations as an exclusive club can be accused of being illegitimate by virtue of those who are affected by its decisions having no say in the deliberative processes. This became particularly so when the G7/8 adopted a focus on international development beginning in the mid-1990s and reaching its zenith a decade later with the 2005 Gleneagles summit.[85]

INGOs' legitimation strategy takes advantage of this particular deficit in the club, contending that it can bring legitimacy to the club by virtue representing excluded constituencies. Larger, better-resourced organisations are especially successful in this move as they have a greater ability to point to a large constituency of members who support their position. The larger the membership of the INGO, the greater the ability it has to make this claim.[86] Moreover, larger INGOs have a greater ability to mobilise its membership as part of its advocacy campaigns – Oxfam and Make Poverty History being two good examples. ONE 'naturally gets a seat at the table' because of its sizeable and active membership.[87] For specific policy initiatives, INGOs may point to evidence of popular support for an issue, be it through online petitions or mass rallies. Regardless of the tactic that is employed, the logic of the strategy relies upon the notion that for decision to be legitimate, those affected by it must have some representation in the process.

It is according to these same principles that the O5's and the G20's membership is composed in the way that it is. The O5 shored up the legitimacy of the G8 at exactly the time that its international development agenda further opened the club up to critiques on these grounds. The logic guiding the G20's composition is distinct from the G7/8 by virtue of the fact that regional and cultural representations were the criteria that were considered when forming the group. The progenitors of the group, Paul Martin and Larry Summers, considered more than economic size when creating the list of those whom would be included, as it was felt that doing so was necessary in order for the group to be effective and legitimate in the post-Asian Financial Crisis context.[88] The G20 is thus not composed of members with alike identities and values, as is the case in the G7, and is not composed of only the top-ranking economies. Argentina, Turkey, Saudi Arabia, and Indonesia are included because of the representative legitimacy they confer upon the club. Because of the importance of representation, Summers was troubled by the exclusion of Nigeria, which he regarded as 'a real African country.'[89] The under-representation of the African continent continues to be a bugbear for the club. Paul Martin has since proposed a new organisation to represent African in the group to shore up this enduring legitimacy deficit.[90]

A legitimation entry strategy is thus a relatively new avenue for entry into status groups by virtue of relatively new norms over what constitutes just governance. What is noteworthy is that legitimation is a highly deferential strategy that serves to reproduce the *status quo*. An outsider seeking entry via legitimation is necessarily not attempting to usurp the club; such an entry strategy does exactly the opposite – offering an ability to help prop up the club in exchange for a degree of inclusion. It is in a large part because of the high degree of deference involved in legitimation strategies that the club

88 *Inclusion*

can stratify to the extent that it has. The 'good' that outsiders offer the club does not buy their way into the club as an equal.

Normalisation

The final relational inclusion strategy is that of normalisation. Like legitimation, it is an entry strategy that is found only in the context of G-summitry as it is the only club under consideration that is predominantly the product of the diplomatic institution.

Normalisation was central to Canada's efforts to secure a spot as a permanent member of the G7. After failing to secure an invitation to the first summit at Rambouillet, Canada was invited to the second summit, in Puerto Rico, by the American hosts.[91] The Americans cited the close ties between the two countries as justification for their inclusion.[92] All the members with the exception of France supported Canada's inclusion (not just at Puerto Rico, but at Rambouillet as well).[93] France objected to Canadian inclusion on the grounds that it would make the club too large and that it would be difficult to continue to exclude other European countries, thus attempting to exclude Canada on grounds of pragmatism.[94] It was only after the Americans sold Canadian participation as a one-off occurrence justified by their prominence on the continent that France ceased to object.[95] Canadian participation, however, was not a one-off. Owing to precedence, they were then invited again to the Downing Street summit the following year as a full member.[96] It was in a Sherpa meeting two years later that Canada's normalisation strategy was explicitly singled out by the German Sherpa during a discussion about the possibility of Australian inclusion. The British Sherpa, John Hunt, recounted that

> [the German Sherpa] Schulmann (trying hard not to look at [the Canadian Sherpa Johnstone) then said that he hoped the Japanese would not think it was a starter to suggest that Australia should come to Tokyo but not to subsequent Summits. This ploy had been tried before.[97]

Spain's inclusion in the G20 as the club's permanent invitee is another case of the normalisation strategy and particularly exemplifies the acceptance of deference in its operation. It also highlights why such a strategy is necessarily one that must be played out in a diplomatic institutional context. Spain had tried (and failed) to join the G7 in its early years.[98] The club denied its membership based on an argument that no further Europeans could be admitted and as they were uncertain about Spain in the immediate post-Franco years.[99] In the mid-1990s, Spanish Prime Minister José María Aznar 'was obsessed' with gaining entry into the G8.[100] While Spain could have been included in the G20 at the finance ministers' level, Anzar did not want inclusion, owing to the G20 at the time being of lower status as a merely ministerial forum. As Spain's economy ranked eighth in the world, he felt Spain unquestionably deserved a spot in the top-tier club at the leaders' level.[101] Little did he realise that if he had accepted Spain's inclusion in the G20 at the ministerial level, owing to precedence, Spain would have almost certainly given an uncontested spot as a full member at the leaders' level in the wake of the Global Financial Crisis.

Spain campaigned for G20 membership at the leaders' level based on its credentials as a country of systematic importance to the global economy, particularly owing to having two of the world's largest banks and its contribution to the short-lived Group of 33 in 1999. At the same time as Spain lobbied for inclusion, so too did the Netherlands. The Dutch similarly argued for inclusion on functionalist grounds citing their systematic importance, especially owing to its Globally Significant Financial Institution (GSIFI), the ING Group. They also successfully lobbied the first three summit hosts – the US, the UK, and Canada – by citing their military contributions as an ally in the war in Afghanistan. The Dutch thus tried to make use of the relationships that it had established with its allies, seeking a spot at a table in return for their war efforts.[102] This particularly complicated Spain's entry bid as the Spanish Prime Minister José Luis Rodríguez Zapatero was elected on a platform pulling Spain out of Iraq. President Bush was deeply opposed to Zapatero, refusing to hold a meeting with him for his entire term in office, and was adamantly opposed to Spain being included at the first leaders' G20 summit in Washington.[103] The Canadian Prime Minister Stephen Harper was closely allied with Bush and the Dutch, and took an 'openly hostile' stance against Spain's inclusion.[104] Australia was likewise opposed to Spain's entry, albeit it for a different reason. While Australian Prime Minister Kevin Rudd was ideologically aligned with Zapatero, he saw Spain's inclusion as opening the door for other entrants to the club. G20 membership at the leaders' level achieved for Australia the status that they had been denied in the G7. Rudd 'did not want the door to be opened for others and water down their status.'[105] Not wanting to have to directly insult Zapatero, though, Rudd refused to take his phone calls.[106] Indeed, as the Spanish Sherpa related, Canada and Australia, as relatively status-insecure powers, were 'the most difficult cases for us.'[107]

While not openly hostile to Spain's petition for entry, Japan and France too were not outright in favour of Spain's inclusion. They were opposed on pragmatic grounds that they wanted to keep the group at the leaders' level as small as possible so as 'not to dilute it.'[108] While France was not inclined to grant Spain membership in the club, they nonetheless held the key to what the Spanish Sherpa had identified as the most important, first move in his normalisation strategy: securing a seat at the Washington summit.[109] While it was the US that was to host the summit, the Spanish wanted the question of Spain's inclusion to be a matter for the club as a whole to decide, not the sole decision of the host. As France held the EU presidency at the time, France was afforded four chairs around the table – two to represent

France, two to represent the EU.¹¹⁰ Spain made the argument that the EU chairs ought to go to the highest-ranked European economy that would otherwise be excluded (i.e. to Spain). The success of this pitch relied heavily on the relationship that Zapatero had developed with Sarkozy, principally owing to their shared vision of a more closely integrated EU.¹¹¹ Given Bush's opposition to Zapatero's inclusion at the summit, though, Spain asked France not to tell anyone – especially the Americans – who would take the EU chair until the latest possible moment.¹¹² While Bush remained adamant, even the week before the summit, that Spain not be included, France was firm that the decision of who would represent the EU at the summit was necessarily one for the Europeans to make regardless of the Bush Administration's preferences. The case was put to the Americans on a phone call between Stephen Hadley, the Bush's National Security Advisor; Jean-David Levitte, the French Sherpa; and Bernardino León Gross, the Spanish Sherpa.¹¹³ In the end, Sarkozy gave both of his EU seats to Spain so that Zapatero and his Finance Minister Pedro Solbes could attend. Sarkozy gave one of his two French seats to the Dutch Prime Minister Jan Peter Balkenende so that the Netherlands too could be represented.¹¹⁴

As the second G20 leaders' summit in April 2009 approached, the British hosts were faced with having to keep European membership in check as a defence against the legitimacy-based critique of the group having too many Europeans. They had to find a way to deal with Sarkozy's move which brought in Spain and the Netherlands. Adding to this problem was that the Czech Republic had taken over the European presidency and also sought inclusion. Switzerland and Poland too continued to lobby for seats at the table. The British Sherpa's solution was to do as Sarkozy had done and play with the number of seats allocated around the table. Invited countries, the Netherlands and Spain, were each given one seat rather than the two allocated to each of the members. The Czech Republic also was given one seat as one of the two representatives of the EU. Spain, thus, held on.

The Obama Administration had taken office by the time of the next G20 summit in November 2009 in Pittsburgh. While Zapatero's relationship with Obama was much better than that which he had with Bush, new American administration nonetheless remained opposed to Spain's continued inclusion. The US Sherpa Michael Froman did not want to invite Spain, as he wanted to use the Pittsburgh summit as the opportunity to permanently institutionalise the G20. He felt that including Spain would make it difficult to refuse others' petitions.¹¹⁵ Nonetheless, owing to the force of precedence, Obama and Froman included the Netherlands and Spain.

It was after the Pittsburgh summit that the Mexicans would host the pivotal meeting that would decide membership of the G20 at the leaders' level. Spain ramped up its already fervent diplomatic campaign to keep its toehold in the club. The meeting was to be held while the US still held the G20 presidency. Spain would soon hold the presidency of the Council of the European Union, but not until the new year. While holding the rotating presidency, Spain could claim a spot at the table; without it, their inclusion remained on shaky ground. While the EU's Treaty of Lisbon came into force in December 2009, it still was not clear who would attend the summit on behalf of the EU. Spain felt that it could take advantage of the unresolved issue, claiming that while it held the presidency it could arbitrate as to whether it would be the President of Commission José Manuel Barroso or the President of the European Council Herman van Rompuy (not to be confused with the rotating President of the Council of the European Union). Nonetheless, Spain could not exploit this opportunity until the new year. The Spanish Sherpa's solution was to call his Mexican counterpart Lourdes Aranda and ask for the meeting to be delayed for couple of weeks, when the US would no longer hold the G20 presidency and Spain would then hold the EU presidency, arguing that it would be most appropriate for the meeting to take place once the Treaty of Lisbon came into force.[116] Mexico delayed the meeting.

Spain's strategy at the meeting was to make the case to the Americans and their allies that, as a Western democracy, they could be relied upon; while concurrently making the case to the non-Western members of the club, Spain would 'not just be a follower naturally aligned to the US.'[117] In advance of the Mexico meeting, the Spanish Sherpa, León Gross, met with Obama's National Security Advisor Jim Jones, arguing that Spain would help maintain the West's dominant position in club, "you need 'us' because you might lose your allies – Mexico, Brazil, Argentina…"[118] While Jones was persuaded by the argument, León Gross next met with Froman, who remained 'dead set on not increasing the number of members.'[119] Meanwhile, Spain made the case to the wider membership of the G20 that Spain could act as a pivot state within the club. Spain pointed to Zapatero's anti-Bush, anti-Iraq positions, and the country's strong relationships with both the Arab world and Latin America, all while opening as many embassies as possible in Africa and trying to increase its development aid to 0.7% GDP.[120] Politically, Spain made the case that they were friends with everyone.

Nonetheless, the prevailing opinion was that Europe ought not to be further over-represented in the club, a sentiment which Spain shared.[121] Spain thus emphasised the economic and functional justifications for its inclusion. While they agreed that the exclusion of further Europeans was justified; they argued that the exclusion of a top-ranked economy, irrespective of geography, could not be justified – the G20 needed Spain in the group in order for the club to achieve its managerial function of stabilising and steering the global economy. Beyond appealing to their economic rank and the significance of their financial institutions, Spain demonstrated its value by being as active as possible, much as Mexico had done as part of the O5. Spain was sure to make proposals at every meeting and summit so as to be seen as a vital and useful.[122] Indeed, after Mariano Rajoy won a landslide victory in the snap 2011 election, Zapatero and the León Gross met with their successors to outline what they believed to be the five priorities for the Rajoy's new government. Included in this list was the import of the G20 for Spain, and they stressed that Spain must continually demonstrate its functional value to the club, 'this works, but only if Spain contributes. If not, Spain is out. Spain has to be active; the most active.'[123]

It was a diplomatic campaign that secured Spain's toehold in the club as its permanent invitee. Argentina and Mexico were seen by the Spanish Sherpa as natural allies. As Japan sought a free trade agreement with the EU, Japanese support for Spain's inclusion was given as a *quid pro quo* for Spain, as the EU president, advancing the trade negotiation. While Russia supported a number of countries for inclusion, Spain used its king's good relationship with Putin to get an agreement that Russia would single out Spain as a special case among those whom they supported. Turkey, Saudi Arabia, South Africa, and Brazil's foreign ministries supported Spain, but their finance ministries were all against.[124] China viewed Spain positively as the 'least American country in Europe' and Zapatero sent missions to China annually to cultivate the relationship.[125] The Chinese Sherpa, though, was dead set against Spain's inclusion based on the pragmatist argument – there were important decisions to make, and they did not want Spain's inclusion to open the door to others so as to decrease the efficacy of the club's deliberative process.[126] It was the same argument Giscard made against the Italians and Canadians in 1975. Other Asian countries were against Spain's inclusion, owing to them having no relationship with Spain, with the exception of South Korea who adopted neutral position. León Gross had tried to cultivate a relationship with his South Korean counterpart by arguing that the two countries were too alike not to be friends, 'Spain is the Korea of Europe... civil wars in the fifties; both peninsulas at the extreme ends of their continents; both the fastest growing economies of the twentieth centuries; both opened up to the world in the 1990's....' As above, Australia was opposed to Spain's inclusion on the grounds that enlarging the club would dilute their new-found status. Just prior to the Mexico meeting, León Gross spoke with his Australian counterpart, reminding him that 'our bosses are good friends. If it swings in Spain's favour and Australia opposed, your boss won't be happy.'[127]

At the Mexico meeting, León Gross asked his counterpart, Lourdes Aranda, the Mexican Sherpa, to speak first in her capacity as co-chair of the meeting and 'to make the argument Spain was there as the representative of all of Europe.'[128] Notably, this was the argument that G7 members who held the rotating EC presidency in the 1970s wanted to avoid as being the basis of their inclusion. León Gross and Aranda 'fixed it up' for Spain to speak immediately after and then have her invite non-Europeans to follow León Gross' intervention on the grounds that 'there was no reason to hear the other European's because Spain was to speak for all of Europe.'[129] The Spanish Sherpa wanted his European counterparts to speak last as they would support the Netherlands' inclusion (the Spanish Sherpa said in his intervention that Spain supported the Dutch too). León Gross got the Saudi,

South African, Turkish, and Brazilian Sherpas to agree that if there were a positive feeling about Spain in the room, they would throw their support behind Spain. The Spanish Sherpa had a close, personal relationship with the Turkish Sherpa and had developed a relationship with the South African Sherpa, thanks to the diplomatic practice of seating according to English alphabetical order, which placed them next to one another in meetings. He relied on the close relationship between the Spanish and Saudi Arabian monarchies to get their agreement. 'With those deals in the bag,' the Spanish Sherpa could then 'get Brazil.'[130]

The meeting unfolded as planned. León Gross followed Aranda, ending his intervention citing Spain's support for the Netherlands. Argentina and Japan spoke next, both supporting Spain. Russia followed, singling out 'Spain's special reason to be supported.'[131] Aranda then spoke to formally support Spain. Turkey, Saudi Arabia, and China spoke next, though without comment on the prospect of Spain's inclusion. The UK Sherpa John Cunliffe then intervened to note that while the UK was against broadening membership, Spain's contributions at the London and Pittsburgh summits gave them a case for inclusion. Jean-David Levitte, the French Sherpa, then spoke in support of Spain. Those who remained against Spain's inclusion were forced to intervene, but did so tepidly. India and Indonesia both spoke for fifteen seconds each, reiterating the position against adding new members. The US Sherpa Michael Froman spoke, saying that, like the UK, the US was not in favour of adding members, but said, as co-chair, that he could see a consensus emerging, a sentiment immediately seconded by Australia. China then spoke last and came out in support.[132] The meeting came to a close with the agreement that Spain would be the G20's permanent invitee, with each year's summit host free to invite two other, non-European guests.

According to the host Sherpa of the following Toronto G20 summit in 2010, the Canadians were left with the '*de facto* situation where Spain and the Netherlands were present.'[133] At the same time, South Korea, the next summit hosts, were pressuring Canada not to invite them because they did not want to feel forced, by virtue of precedence, to invite them to the Seoul summit.[134] Canada announced in the days before the Toronto summit that they would invite the Netherlands, owing to the strong historical ties between the countries. The other Sherpas were dismayed, 'it was as if everything negotiated at Mexico was useless. If we couldn't stick to our own agreements, this would not look good to the rest of the world.'[135]

By the time of the Seoul G20 summit in November 2010, Columbia, Singapore, the UAE, Egypt, Algeria, and Nigeria were all still trying to gain entry to the club.[136] No member of the club wanted to further revisit the question of membership after the Mexico meeting, but the South Korean hosts were left with the awkward question of the Netherlands. While exclusion was the focus of the previous chapter, it is worthwhile to examine the Netherlands' exclusion here as it is a case that reveals more about inclusion than it does about exclusion. The Netherlands were the most vulnerable European country included in the summit. Spain could rely on the diplomatic allies that its Sherpa had cultivated to keep it in the club, whereas the Netherlands could not.[137] The Netherlands' European identity and its relative vulnerability made it a prime target for South Korea, a newly included former-outsider, to claim status for itself by 'shooting a European.'[138] The South Koreans in part excluded the Dutch because they sought to claim greater status for themselves, particularly vis-à-vis the other newly included, non-G8 participants in G-summitry. The French, who were to host the following summit, aided them in this move, as French President Sarkozy did not want to be in a position a year later as the summit host to be forced to exclude an invitee that had precedence on its side, particularly as that invitee was a European ally. Not wanting to have to grapple with the issue of European over-representation and have to combat the strength of precedence in influencing inclusion as previous hosts had, France withdrew its support for the Netherlands' inclusion.[139] Citing the decision of the Mexico meeting and being free of the ties that the Canadian government had with the Dutch, South Korea cut the Netherlands loose. What is worth highlighting is that the Netherlands' and Spain's cases for entry were largely the same. What differentiates them is that Spain was better positioned to advance a sufficiently effective diplomatic strategy than the Netherlands were. Indeed, this speaks to a broader point: actors with well-developed diplomatic capacities in the Western European tradition are significantly advantaged in playing the contemporary closure game. International society might now be globalised, but those from the 'Old World' remain best enabled and positioned to thrive in the status competition within it.

Another failed entry bid to note here is that of Switzerland. Like Spain and the Netherlands, Switzerland sought inclusion in the G20 based on its international economic and financial credentials. The Swiss mobilised their well-developed central banking and treasury networks to lobby for inclusion, particularly at the IMF. The Swiss Finance Minister Hans-Rudolf Merz personally made the case to Gordon Brown at every opportunity available to him.[140] The Swiss made their case based on the functional contributions that they would bring to the club: first, in terms of their strength and experience in financial regulation, and second, in terms of their contributions to international development as donors.[141] Switzerland was unsuccessful in gaining inclusion at Washington, and when it became clear that they would also be excluded from the London summit, they changed their strategy in a significant way. Instead of continuing to seek full membership, they changed tack to seek inclusion only as an invitee.[142] This was a deliberate shift in inclusion strategy towards a more deferential normalisation strategy. The Swiss changed to a strategy that would abandon their chances of entering the club as an equal in favour of one that might get them in, albeit with a lesser status. Despite this shift, however, they remained unsuccessful as they could not overcome the desire of the club not to further exacerbate the over-representation of Europe.

INGOs' normalisation strategy is the same as that practised by state actors. When the G20 was elevated to the leaders' level, there was no precedence for civil society inclusion.[143] They thus worked to establish precedence as a first move in the strategy. There was precedence for the inclusion for advocacy organisations in the G7/8 process that actors could point to as a basis for their engagement. INGOs with a history of engagement with the G7/8 were best able to engage with the larger G20. This was particularly the case for the British Overseas Aid Group (BOAG), the group comprised of the largest UK INGOs: Oxfam, Save the Children, Christian Aid, ActionAid, and CAFOD.

To begin with, INGO representatives had to renegotiate their inclusion with every new G20 host, aiming to establish and normalise a routine for inclusion, regardless of prior inclusion in the G7/8.[144] As Bond's Policy and Government Relations Manager related, 'the strategy is to set precedence for our presence.'[145] At the 2011 Cannes summit, civil society deliberately tried to formalise the accreditation process in hopes that it would set precedence for the 2012 Los Cabos summit and all subsequent summits.[146] This was especially important following the 2010 Toronto summit, from which INGOs were almost entirely excluded.[147] The move was successful as the Mexican government based their accreditation process entirely upon that which was negotiated with the French government.[148] With the exception of the 2016 Hangzhou summit, the process has held.

The same was true for INGOs' inclusion in the preparatory process. With no established process, they created one. There is an interesting discursive move to this element of the normalisation strategy, wherein INGOs point to authoritative statements made by those superiorly positioned to gain and maintain inclusion. In interviews, INGO representatives repeatedly pointed to paragraph seventy three of the Seoul Summit Document as the textual basis on the justification for their inclusion.[149] The paragraph asserts that the G20 leaders recognise 'the necessity to consult with the wider international community' including 'international organisations, in particular the UN, regional bodies, civil society, trade unions and academia.'[150] The paragraph also committed the leaders to 'increase [their] efforts to conduct G20 consultation activities in a more systematic way.'[151] The leaders' statement and commitment gave INGOs a foundation upon which to build future claims for inclusion.[152]

INGO representatives also pointed to the extraordinary inclusion afforded to the Gates Foundation at the 2011 Cannes summit as another precedence setting and inclusion legitimating phenomenon. Sarkozy asked Bill Gates to write a report on development financing to present to the leaders at the 2011 Cannes summit.[153] Like Bono, Gates had his own (pseudo-)Sherpa Geoff Lamb who managed the development of the report which involved civil society consultation in its drafting. The consultation involved face-to-face meetings in Washington, Brussels, and Cape Town with written submissions also having been presented.[154] After the report was tabled to the leaders at the summit, Lamb met with the accredited INGO representatives to brief them on what happened in the private meeting between Gates and the leaders. Gates reported to the leaders how useful the input from INGOs was, particularly the "time and capacity" for research that INGOs could offer.[155] As Bond's Policy and Government Relations Manager related, this served as a 'proof of concept' for civil society engagement.[156] The same move was being made here as with the references to the Seoul Summit Document, with actors pointing to an authoritative statement made by the club as a way to set precedence and demonstrate their value in functionalist terms.

INGOs had been aided in their normalisation strategy by sympathetic states. The nature of the relationship between INGOs and G20 governments varied considerably from country to country, just as the degree of inclusion afforded to them varied from summit to summit. The aim of the normalisation strategy was to condition the process so that a greater degree of inclusion was achieved at each subsequent summit. The 2010 Toronto summit was widely seen as 'disastrous' and 'a huge step backward' for advocacy organisations because they were relatively more excluded from the preparatory process and from the summit itself.[157] At the summit, for example, INGO representatives were barred from the media centre. This was especially problematic as it denied civil society the ability to use the summit as an opportunity to engage in their public messaging, which necessarily involves the media. It is for this reason that so much effort went into re-establishing precedence at Cannes the following year. By 2012, the Los Cabos preparatory process and summit was regarded by INGOs as the being the most transparent and open.[158] In addition to regular and substantive consultations in the preparatory process, INGOs were given daily briefings at the summit by the sous-Sherpa responsible for INGOs and themselves gave daily press conferences. What is significant is that the Mexican government afforded a greater degree of inclusion to INGOs, not just because of a subscription to the idea that their input was necessary for the legitimacy of the process and outcomes, but, critically, also because they hoped that it would set a precedence that future summit hosts could not deviate from, wanting it to be a part of their presidency's legacy, marking Mexico out as a governance innovator.[159]

Labour groups engaged in the same strategy. As with INGOs, labour groups too pointed to summit communiqués as being a critical element of their normalisation strategy. As the International Trade Union Confederation's (ITUC's) Director of Economic and Social policy and (pseudo-)Sherpa James Howard reported, "having the L20 in Cannes that was on the first page of the leaders' declaration was very important for us."[160] Their strategy was incremental with the aim of establishing a precedence.[161] ITUC first received an invite for consultation at the Washington G20 and advanced from there a deliberative normalisation strategy, "what we're trying to do with G20 is create a pattern to make it part of the process."[162] Helping this process was a request by the leaders at London for the International Labour Organisation (ILO) to produce a report, with the implication being that they would present it at the following summit in Pittsburgh. The leaders' request, in short, guaranteed a return invitation.[163]

The G20 again made the request at Pittsburgh for a report to be tabled at the following summit, thus continuing to cement the pattern of interaction.[164]

Precedence is a norm of inertia. Whether an actor is included or excluded, precedence has the tendency for that condition to remain so. As such, an actor that is included, however marginally, tends to remain included. It is relatively more difficult for an actor that is excluded to gain inclusion by virtue of this same inertia, this is why normalisation strategies advance in gradual steps. It is for this same reason that a move made by a host to exclude others to a greater degree than a previous host is so vigorously opposed, as it is a move that directly undercuts the normalisation strategy and the likelihood of future inclusion.

Identity adaptation

This chapter has so far analysed how outsiders seek entry by advancing strategies that directly insert themselves in a particular position within a club. There is a second category of inclusion strategy that may be employed in tandem, that of identity adaptation; or, more colloquially, mimicry, which is less direct in its approach.

The analysis below is divided into international mimicry and internal mimicry. This categorisation matches Neumann and Welsh's distinction between international values – those explicated by Bull – and domestic values.[165] Here, the term 'domestic' is revised to 'internal' so as to allow for an account of the identity adaptation practices of non-state actors, who have no 'domestic' of which to speak. In general, international mimicry involves the adaptation of the ways in which as an actor relates to others in the international domain, while internal mimicry involves the organisation of an actor's internal structures and practices to match those of insiders. There is elision between the two, but it is useful for our purposes of analysis to divide them ideo-typically here. While there is a well-developed literature on mimicry that need not be rehearsed here, the illustrative sketches below, drawing on the cases of Russia and Japan's entry bids, are used to highlight that (i) just as mimicry was a key dimension of outsiders' bids for entry into international society, so too is it instrumental to INGOs seeking inclusion in the management of international society today; and (ii) that because of the deferential nature of mimicry, outsiders contribute the reproduction of the *status quo* order.[166] Additionally, as the dimension of social differentiation is relatively downplayed in the established literature, the examples below are presented in such a way as to emphasise this aspect of mimicry.

International mimicry

Geopolitical mimicry

Geopolitical mimicry mostly features as an inclusion strategy in the context of the Family of Civilised Nations and the Great Powers' club, as questions

98 *Inclusion*

territorial control matter little in G-summitry.[167] The acquisition of territory is primarily a feature of entry into the Great Powers' club, though there is overlap with entry into international society during its 'expansion' period, as is exemplified by the cases of Russia and Japan who both were actors that concurrently sought entry into international society as well as into the Great Powers' club.[168] Suzuki similarly relates this point with reference to Keal, "[a]s the guardians of the Society are great powers, this often means that aspirant members have to recast themselves 'in the image of the dominant power or group of powers at the time.'"[169]

To be a great power, a state needs to *act* like a great power. Territorial conquest was a central part of signalling this identity.[170] Territorial expansion, as above, contributed materially and functionally to achieving entry into the club; but the concern here is the way in which doing so is a conspicuous act that signals belonging. The acquisition of colonies, Anderson relates, was a "striving for national status."[171] This was especially so for those precariously positioned at the margins of the club, as taking territory was a conspicuous way of signalling belonging in the club. Moreover, because the possession of territory is zero-sum, its possession necessarily denied it to others.[172] It is thus an efficient entry move in that at once signalled alikeness to insiders while concurrently denying others the ability to improve their position by having that territory.

Russia was ascribed by international society's insiders, as well as the exclusive Great Powers' club within it, as being at the margins of both clubs. For the entirety of the European states-system's creation, Russia was the constant 'peripheral presence.'[173] As Russia was held as a barbaric (or, at best, semi-barbaric) entity, much of its entry bid focused on overcoming this ascription. As Neumann details, a significant motivation behind Muscovy's campaign against the Mongols and the conquest of their territory was to overcome this dual identity of being neither quite civilised nor quite great.[174] "Muscovy actually started propping up its claims to being an imperial power on par with the Holy Roman Empire by invoking its conquests of the successors states of the Golden Horde, notably Kazan' and Astrakhan."[175] Russia's desire to take Poland at the Congress of Vienna continued this strategy. Poland was seen as being more developed, civilised, and European than Russia. By subsuming it, "Poland would be Russia's foot in the European door."[176] Indeed, as Talleyrand wrote to Louis XVIII quoting a Russian minister, "They wanted to make an Asiatic power of us [Russia]; Poland will make us European."[177]

Italy's attempts to take Abyssinia was a reaction to its second-class status at the periphery of the Great Powers' club. Wight relates that Italy's status as a great power was a 'courtesy' after its unification in 1860 and "developed a national inferiority complex through never having proved her place among her peers by war."[178] Its attempted conquest of Abyssinia "was a desperate act of self-assertion" in reaction to this feeling of inferiority.[179] Note that this mimetic move appeals directly to the particular type of credentialism governing entry into the Great Powers' club, with the feeling of inferiority being a result of Italy not having been admitted to the club according to this credentialism.

Likewise, French colonialism after 1815 was a reaction to its precarious status, seeking to solidify its position within the club, which Bridge and Bullen assert they achieved with the occupation of Algiers in 1830.[180] The humiliating defeat in the Franco-Prussian War which severely threatened France's great power status later prompted "a renewed emphasis on colonial expansion" in the 1870s.[181] As Anderson argues, France's colonial drive in this period was a mostly symbolic act to signal prestige, especially in the face of Britain's naval domination.[182] This assertion is especially important for the claim being made here that, *contra* Hobson, Lenin, and Brailsford, colonial expansion was not just – or even not at all – rationalist materialism.[183] The acquisition and possession of colonies was, at least in part, a signalling move to claim status in the international social hierarchy.

Japan's imperial activities were equally a part of this game and motivated by their precarious position in the club, particularly as a reaction to the inferiority affirmed by the imposition of unequal treaties and the racial inferiority that endured even after their overturning.[184] Japan wanted to be an equal in international society and a ranking member as a great power, and so began to act as such through Japan's subordination of Korea and its military campaigns against China. Indeed, Japan's contribution of forces towards putting down the Boxer Rebellion was a critical move in signalling its belongingness to both the club of civilised states and the even more exclusive Great Powers' club within it. What set Japan's imperial mimicry apart from the imperialism of those whom it emulated was that Japan was relatively late to the imperial game.[185] As Zarakol quips, 'Japan seemed to have missed the memo about overseas imperial enterprises being on their last legs.'[186] By the time Japan began playing this geopolitical dimension of the entry game, the international norms surrounding imperialism had shifted, delegitimised by Wilsonian norms of self-determination.[187] Playing the right game at the wrong time came with significant consequences for Japan, actually pushing it out of the club rather than winning them an improved position within it.[188] Zarakol makes the same point about Russia's entry to the club, arguing that Russia sought entry to the Great Powers' club based on 18th-century principles of dynastic legitimacy and reciprocity, which were soon to be rendered obsolete elsewhere in Europe in the 19th century by the effects of the French Revolution.[189] Like Japan being late to the imperial game after it had been delegitimated in/by international society, Russia played the dynastic game too late and likewise was marginalised and subordinated as a result.

In each case, these actors were 'frustrated powers', states whose positions were not recognised by others as being what they perceived themselves to be based on a self-assessment of their attributes and a belief in having achieved the criteria necessary for entry as an equal.[190] "'Frustrated great powers' are particularly likely to be sensitive to their lack of recognition as 'legitimate great powers' because they may already have sufficient material power, and some may also have been great powers in the past."[191] The following chapter discusses frustrated powers in detail. For now, though, what is important to note is that frustration with status is a particularly strong motivation behind geopolitical mimicry.[192] Furthermore, the discussion here details the material, hard-power dimension of how frustrated powers respond to their position, whereas Suzuki's treatment emphasises the ideational, soft-power dimensions.[193]

As in domestic societies, it is those precariously positioned who tend to signal and affirm their belongingness most regularly and conspicuously. It is for this reason that Canada invests as heavily in G-summitry and touts its membership in it as much as it does, given that Canada, with the possible exception of Italy, is placed most precariously within the club. In the absence of its inclusion, Canada largely lacks other means to claim status as a ranking power. Canada's inclusion allows it to at least claim to be able to 'punch above its weight' in international affairs.[194] As Osiander relates about Russia in the 19th-century concert system, as a 'relative outsider,' the country invested heavily in the system. Without it, the Europeans could band together against, such that 'Russia could not play the role in Europe to which it aspired, but would be relegated yet again to the sidelines.'[195] For this reason Russia invested greatly in assuming a coordination role within the system, just as Mexico did in order to assure itself a position within the O5.[196]

Such mimicry involved more than just taking territory by force – how that force was exercised also mattered. At the macro level, this concerned the rules by which war was fought – violence was to be applied within the bounds of international law, thus signalling adherence to one of the international society's primary institutions.[197] As the West was not convinced that Japan that would actually honour the Treaty of Geneva in warfare, despite signing it in 1886 as a signal of their adoption of Western civilisation,[198] deliberate steps were taken to ensure compliance, "[i]n their victorious war against China, Japanese soldiers were instructed to observe international law faithfully and to avoid any conduct that might invite accusations of violating these codes."[199] At the micro level, this mimicry concerned the more performative dimensions of military life. While it made rational sense to adopt the superior weapons technologies and battlefield tactics of Europeans, the same cannot be said as concerns the abandonment of traditional martial dress in favour of European uniforms.[200]

Cooperative mimicry

International mimicry need not be violent. The adoption of particular diplomatic, legal, trade, and cultural institutions and practices were critical to meeting the Standard. This is not to say that interaction through these institutions may not be conflictual or coercive, as the imposition of the Treaty Ports system makes clear. The focus here, though, is on the manner in which interaction is practised, with the claim being that it is mimetic in order to gain relative positional advantage within and through that interaction. A particular kind of conquest and warfare is reproduced by outsiders mimicking the practices of insiders in the ways described above. So too are other international institutions likewise reproduced.

Actors seeking entry mimic the diplomacy of insiders. Practising the European conception of diplomacy was necessary for meeting the Standard of Civilisation. English School scholarship is rich with accounts of how outsiders established and mobilised diplomatic assets and techniques modelled after those of the Europeans to meet the Standard in order to gain entry. Examples here are not rehashed for their own sake, but rather to emphasise the extent to which the adoption of European diplomacy was not just to gain relational advantages in interaction, such as reducing transaction costs by conduction relations through a common institution, but was also mimetic – emulating insiders to signal belongingness. Beyond signing treaties, sending and receiving embassies, attending international conferences, sending government missions, and establishing foreign ministries, outsiders seeking entry adopted the habitus of Western diplomats. Events during and resulting from Japan's Iwakura Mission nicely exemplify such mimicry. The Iwakura Mission travelled through America and Europe between 1871 and 1873 with three aims: to gain recognition for the newly reinstalled Meiji dynasty, to begin negotiations to overturn the unequal treaties imposed upon Japan, and to study the structures and systems of the modernised West. The mission, in other words, was designed to navigate Japan's entry into the club, with its ultimate aim to affect 'the perceptions of the Japanese leaders concerning international politics and *on how Japan should act in order to enter the European club of international society.*'[201] The importance of the mission at the time and its historical significance cannot be overstated. The mission 'virtually empt[ied] the Japanese government for two years, with important national issues deferred' until the return of 'almost all prominent young Japanese statesmen' who originally left the country to negotiate treaty revisions.[202]

Moreover, the mission did not just figure out how to act like a club member, but was also a means of social differentiation. As Okagaki writes, citing Nish, "[t]he Iwakura Mission functioned as a measurement of Japan not only against the West, but also against Asian countries, China in particular, in the degree of modernisation and civilisation."[203] Notable mimicry during the mission itself includes the delegation's ditching of their kimonos upon arriving in the US and Iwakura himself cutting off his traditional Japanese topknot after being criticised in the US press for adhering to Japanese style.[204] As detailed previously, outsiders did not just mimic insiders in their relations with insiders; critically, they did so in their relations with other outsiders. After the Iwakura Mission, for example, Japan began concluding treaty negotiations with Korea and China in English and according to European international law.[205]

102 *Inclusion*

This is equally observed through the institution of international law. Just as with diplomacy, outsiders adopted international law to meet the Standard.[206] Moreover, they used it in relations with other outsiders and they eventually used it against insiders to improve their own position. As above, the adoption and observance of the European laws of war serve as good examples. This is especially so in the case of the Sino-Japanese War wherein Japan signalled belonging through mimicry by conducting themselves within the bounds of what Europeans considered to be just warfare in conflict.[207] Those seeking to improve their position could come to use international law to their own advantage, most notably by using it to overturn the unequal treaties that had previously and effectively prevented them from achieving full membership. Other illustrative examples include China's use of Vattel to claim the illegality of the opium trade[208] and the nature of the treaty Japan imposed on Russia at the end of the Russo-Japanese War.[209] As Gong relates, Japan used the same punishing language in dictating the terms of the Treaty of Portsmouth in 1905 as Russia had previously used in the Triple Intervention when victorious over Japan in 1895.[210]

In the context of G-summitry, excluded states employed the same means to gain inclusion as incumbents use to coordinate their activities among themselves – namely, their diplomats. This is neither interesting nor surprising so will not be much dwelled upon here other than to say that the extent to which those seeking entry flex their diplomatic muscles in a mimetic manner is noteworthy.[211] The Italians, for example, were initially excluded from the club and engaged in a vociferous diplomatic campaign to gain inclusion. More than this demonstration of international diplomatic capacity, however, the Italians self-appointed their own Sherpa even before they had been granted entry to signal their readiness for the summit's preparatory meetings.[212] Spain in the context of the G20 did likewise, with its Sherpa attending preparatory meetings in the early years of the club's elevation to the leaders' level even without formally being invited.[213] The O5 made the similar mimicry moves. Not only did they also appoint their own Sherpas, at the 2009 summit, they produced a communiqué independent of the G8 on "G5" letterhead, which was met with raised eyebrows by the G8 leaders.[214] The O5 thus attempted to signal that they were not just an auxiliary, O5, but a *Group* of 5. It was a calculated discursive move to shift the perception of the marginalised actors' identities. Cooper relates a similar story wherein "[i]n a significant symbolic display President Lula de Silva handed out Brazilian football jerseys with the number '5' jersey at the l'Aquila summit as a display of apartness from the G8."[215] States thus did not just seek entry relationally; they adopted particular practices to signal belonging in the club.

Internal mimicry

Those seeking entry do not only mimic others in their interactions with others, but they mimic others in terms of how they organise themselves.[216] For state actors, internal mimicry is domestic mimicry, constructing domestic institutions to be alike those of club members. For non-state actors, internal mimicry predominantly manifests in how they organise and manage their engagement in the summitry process. As with international mimicry, there are functional benefits to be derived from an actor adapting itself in this way, but mimicry is more than just functional, it also serves to help recast an actor's identity so as to appear more like insiders and less like outsiders.

We have already seen how dynastic monarchies reformed themselves to mimic European nation-states to overcome the primary collectivist barrier set by the Standard. They, and others seeking entry, reformed their domestic political and bureaucratic structures to fit the Western mould, a mimicry move that aided entry into both the Family of Civilised Nations and the Great Powers' club. States seeking entry sent and received scholars to learn what reforms to make and how to accomplish them. In the legal dimension, they learned and adopted liberalism (however unevenly), constitutionalism, and courts systems. Furthermore, they outlawed traditional practices deemed uncivilised by the club – namely, slavery, polygamy, and suttee.

Mimicry to meet the Standard extended into the cultural realm too. Here, practices may be most clearly identified as mimetic as there is no (or, little at best) relational, functional value to their adoption. A description of the mid-1870s Japan captures the totality of its mimicry of the West well.

By 1873 soaps, watches, gold chains, umbrellas, Western hats, jackets, trousers, and shoes were the veneer of an adoration of things Western that went deeper to include Western literature, philosophies, politics, religion, architecture, painting, sculpture, and music. By 1875 gas lamps flickered at the Imperial Palace gates and the first brick buildings had been erected on the Ginza. In short, the changes in Japan's political organisation and its diplomatic and legal sectors were part of a much larger movement to emulate the general civilisation of the West.[217]

Sartorial habits changed, either by convention or decree, recasting everything from people dressed to how men trimmed their beards. Entertainment became Western and so too did calendars. Even the honorific social order was reformed to match that of the Europeans, as in Russia and Siam with the introductions of knighthoods, and in Japan, with the abolition of clans. To enter the club, mimicry was totalising, leaving no facet of life unreformed.

It is much the same with INGOs today in order to demonstrate that they are 'functional equivalents' of states worthy of being included in the management of international society. INGOs particularly mimic states in terms of how they organise and manage their engagement in the summitry process.[218] While the popular conception of civil society at international summits is as protestors, such an image captures a very narrow band of activity and almost entirely misses the substantive interaction between governments and INGOs.[219] A key role that mimicry plays for INGOs is to socially differentiate themselves from protestors and demonstrate that they are worthy of substantive inclusion in summitry and its preparatory processes – the same motivation for social differentiation in which Japan engaged to 'leave Asia.'

104 *Inclusion*

The large, development-focused INGOs – the likes of the Gates Foundation, ActionAid, Oxfam, World Vision, and ONE – are illustrative. Such advocacy organisations particularly rely on their experts and policy units that match – if not supersede on specific issues – those of state ministries. INGOs are staffed by the same cadre of people whom one might otherwise expect to find working in government and are tasked with the same sort of policy development aims.[220] Of particular note, both Bill Gates and Bono appointed their own Sherpas – Geoff Lamb and Lucy Matthews, respectively – to manage their inclusion in the summit process, directly mimicking government members of the club. As one INGO representative put it, 'the aim for civil society organisations is to figure out how to prove our relevancy, we need to show that we have something useful to say.'[221] Sartorially mimicking established the habitus of state representatives, INGO representatives also tend to wear formal suits at summits and in preparatory meetings, matching the garb of their governmental interlocutors and distancing themselves from the habit of protestors on the street. Particularly telling, representatives tend to dress informally in the days leading up to the summit, swapping casual clothing for dark suits only once the leaders arrive and the summit becomes formally constituted. While not as dramatic as cutting off a topknot and ditching a kimono, an analogous mimetic move is being made. All of this is critical for overcoming the collectivist stereotype that lumps them together with protest groups.

Mimicry is thus a key dimension of INGOs' bids to achieve inclusion, despite the legal-collectivist rule that outright excludes them from the status of membership. What is significant about this is twofold. First, it demonstrates that mimicry is as much a dimension of today's outsiders' inclusion strategies as it was for those seeking entry when faced with the Standard of Civilisation. Moreover, its effect of buttressing the dispositional order of international society likewise holds constant. Mimicry entrenches the values, beliefs, norms, practices, and institutions of the incumbent, superiorly positioned insiders. As concerns state actors, this perpetuated the ideational dimensions of Western European international society, safeguarding it in the face of the entry of non-Western actors during its globalisation. In contemporary international politics, it safeguards the centrality of sovereign states, their institutions, and practices, despite being faced with the necessary inclusion of non-state actors in today's global governance landscape. In both contexts, the *status quo* is threatened by the inclusion of outsiders, but in both instances order is actually in part maintained by the very ways that those outsiders seek inclusion.

Conclusion

This chapter has argued that the very ways that outsiders seek entry into international clubs serve to in part perpetuate the *status quo*. Owing to the prevalence of deference in the strategies that outsiders adopt to seek entry, ascendant actors by and large do not seriously threaten to the status position of superiorly positioned insiders, with only the exception of assertive strategies used to gain entry into the Great Powers' club. Moreover, because of the relatively greater deference required to gain inclusion in G-summitry and the fewer possible means of inclusion, insiders' positions are even more secure than of those in other groups. Despite G-summitry – particularly the G20 – ostensibly being part of a more open, representative governance order, those seeking inclusion are actually less able to gain inclusion as equals in the club. Critically, this is so not because of the way that the club excludes, but because of the ways that outsiders seek inclusion and because of the diplomatic institutional context in which they must do so.

This chapter has also served to further reform closure theory, offering a more complete account of the types of strategies that outsiders may adopt in the closure game. What has been demonstrated is that usurpation is not the only possible strategy available to those seeking to improve their position. Indeed, in the international domain it actually features relatively little. Rather, those seeking inclusion predominantly do so not by trying to overthrow the existing order but by trying to improve their position within it. The particular norms, values, ideas, beliefs, institutions, and practices of international society are thus reproduced and perpetuated because ascendant actors largely are not trying to be revolutionary. Even if new actors manage to assume dominant status positions, they do so within a context that predated their inclusion. While the members of the in-group may not be able to maintain their positional dominance in the order indefinitely, because of the way that international social closure works, they are at least able to be more sure that the ideational dimensions of the *status quo* order will.

Notes

1 Parkin, F. (1979). *Marxism and Class Theory: A Bourgeois Critique*. New York: Taylor & Francis, 74.
2 Bremmer, I. (2012). *Every Nation for Itself: Winners and Losers in a G-Zero World*. London: Portfolio.
3 Martin, P., Interview in Person, 23 August 2012.
4 Thus refining Wight's headhunter analogy of great power status. A headhunter becomes a headhunter not when (s)he has taken any head, but that of another headhunter [Wight M. (1946). *Power Politics*. London: Leicester University Press, 46].
5 Zarakol notes, when "Japan struck the Russia fleet in 1904; the Russians were completely unprepared as they thought the Japanese would never dare to attack a major Western power" [Zarakol A. (2010). *After Defeat: How the East Learned to Live with the West*. Cambridge; New York: Cambridge University Press, 167].
6 Levy, J. S. (1984). *War in the Modern Great Power System: 1495–1975*. Kentucky: The University Press of Kentucky, 29; see also: Petrie, S. C. (1949). *Earlier Diplomatic History, 1492–1713*. Hollis and Carter.
7 Levy, *War in the Modern Great Power System*, 1984, 38–40. The formal date given is 1721 with the signing of the Treaty of Nystadt.
8 C.f. Bull, H. (1977). *The Anarchical Society: A Study of Order in World Politics* (4th edition). Basingstoke: Palgrave Macmillan, 51–73.
9 C.f. Dunne, T., & Reus-Smit, C. (Eds.). (2017). *The Globalization of International Society*. Oxford: OUP.

106 *Inclusion*

10 Which Webster describes as being a "sham" [Webster, S. C. (1950). *The Congress of Vienna 1814–1815* (Later edition). London: OUP, 81].
11 Simpson, G. (2004). *Great Powers and Outlaw States: Unequal Sovereigns in the International Legal Order.* Cambridge; New York: Cambridge University Press, 98–99; Webster, *The Congress of Vienna*, 1950, 80.
12 Reus-Smit, C. (1999). *The Moral Purpose of the State: Culture, Social Identity, and Institutional Rationality in International Relations.* Princeton, NJ: Princeton University Press, 136.
13 For well-presented accounts, see Webster, *The Congress of Vienna*, 1950; Reus-Smit, *The Moral Purpose of the State*, 1999.
14 Webster, *The Congress of Vienna*, 1950, 81. France won Britain and Austria's support for inclusion because France would side with them against Russia and Prussia over the Polish-Saxony question. They were excluded to prevent this critical division amongst the Four being exploited for France's gain, but then won support for inclusion because France's interests aligned with Britain and Austria's.
15 Webster, *The Congress of Vienna*, 1950, 84.
16 Ibid. See also: Pallain, G. (1881). *Correspondance inédite du prince de Talleyrand et du roi Louis XVIII pendant le Congrès de Vienne.* Paris: E. Plon et Cie (cited in Webster, *The Congress of Vienna*, 1950).
17 Webster, *The Congress of Vienna*, 1950, 93.
18 Mexico's assumption of leadership within the G8's "Outreach 5" is a comparable contemporary case.
19 Gulick, E. (1967). *Europe's Classical Balance of Power: A Case History of the Theory and Practice of One of the Great Concepts of European Statecraft.* New York: W. W. Norton & Company, 230.
20 Gulick, *Europe's Classical Balance of Power*, 1967, 230.
21 Ibid., 230; Osiander, A. (1994). *The States System of Europe, 1640–1990: Peacemaking and the Conditions of International Stability.* New York: Clarendon Press, 171–172; Webster, *The Congress of Vienna*, 1950, 93.
22 Webster, *The Congress of Vienna*, 1950, 85.
23 Nicolson, H. (1946). *The Congress of Vienna: A Study in Allied Unity, 1812–1822.* New York: Grove Press, 142; Osiander, *The States System of Europe*, 1994, 233–234.
24 Prussia wanted to annex Saxony as doing so would increase its power through an increase in population and territory.
25 See discussion below on Geopolitical mimicry.
26 Osiander, *The States System of Europe*, 1994, 181.
27 Ibid., 180. Indeed, Osiander relates that Russia's own leaders also saw the country in these terms. See also: Osiander, *The States System of Europe*, 1994, 178 and 225.
28 Webster, *The Congress of Vienna*, 1950, 91, 225–234.
29 Osiander, *The States System of Europe*, 1994, 178–179.
30 Webster, *The Congress of Vienna*, 1950, 132.
31 As was particularly successful when dealing with climate change policy.
32 Interview: Anonymous subject 1.1.
33 Ibid.
34 One difference to note about Mexico's banding strategy in the O5 from that of France at Vienna is that Mexico was the most vulnerable member of the excluded lot while France was the strongest.
35 León Gross, B., 18 May 2018, In-person, London.
36 Bond UK. (2013, April 17). About us | Bond. Retrieved 17 April 2013, from www.bond.org.uk/about-us; I InterAction. (2013, April 17). About InterAction. Retrieved 27 July 2014, from www.interaction.org/about.

37 Khatchadourian, R., Interview in Person, 8 February 2012, R., Interview in Person, 8 February 2012; Price-Thomas, S., Interview by Skype, 1 August 2012; Rea, J., Interview in Person, 9 February 2012; Reynoso M., Interview in Person, 19 June 2012; Ruthrauff, J., Interview by Telephone, 2 August 2012.
38 ONE itself began as a campaign involving the partnership of 11 civil society organisations. See: Onea, T. A. (2014). Between Dominance and Decline: Status Anxiety and Great Power Rivalry. *Review of International Studies, 40* (1), 125–152.
39 Ruthrauff, J., Interview by Telephone, 2 August 2012.
40 Ibid.
41 There is one exception to this, which is a media release from 2012 by Save the Children which does mention contraception and family planning. See: Save the Children. (2012). Save the Children Says Pregnancy Kills or Injures One Million Girls a Year. Retrieved 27 July 2014, from www.interaction.org/document/save-children-says-pregnancy-kills-or-injures-one-million-girls-year.
42 Armstrong to Whitmore, 25 April 1980.
43 Howard, J., Interview in Person, 2 April 2012.
44 Ibid.
45 Webster, *The Congress of Vienna*, 1950, 93.
46 Cooper (2001); Nicolson, *The Congress of Vienna*, 1946, 143.
47 Hunt to Callaghan, 29 May 1978, in *Bonn Summit*; Bayne, N., Interview in Person, 9 October 2012.
48 Kahler, M. (2013). Rising Powers and Global Governance: Negotiating Change in a Resilient Status Quo. *International Affairs, 89* (3).
49 Neumann, I. B., & Welsh, J. (1991). The Other in European Self-definition: An Addendum to the Literature on International Society. *Review of International Studies, 17* (4), 327–348, 329–330.
50 Ibid., 334.
51 Ibid., 345. See also: Weisensel, P. R. (1991). Russian Self-identification and Travellers' Descriptions of the Ottoman Empire in the First Half of the Nineteenth Century. *Central Asian Survey*, 65–85. (cited in Neumann and Welsh).
52 C.f. Okagaki, T. T. (2013). *The Logic of Conformity: Japan's Entry into International Society*. Toronto: University of Toronto Press, 73; Suzuki, S. (2013). *Civilization and Empire: China and Japan's Encounter with European International Society*. London: Routledge, 161–176, see especially 176.
53 Okagaki, *The Logic of Conformity*, 2013, 78.
54 Neumann, I. B. (2008). Russia as a Great Power, 1815–2007. *Journal of International Relations and Development, 11* (2), 129.
55 Suzuki, *Civilization and Empire*, 2013, 161–176; Suganami, H. (1984). Japan's Entry in International Society. In Bull, H., & Watson, A. (Eds.), *The Expansion of International Society*. Oxford: OUP, 185–199.
56 Suzuki, *Civilization and Empire*, 2013, 183.
57 Gong, G. (1984). *The Standard of Civilization in International Society*. Oxford: OUP, 183; Jansen, M. B. (1974). Modernization and Foreign Policy in Meiji Japan. In Ward, R. E. (Ed.), *Political Development in Modern Japan: Studies in the Modernization of Japan* (New edition). Princeton, NJ: Princeton University Press, 186.
58 Okagaki, *The Logic of Conformity*, 2013, 86. The Treaty of Geneva (1864) was the precursor to the Geneva Conventions, comprising its first ten articles.
59 Okagaki, *The Logic of Conformity*, 2013.
60 Gong, *The Standard of Civilization in International Society*, 1984, 23; Okagaki, *The Logic of Conformity*, 2013, 88.
61 Okagaki, *The Logic of Conformity*, 2013, 87.

108 *Inclusion*

62 Ibid., 88. The same differentiation may be observed in Italy's campaign in Abyssinia as part of its bit for entry into the club. Italy was accused of treating prisoners poorly (c.f. Gong, *The Standard of Civilization in International Society*, 1984, 122).
63 Gong, *The Standard of Civilization in International Society*, 1984, 184; Okagaki, *The Logic of Conformity*, 2013, 78.
64 Suzuki, *Civilization and Empire*, 2013.
65 Cooper, A. F. (2013). Civil Society Relationships with the G20: An Extension of the G8 Template or Distinctive Pattern of Engagement? *Global Society, 27* (2), 179–200.
66 Reynoso M., Interview in Person, 19 June 2012.
67 Price-Thomas, S., Interview by Skype, 1 August 2012; Rea, J., Interview in Person, 9 February 2012.
68 This is an imprecise characterisation of protest groups' activities but highlights the main difference between advocacy and protest groups. Protest groups may not want to disrupt the club's discussions, rather they question the content of those discussions, the legitimacy of the group to discuss them, or take advantage of the presence of the media at a summit to communicate their message.
69 Leo, B., Interview by Telephone, 15 May 2012; Price-Thomas, S., Interview by Skype, 1 August 2012.
70 Cooper, A. F. (2008b). Introduction: Diplomacy and Global Governance: Locating Patterns of (Dis)Connection. In A. F. Cooper, B. Hocking, & W. Maley (Eds.), *Global Governance and Diplomacy: Worlds Apart?* (pp. 1–14). Basingstoke: Palgrave Macmillan, 11.
71 Cooper, A. F. (2007). *Celebrity Diplomacy and the G8: Bono and Bob as Legitimate International Actors* (CIGI Working Papers). CIGI. Retrieved from www.cigionline.org/publications/2007/9/celebrity-diplomacy-and-g8-bono-and-bob-legitimate-international-actors; Cooper, Diplomacy and Global Governance, 2008; Pigman and Kotsopoulos (2007).
72 While legitimacy is a central topic in social IR theory [Clark, I. (2005). *Legitimacy in International Society*. Oxford: OUP; Clark, I. (2007). *International Legitimacy and World Society*. Oxford: OUP; Coicaud and Heiskanen (2001); Finnemore and Toope (2001); Hurd (1999); Steffek (2003)]. The relatively brief discussion of legitimacy and legitimation here is not meant to make a substantive contribution to this topic but rather to offer a way of looking at it from the perspective of social closure.
73 C.f. Gong (1984, p. 7); Okagaki, *The Logic of Conformity*, 2013, 110.
74 Lake, D. (1996). Anarchy, Hierarchy and the Variety of International Relations. *International Organization, 50* (1), 1–33; Lake, D. (2011). Hierarchy in International Relation. In M. Larionova (Ed.), *The European Union in the G8: Promoting Consensus and Concerted Actions for Global Public Goods* (1st edition). Farnham: Ashgate.
75 G6, 17 November 1975, in The Declaration of Rambouillet; Bayne to Fogarty, 11 July 1975, in *Giscard's Proposal For A Monetary Summit Conference*; Schmidt, 31 July 1975, *Private Memorandum on International Concertation of Economic Action*.
76 Martin, P., Interview in Person, 23 August 2012.
77 UK Foreign and Commonwealth Office, 12 February 1976.
78 Ibid.
79 Morris to Kissinger, 7 August 1975, in *Proposed Five Power Economic Conferenc*. At this time Italy's inclusion had not be secured in the club. The first occasion where a common EC position could be formed was at a meeting of EC Finance Ministers in Venice on the 24th of August, 1975.
80 Morris to Kissinger, 7 August 1975, in *Proposed Five Power Economic Conference*.

Inclusion 109

81 Greenwald to Kissinger, 30 October 1975 in *Reluctance of the Member States to Assume Community Budgetary Obligations Signals Setbacks in EC Solidarity.*
82 Ibid.
83 See Chapter 5
84 See Clark, *International Legitimacy and World Society*, 2007. Oxford: OUP; Van Rooy, A. (2004). *The Global Legitimacy Game: Civil Society, Globalization and Protest.* Basingstoke; Hampshire; New York: Palgrave Macmillan, Print; for further discussion.
85 Leo, B., Interview by Telephone, 15 May 2012; Ruthrauff, J., Interview by Telephone, 2 August 2012.
86 Leo, B., Interview by Telephone, 15 May 2012; Price-Thomas, S., Interview by Skype, 1 August 2012.
87 Leo, B., Interview by Telephone, 15 May 2012.
88 Martin, P., Interview in Person, 23 August 2012; Summers, L., Interview by Telephone and Skype, 13 October 2012.
89 Summers, L., Interview by Telephone and Skype, 13 October 2012.
90 Martin, P., Interview in Person, 23 August 2012.
91 Callaghan to Ford, 1 June 1976; Ford to Callaghan, 30 May 1976; Ford to Callaghan, 31 May 1976; Ford to Callaghan, 5 June 1976.
92 Ford, G. (1976, May 30). Telegram. Retrieved from www.margaretthatcher. org%2Fdocument%2FE3B62FE35047403F8286B59CD45FB666.pdf.
93 Kissinger to Sonnenfeldt, 25 September 1975, in *Proposed Economic Summit.* Contrary to what is the now popular and accepted account of G-summitry's origins.
94 Enders to Kissinger, 26 November 1976, in *Canada and Next Economic Summit.*
95 Bayne, N., Interview in Person, 9 October 2012.
96 Carter to Callaghan, 12 February 1977.
97 Hunt to Callaghan, 29 May 1978.
98 Bayne, N., Interview in Person, 9 October 2012.
99 Ibid.
100 León Gross, B., 18 May 2018, In-person, London.
101 Ibid.
102 Edwards, L., Interview by Telephone and Skype, 15 March 2012; Anonymous subject 1.1.
103 León Gross, B., 18 May 2018, In-person, London.
104 Ibid.
105 Ibid.
106 Ibid.
107 Ibid.
108 Ibid.
109 Ibid.
110 The EU had not yet passed the Treaty of Lisbon which created the post of the President of the European Council, who would be tasked with representing the EU at the G20 alongside the President of the European Commission.
111 Sarkozy, N. (2007). *Testimony: France, Europe, and the World in the Twenty-First Century.* New York: Harper Perennial.
112 León Gross, B., 18 May 2018, In-person, London.
113 Ibid.
114 Summit records indicate that the Netherlands were representing the EU (G20 Information Centre 2014). Indeed, the Dutch representative sat behind an EU flag at the summit table. However, the seat itself belonged to France and was meant to be occupied by French Finance Minister Christine Lagarde who was relegated to the back row with the Sherpas and deputies so that Balkenende could sit with the other leaders. This did not sit well with Legarde, particularly when Balkenende sent his State Secretary Jan Kees de Jager to the summit in

his place so that Balkenende could return to the Netherlands due to the death of his father.
115 León Gross, B., 18 May 2018, In-person, London.
116 Ibid.
117 Ibid.
118 Ibid.
119 Ibid.
120 Ibid.
121 Ibid.
122 Ibid.
123 Ibid.
124 The Spanish Sherpa, León Gross, noted that Argentina and Mexico in part were such clear allies because their G20 engagement was led by their foreign ministries rather than their finance ministries. Their support for Spanish inclusion was not just viewed as being about the G20 in and of itself, but as part of a broader diplomatic strategy.
125 Ibid.
126 Ibid.
127 Ibid.
128 Ibid.
129 Ibid.
130 Ibid.
131 Ibid.
132 Ibid.
133 Edwards, L., Interview by Telephone and Skype, 15 March 2012.
134 Ibid.
135 León Gross, B., 18 May 2018, In-person, London.
136 Ibid.
137 Kobele, F., Interview by Telephone and Skype, 13 February 2012; Martinez, R., Interview by Telephone, 16 March 2012; Anonymous subjects 2.2. and 3.3.
138 Interview: Anonymous subject 1.1
139 Ibid.
140 Ibid.
141 Ibid.
142 Ibid.
143 Edwards, L., Interview by Telephone and Skype, 15 March 2012.
144 Burnley, J., Interview in Person, 30 January 2012; Rea, J., Interview in Person, 9 February 2012; Ruthrauff, J., Interview by Telephone, 2 August 2012.
145 Rea, J., Interview in Person, 9 February 2012.
146 Ibid.
147 Edwards, L., Interview by Telephone and Skype, 15 March 2012; Khatchadourian, R., Interview in Person, 8 February 2012; Rea, J., Interview in Person, 9 February 2012.
148 Gomez, A., Interview in Person, 19 June 2012; Ramirez, L., Written Correspondence, 19 June 2012; Rea, J., Interview in Person, 9 February 2012; Reynoso M., Interview in Person, 19 June 2012.
149 G20, 12 November 2010, in *The Seoul Summit Document*.
150 Ibid.
151 Ibid.
152 Rea, J., Interview in Person, 9 February 2012. As one Sherpa related, the Sherpa group is perfectly aware of the game being played,

> you always have a few words at the end of the communiqué that NGOs like so as to appeal to them, they get to say to their membership 'look, we had an

effect.' We have to do it because without civil society engagement the whole thing looks illegitimate.

(Interview: Anonymous subject 1.1)

153 See: Gates (2011).
154 Rea, J., Interview in Person, 9 February 2012.
155 Ibid.
156 Ibid.
157 Burnley, J., Interview in Person, 30 January 2012; Rea, J., Interview in Person, 9 February 2012; Ruthrauff, J., Interview by Telephone, 2 August 2012.
158 Ibid.
159 Bezaury, A., Interview by Skype, 21 August 2012; Gomez, A., Interview in Person, 19 June 2012; Reynoso M., Interview in Person, 19 June 2012.
160 Howard, J., Interview in Person, 2 April 2012; see the 2011 Cannes Summit Communiqué: G20 2011.
161 Pursey, S., Interview by Skype, 28 March 2012.
162 Howard, J., Interview in Person, 2 April 2012; the notion was echoed by the ILO's Sherpa, Stephen Pursey, "the L20 is likely to carry on because it becomes an established thing. These things have inertia." (Pursey, S., Interview by Skype, 28 March 2012).
163 Pursey, S., Interview by Skype, 28 March 2012.
164 Ibid.
165 Neumann and Welsh, *The Other in European Self-Defintion*, 1991, 328.
166 Johnston, A. I. *Social States: China in International Institutions, 1980–2000*. Princeton, NJ: Princeton University Press, 2008. See also: Bhabha, H. Of Mimicry and Man: The Ambivalence of Colonial Discourse, 28 October 1984, 125–133; Suzuki, *Civilization and Empire*, 2013; Okagaki, *The Logic of Conformity*, 2013; Zarakol, *After Defeat*, 2010; Neumann, I.B. (2011). Entry into International Society Reconceptualised: The Case of Russia. *Review of International Studies*, 37, 463–484; Gong, *The Standard of Civilization in International Society*, 1984; Stivachtis, Y. (2006). Democracy: The Highest Stage of Civilized Statehood. *Global Dialogue*, 8 (3–4), 87–99.
167 Control of territory does matter in G-summitry in so far as territory and its population contributes to a state's economic power.
168 Taking territory in the G-summitry context is disadvantageous to an actor, as is evidenced by Japan's opposition to Russia'a entry on grounds of its annexation of the Kuril Islands and Russia's 2014 censure by the G8 for annexing the Crimea.
169 Keal, P. (2000). An 'International Society'? In G. Fry & J. O'Hagan (Eds.), *Contending Images of World Politics*. Macmillan, 72; Suzuki, *Civilization and Empire*, 2013, 12.
170 C.f. Zarakol, *After Defeat*, 2010, 164.
171 Anderson, M. S. (2003). *The Ascendancy of Europe, 1815–1914* (3rd edition). Harlow: Pearson Longman, 277.
172 Ibid., 292.
173 Neumann, Entry into International Society Reconceptualised, 2011.
174 Ibid., 481–483.
175 Ibid., 483.
176 Osiander, *The States System of Europe*, 1994, 101.
177 Ibid., 181.
178 Wight, *Power Politics*, 1946, 47.
179 Ibid.
180 Bridge, F. R., & Bullen, R. (2005). *The Great Powers and the European States System 1814–1914*. Pearson Education, 5.

112 *Inclusion*

181 Ibid.
182 Anderson, M. S. (2003). *The Ascendancy of Europe, 1815–1914* (3rd edition). Harlow: Pearson Longman, 277.
183 Ibid., 283–292; esp. 291–292.
184 C.f. Okagaki, *The Logic of Conformity*, 2013; Suzuki, *Civilization and Empire*, 2013.
185 The same can be said of Fascist Italy.
186 Zarakol, *After Defeat*, 2010, 192.
187 Marks, S. (2002). *The Ebbing of European Ascendancy: An International History of the World 1914–1945*. London: New York: Hodder Arnold, 208–213; Okagaki, *The Logic of Conformity*, 2013, 118–119; Zarakol, *After Defeat*, 2010, 192–193.
188 Neumann makes a similar point with respect to Russia's current foreign policy. Neumann, I. B. (2008). Russia as a Great Power, 1815–2007. *Journal of International Relations and Development*, *11* (2), 128–151.
189 Zarakol *After Defeat*, 2010, 204–205.
190 C.f. Suzuki, *Civilization and Empire*, 2013; Wallace (1973).
191 Suzuki, *Civilization and Empire*, 2013, 49.
192 On what motivates status moves see: Towns, A. E., & Rumelili, B. (2017). Taking the Pressure: Unpacking the Relation between Norms, Social Hierarchies, and Social Pressures on States. *European Journal of International Relations*, *23*, 756–779; Towns, A. E. (2010). *Women and States: Norms and Hierarchies in International Society*. New York: Cambridge University Press; Larson, D. W., & Shevchenko, A. (2010). Status Seekers: Chinese and Russian Responses to U.S. Primacy. *International Security*, *34*, 63–95.
193 See esp. Suzuki, *Civilization and Empire*, 2013, 50.
194 Heinbecker, P. (2011). The Future of the G20 and Its Place in Global Governance. *CIGI G20 Papers*, (5), 20, 9; Penttilä, R. (2013). *The Role of the G8 in International Peace and Security*. Routledge, 61 and 64.
195 Osiander, *The States System of Europe*, 1994, 241.
196 Ibid., 242; Interview: Anonymous subject 2.2.
197 Japan conspicuously portrayed itself as conducting itself justly in the Sino-Japanese War while accusing China of not adhering to the rules. C.f. Okagaki, *The Logic of Conformity*, 2013; Suzuki, *Civilization and Empire*, 2013.
198 Okagaki, *The Logic of Conformity*, 2013, 86.
199 Ibid., 86–87. The Treaty of Geneva (1864) was the precursor to the Geneva Conventions, comprising its first ten articles. Japan did likewise in the Russo-Japanese war, see: Gong, *The Standard of Civilization in International Society*, 1984, 183; Jansen, M.B. (1974). Modernization and Foreign Policy in Meiji Japan. In Ward, R. E. (Ed.), *Political Development in Modern Japan: Studies in the Modernization of Japan* (New edition). Princeton, NJ: Princeton University Press, 186.
200 Gong, *The Standard of Civilization in International Society*, 1984, 101–105. See also: Stivachtis, Democracy: The Highest Stage of Civilized Statehood, 2006; Zarakol, *After Defeat*, 2010, 208–209.
201 Okagaki, *The Logic of Conformity*, 2013, 66. (Emphasis mine.)
202 Ibid., 65–66.
203 Nish, I. (1977). *Japanese Foreign Policy, 1869–1942: Kasumigaseki to Miyakezaka*. Routledge, 24; Okagaki, *The Logic of Conformity*, 2013, 64.
204 Okagaki, *The Logic of Conformity*, 2013, 108.
205 Dudden, A. (1999). Japan's Engagement with International Terms. In L. H. Liu (Ed.), *Tokens of Exchange: The Problem of Translation in Global Circulations* (pp. 165–191). Duke University Press, 165; Okagaki, *The Logic of Conformity*, 2013, 70.

206 More or less willingly, depending on the case- Japan more so; China, less so.
207 C.f. Okagaki, *The Logic of Conformity*, 2013; Suzuki, *Civilization and Empire*, 2013.
208 Gong, *The Standard of Civilization in International Society*, 1984, 152–153.
209 Ibid., 197
210 Ibid. This sort of vengeance recalls the view that the severity of the Treaty of Brest-Litovsk paved the way the severity of The German Treaty at Versailles.
211 Archival records documenting Canada and Italy's entry bids are particularly rich. See bibliography.
212 Kissinger to Volpe, 30 September 1975, in *Secretary's Meeting with Italian Foreign Minister Rumor*.
213 León Gross, B., 18 May 2018, In-person, London.
214 Interview: Anonymous subject 1.1. The G5 also issued a separate Leaders' Statement at the 2008 Sapporo summit.
215 Cooper, A. F., & Thakur, R. (2013). *The Group of Twenty*. New York: Routledge, 64.
216 The two dimensions are, of course, interrelated.
217 Gong, *The Standard of Civilization in International Society*, 1984, 187; Zarakol, *After Defeat*, 2010, 163.
218 C.f. Hopgood, S. (2006). *Keepers of the Flame: Understanding Amnesty International* (1st edition). Ithaca, NY: Cornell University Press.
219 C.f. Cooper, A. F. (2013). Civil Society Relationships with the G20: An Extension of the G8 Template or Distinctive Pattern of Engagement? *Global Society*, *27* (2), 179–200.
220 C.f. Rani, R. S. The Management Set. *BRIGHT Magazine* (blog), 2 March 2016. Retrieved from https://brightthemag.com/the-management-set-699e186469c3#.uquc27mab.
221 Rea, J., Interview in Person, 9 February 2012.

6 Incorporation

Introduction

Much of the way that we have so far analysed international social closure gives us a relatively static description of the system: insiders guard their positions through exclusion strategies and mobility dampeners; outsiders try to overcome closure barriers, but mostly do so in such a way that the *status quo* is largely perpetuated. This chapter places a greater emphasis on change, examining how insiders bring outsiders into status groups, albeit by placing them in stratified, subordinate positions.

Club membership, and the rise and fall of status groups themselves, mostly changes through incorporation, wherein outsiders are included as a response to a group's functionalist needs. For a club to survive as a ranking status group, it must be effective in achieving its role in international society; otherwise, by a sort of Darwinian logic, it will not. If its incumbent membership cannot achieve the club's objectives, incorporation is the means by which newer members can be included so as to shore up the club's functional deficit. It is useful here to recall Bull's observation about the goals of international society, chief among being the preservation of the society itself.[1] An outsider may be included if it contributes to this function of the club. Closure rules are the means of ensuring entrants satisfy both of these requirements. That insiders may incorporate outsiders to suit their own needs is straightforward and not particularly interesting. What is worthy of analysis, though, is *how* the club ostensibly includes outsiders as equal members but substantively incorporates them into lower order positions.

The focus of this chapter is thus on intra-group closure and stratification. The focus returns to that of Chapters 3 and 4, looking mostly at moves made by the superiorly positioned; here, though, their closure moves are exercised not against outsiders but against other insiders who have at least some degree of inclusion in the club. While earlier chapters demonstrated how insiders broadly stratify the international domain through exclusion strategies and mobility dampeners, and Chapter 5 demonstrated how the inclusion strategies of insiders also contribute to stratification, this chapter examines the final closure dynamic that produces stratification within groups. This chapter is thus principally about how the status game continues to be played when outright exclusion is not possible. That is, if the status of incumbents cannot be maintained by outright excluding aspirant outsiders, how can it be protected as best as possible? In short, insiders bring in new members according to a particular mode of closure: incorporation. Whenever possible, outsiders are not brought in as equals to incumbent members – incorporation is stratified inclusion.

Insiders justify stratification according to *functionalist* necessity. More than this, though, when functionalist necessity fails to keep others in a relatively lower position, insiders will stratify according to a more *collectivist* logic. Insiders guard their status positions against emerging/rising others by pointing to collectivist traits as justification for a continued inequality of status. Thus, while the contemporary G-summitry status game seems more just and open, it is not, owing to persisting collectivism. Chapter 4 demonstrated how legal-collectivism endures as a strategy of closure and below the case is made for adding a 'Logic of Culture' as another enduring collectivist means of closure. While a collectivist Logic of Culture stratifies rather than outright excludes, both involve the superiorly positioned protecting their status positions. Collectivism thus endures in two ways in the international domain: through legal-collectivism, which maintains international society as a society of states, and through a Logic of Culture, which maintains the superior position of incumbent (predominantly Western) club members.

There are two means of achieving such intra-group stratification: functional stratification and cultural stratification. Functional stratification involves the incorporation of an actor where their marginalisation is justified on grounds of practicality. For example, stratification is justified because it makes functional sense for the Great Powers' club or the leading industrial economies to manage the international system. Cultural stratification, in contrast, involves stratification within the club wherein the marginalisation of an incorporated actor arises from a more collectivist means of closure. Actors are positioned into lower strata because of dissimilarity in their attributes with incumbent club members. Functional stratification results from a status game grounded (at least ostensibly) in pragmatism or practicality; cultural stratification has no such justifiable cover.

There are two dimensions of change captured here. First is change in club composition – how new members are incorporated owing to functional necessity. The second dimension of change is that of international society's fundamental values. In contemporary globalised international society, a ranking governance group must now be seen to be representative. The change in membership criteria from the G5 in 1975, in which inclusion was entirely a matter of economic power, to the G20 today, in which inclusion is partially based on ensuring that its membership is regionally and culturally representative, illustrates this shift. The new normative requirement for group legitimacy is still functionalist, but it is functionalism tempered differently than in the Family of Civilised Nations, the Great Powers'

116 *Incorporation*

club, or even G-summitry when it was first established. In order for the club's actions to be legitimate and therefore accepted (or, at least, tolerated) by those excluded, it must be seen as a representative group. This normative shift in the values underpinning group composition in international society should not be underemphasised. The need for representative legitimacy marks the G20 as being distinctly different.

This chapter proceeds in two stages. It first looks at how clubs incorporate and stratify according to functional necessity, focusing on inclusion at the Congress of Vienna and the early formation of G-summitry. The main point advanced is that stratification can be used to achieve a club's functional purpose. It is not just about protecting the status of insiders, but also ensuring that the club is able to perform its broader role within international society effectively. The chapter then examines how the club achieves stratification according to more collectivist means, making the argument that the same sort of cultural logic that stratified the Family of Civilised Nations and the Great Powers' club stratifies contemporary G-summitry. In contrast to functional stratification, this more collectivist – or cultural – stratification is entirely about protecting the status of insiders.

Functional stratification and incorporation

It is difficult to analytically separate incorporation and stratification, as the two go hand in. They are divided here as best as is possible in order to accentuate the critical dimensions of how international social closure works. How clubs functionally stratify is first examined before turning to how they functionally incorporate. This labelling is inaccurate as incorporation *is* stratification, but it is useful because it allows us to analytically isolate these two dimensions of closure. The first examines how and why club insiders *construct* a stratified structure and the second examines how and why insiders permit a *change* in the status positions of others. Stratification focuses on *how* insiders bring outsiders into the club in such a way as to protect, as best as possible, the status of incumbents despite the enlargement of a club. Incorporation focuses on *why* they do this, which is to protect the existence of the club itself.

Functional stratification

Great Powers

Two hundred states, cities, associations, and individuals attended the Congress of Vienna.[2] As we saw in Chapter 4, only four (later, five) participants, however, really mattered in influencing the Congress and the Concert system to which it formally gave birth. As Webster relates, "[n]o appreciable difference would have been made in the final settlement at Vienna if the large majority of the plenipotentiaries had never appeared there at all."[3] The Congress was a highly stratified affair, with multiple gradations of standing. The uncertainty over how to constitute the Congress and contestation over the issue had the effect of continually delaying its formal start. After months of delay, the ranking powers eventually concluded their closure game to stratify the Congress as they needed and desired. They achieved closure so completely that the lesser powers were entirely excluded from the decision-making process – the Congress of Vienna was never actually called together at all.[4] The result of the closure game was to ensure that no one save the Great Powers' club had any substantive role in the management of the European system.

There were two imperatives driving this stratification. The first was a matter of practical concern. With so many actors included at Vienna, it was seen as impossible to come to any sort of comprehensive agreement, let alone constitute a way to negotiate any agreements that included all concerned equally.[5] "The idea of a constituent assembly, imagined by some… was found to be impossible. The large number of small States made such an assembly impracticable in any case."[6] Stratification of the Congress could thus be justified as a pragmatic exercise. This allowed the second motivation for stratification to be at least somewhat masked by an ostensibly functional necessity. The ranking powers – those who were to be formally ascribed as the great powers – wanted to maintain control of the Congress and its decisions.[7]

The Four – Britain, Austria, Prussia, and Russia – faced difficulty in constituting the Congress because there was no just means by which to base the stratification that they practically needed and self-interestedly desired. The relevant treaties provided neither a guide for how to constitute the Congress nor a legal basis upon which stratification could be justified. Moreover, there was no historical precedence to rely upon as the Congress of Vienna was a new type of summit. Previous international conferences of a similar nature were called to sign peace treaties. Stratifying peace conferences was relatively straightforward as the primary combatants could easily and justifiably assume superior, advantageous positions in the proceedings. The Congress was different because its purpose was oriented more towards managing the future peace of Europe than it was towards just ending past hostilities. While the Treaty of Paris ended the Napoleonic Wars, the Congress of Vienna sought to ensure hostilities could never resume. While the Congress was about the future of all of Europe, it was nonetheless solely the major combatants in the final coalition against Napoleon who served as the directorate of the Congress' Inner Committee, thus grounding the Congress in the *status quo*. It was a situation ripe for stratification. In the end, the Four used precedence set by peace conferences to base their claim for special status. "There came to Vienna an enormous number of plenipotentiaries… only to find no principle which should govern their procedure and no machinery by which they could be made into a coherent body."[8]

The Four communicated and met informally and secretly, mostly in Metternich's apartment, to devise how to constitute the Congress.[9] Most problematic was figuring out a way to stratify the other ranking powers who ostensibly were regarded as equals as ranking powers, but who were effectively considered as inferiors by the Four. Spain, Sweden, Portugal, and France were all signatories to the Treaty of Paris and along with the Four were considered to be the Eight great powers. Moreover, with the Treaty of Paris, which formally called for the Congress to be convened to settle European affairs via Article XXXIII, providing the closest approximation to a legal basis for the constitution of the Congress, their inclusion in the directing committee was warranted. The Treaty of Paris had secret articles, however, that were unknown to all except France, Great Britain, Austria, Prussia, and Russia. The first of the secret articles, which France was also unaware of, called for the members of the Quadruple Alliance to maintain control of the Congress for themselves.[10] This was affirmed on the 13th of September, 1814 when the ministers of the four allies – Great Britain, Austria, Prussia, and Russia – met in Vienna and agreed to "the necessity of keeping control of the discussions in their own hands."[11] For the Four to meet and affirm this among themselves already marks out stratification amongst Europe's ranking powers and signatories to the treaty. Spain, Portugal, and Sweden were also allied signatories who were excluded from this inner club.[12] They were seen by the Four as being relatively lesser powers, which is reflected in them having signed the Treaty of Paris *after* the Four had and having not been party to the Treaty of Chaumont. Moreover, they were not the principal contributors to the military efforts against Napoleon, particularly the 1814 campaign that drove him from power after the Battle of Leipzig.

At first, the Four came to the decision that they themselves would decide the most important matters – those concerning territory. The Four decided that the decisions that they took on these issues would first be communicated to Spain and France, and then to the rest of the Congress.[13] This arrangement was communicated to France and Spain "in as palatable a fashion as possible."[14] Despite the sugar coating of the Four, the idea was strongly objected to by Talleyrand. The idea of the Six was then abandoned in the face of Talleyrand's opposition and manoeuvring, accepting the Eight signatories of the Treaty of Paris as the Congress' directing Committee. Even still, though, the Four sought to maintain their privileged position. They continued to meet and correspond secretly at the exclusion of the others.[15]

Spain's, Portugal's, and Sweden's positions in a relatively lower stratum could be somewhat justified on credentialist grounds, owing to not participating in the decisive campaign against Napoleon. Casting France into a similarly lower position was comparatively more difficult and was ultimately impossible for the Four to achieve. As we saw previously, France was seen as an equal to the Four. Even when the Four ultimately had to concede and admit France into the inner club, they nonetheless continued to try to keep control. Without a sound argument to continue to justify France's exclusion, they instead just relied on secrecy, hiding their meetings from France (and the others).

In their secret interactions, the Four also discussed how to win the consent of the lesser powers for the stratified structure that they sought for the Congress. At first they agreed that the Six, including Spain and France, would constitute the directing Cabinet of the Congress and that the distinction between the Six and the rest of Europe constituted the distinction between the greater and lesser powers. It was in a series of meetings amongst the Four between the 15th and 19th of September 1814 that this social division, which would form the basis of the European international society throughout the long 19th century, was first articulated.[16] Beyond this giving birth to the Great Powers' club, it is also significant to note that this club had no legal grounding, having been self-selected and self-appointed by the in-group itself and having been so without any relation to even the Treaty of Paris. This club, in short, was formed in the exact same way as the Family of Civilised Nations and, as is detailed below, G-summitry. The Six, however, "was then to be a sham directing committee... with a real inner Committee of the four Powers..."[17] The Six could be socially divided from the rest according to a rationale based on the notion of there being a gradation of power, the superiorly positioned of whom had special responsibilities which justified their special status. The exclusion of France and Spain from the real inner Committee could not be so justified, so they continued to effectively exclude them by meeting secretly, even after formally declaring an equality of standing with them.[18]

G-summitry

Like the Great Powers' club, G-summitry formed to respond to a functional need for system-wide management and stratified the global economic governance order to accomplish that function. As detailed in Chapter 3, the origins of the club are to be found in a pragmatic solution devised by US Treasury Secretary George Shultz to respond to the crisis facing the Bretton Woods system in concert with the UK, France, West Germany, and Japan. It led to a series of regular, largely secret interaction until, in March 1973, Shultz suggested a more formal meeting amongst the Five. Shultz cleared the idea for the meeting with Nixon who said that as he was out of Washington on the weekend that the meeting was planned and suggested that Shultz give it 'a little class and have it in the White House.'[19] The group met over lunch in the White House library. Seeing practical value in continuing to meet and collaborate but needing to maintain the secrecy of the group, the emerging club decided to call themselves, "The Library Group," choosing something that would have meaning for those who were included but would not mean anything for those who were excluded.[20] The Library Group continued to meet on the sides of IMF meetings as well as at other times.[21] The group increasingly made itself more formal and its interactions more regular, but continued to hide its existence from the rest of the IMF as its exclusivity and the control it exercised could not be justified, being entirely of devoid of any legal basis or any other source of legitimacy. After Giscard mused about the possibility of holding an economic summit, the Library Group became his model for what the summit could be, based on his experiences in the group as the French finance minister up until he assumed the French presidency in May 1974.[22]

The interactions of the leaders and their representatives over the following months were all practical in nature, focused on how best to constitute a summit that could make a significant contribution to solving the economic crisis. Giscard, US President Gerald Ford, and the West German Chancellor Helmut Schmidt, who also was in the original Library Group with Giscard, discussed the idea of a summit later that month.[23] The French claimed that Ford was favourable to the idea, but US Secretary of State Henry Kissinger was doubtful, and US Assistant under Secretary of State for Economic and Business Affairs Thomas Enders indicated to Giscard earlier that month that the US would be opposed.[24] The British government's assessment was that the Americans were deeply sceptical of the idea.[25] Nonetheless two months later the relevant actors all agreed for the need for a high-level discussion on economic and financial matters. Ford, Schmidt, Giscard, and Wilson – "The Four" – agreed to meet on the side of the Conference on Security and Co-operation in Europe (CSCE) summit in Helsinki over lunch on the 31st of July 1975. Kissinger and the British Prime Minister James Callaghan were also present.[26] Just prior to the meeting, Schmidt circulated a memorandum detailing his argument in favour of a summit and suggested that the idea be formally adopted at "the luncheon of the four."[27] After outlining the problems affecting the world economy and the German position, he presented a specific proposal for a preparatory process. Schmidt suggested that the central bank governors should meet, ideally within a month, to agree to a coordinated policy to lower interest rates.[28] He stated that "The Conference should be prepared by the personal representatives of the heads of State and Government" and stressed the need for a summit amongst the US, the UK, France, Germany, Japan, "and possibly also Italy" before the end of the year.[29] At the lunch, the Four agreed on the utility of the summit and agreed on a process for preparing for the summit by coordinating things through a high-level group of experts, the group which would later become known as the Sherpas. Wilson suggested that, The Five's finance ministers (including Japan) should also meet to prepare for the Heads of Government meeting.[30]

What is important to stress here is that the club formed in response to the necessity to fix the world's economic system and did so adopting a governance model of that of the Great Powers' club, wherein the need for exclusivity was justified because of functional imperative and superior status was one reward for assuming systemic responsibility.[31] The group thus cast themselves as the great economic powers who as such shouldered the responsibility of managing the international economy.[32] US President Ford's opening remarks at the first summit at Rambouillet emphasised this notion of great economic power responsibility clearly,

[o]ur nations have for three decades been the foundation of human progress and the cornerstone of global peace. We are of central importance to one another – economically, politically, and militarily. The cohesion and vitality of our societies is of central importance to the rest of the world.[33]

So cast, a stratified global economic governance order could be justified in the same way that the European states system was under the stewardship of the Great Powers' club.

This is evident not just in the declarations that the group members made in calling for the establishment of the summit, but also in the way that they justified the exclusivity of the group's membership to those actors who felt they should be included. The club justified their exclusivity and the subordination of others on the grounds that doing so made it possible for the largest, industrialised, democratic economies to fix the economic crisis. The inclusion of any superfluous actors would harm the ability of the group to accomplish its function. French President Giscard most obstinately denied inclusion to others according to this argument, particularly Canada.[34]

Despite Giscard's efforts to keep Canada, Italy, and the European Community out of the club, they eventually gained inclusion, with the G5 expanding quickly to become a G7 (+ the EC) by 1977.[35] As quickly as the group expanded, it internally stratified in order for those superiorly positioned within it to remain in control, just as was the case of the Four at the Congress of Vienna. "The Four" – the US, the UK, France, and West Germany – were a club within the club. The archival record is rich with communication amongst the Four from the moment the possibility of a summit is first mused about by Giscard. It was the Four that first met in-person in Helsinki, and it was representatives of the Four who first formed the Carleton Group in Shultz's hotel room on the 16th of September 1975.[36] Japan, Canada, and Italy were marginalised as they were not seen to be of equal political standing to the others. Canada and Italy were relatively more marginalised than Japan as they were also seen as being of sufficiently less economic standing than the others such that further division could be warranted. Again, the Four adopted the same rationale as the leading powers at Vienna for internally stratifying the upper echelons of the Congress as the Four, the Five, the Six, and the Eight.

Stratification on political grounds was present from the genesis of the very idea of the summit. Giscard raised the possibility of Italy's inclusion in the interview in which he first mused about the possibility of holding an economic summit.[37] Italy's place was not secured, though, until relatively soon before the summit began, having been debated by the Four over the course of nearly four months before finally being granted. Italy was eventually incorporated in order to give a symbolic boost to the governing Italian Democratic Party against the Italian communists. Prior to being brought in, Italy was excluded by the Four from the early meetings to form the club, claiming that they were meeting without Italy to discuss Berlin, an issue to which Italy could not claim any responsibility or ability to contribute.[38]

What is significant is not just that they initially excluded Italy on these grounds, but that the Four continued to maintain a superior position by internally stratifying the club even after Italy (and Canada) was incorporated into the club. The Four continued to meet "under the Berlin umbrella" to discuss political topics at the exclusion of the rest of the G7.[39] In a meeting with Callaghan, Giscard said, "in a case of serious crisis or real emergency, it might be useful to have a meeting of the United States, the United Kingdom, France, and West Germany."[40] Callaghan responded highlighting the necessity of excluding others to keep the meetings small and effective, proposing a strategy of, "fix[ing] up crisis meetings at very short notice, before the rats could get at them."[41] Giscard's and Callaghan's use of language is significant. Giscard's language discursively ascribes an identity wherein the marginalised are not fit to deal with "serious" or "real" issues. Callaghan's language equally – though more bluntly – inferiorly positions these actors by relating them undesirably to pests. To Callaghan, the only "valuable meetings" were those from which all but the Four were excluded.[42]

Beyond the significance of this internal stratification, it is also worthwhile to note here that, contrary to what have become the canonical accounts of the G7 summit's history, the early summits were not solely focused on economics. They were publically portrayed as economic summits in order to justify the exclusion of all but the few members of the club; substantively, the summits always had a political dimension. Indeed, at the 1978 Bonn summit the G7 began making formal statements on political topics.

The Four sought to meet privately in advance of the third G7 summit at Downing Street. Carter's Vice President, Walter Mondale, reported after a meeting with Giscard that the French President wanted to reach a formal agreement "hereby certain members of the summit should have separate political discussions."[43] Carter subsequently sent a telegram to Callaghan stating, "I would hope that – as President Giscard suggested and you and the Vice President discussed – we might use the occasion to hold, discretely, a separate, smaller meeting of the four of us with special Berlin interests."[44] In a conversation a few days later, Carter again suggested to Callaghan that the Berlin cover be used as a cloak for a discrete meeting of the Four at the Downing Street Summit.[45] Schmidt also agreed to Giscard's suggestion "that before the meeting of the Seven we could have a meeting at four [*sic*] *with* the cover, if we need one, of Berlin, for instance."[46] The need for secrecy was emphasised in a telephone conversation between Giscard and Callaghan prior to the summit as they discussed possible venues for the Four to meet that would be, in Giscard's words, "a special place, like a kind of private place, perhaps it would be less offensive."[47] Much discussion was also had about whether or not the Four should meet before or after the formal

G7 meeting.[48] The Four tried to find a time and place that would least attract the attention of the excluded and that would least offend them, should the meeting's existence become known outside of the Four. Callaghan and Giscard discussed the possibility of the Four meeting the evening prior to the summit. Callaghan sent a telegram to Carter a few days later about the summit and Carter responded with a letter in which he suggested that the Four meet after the summit "to avoid embarrassing the others attending the Summit, who might conclude that the purpose of a May 6 meeting among the four was to prepare for the Summit meeting itself."[49]

The French proposed a meeting of the Four in Bonn in 1978, but were opposed by the Americans.[50] The Americans were not as concerned with retaining such exclusivity – their status position was far more secure than that of the Europeans. The US' rank as the largest economy was undisputed, and they lacked any neighbour who might pose a challenge to their position, whereas the Europeans' position was more precarious. Indeed, from the very beginning the US was resistant to France's push for a small directorate, preferring a larger "consultative group" made up of what would eventually become the G7 membership.[51] Having opposed the French proposal for another meeting of leaders of the Four in 1978, the Four's foreign ministers instead met on the sidelines of the Bonn summit where they planned a political meeting amongst the heads of the Four for the following year which would exclude Japan, Canada, and Italy.[52]

A 1979 political meeting of the Four took place in Guadeloupe. This meeting is significant because it cemented the relative positions of the relevant actors. As with their other meetings before, the Four justified the exclusion of others by claiming that the meeting was exclusively to deal with political topics. In so doing they co-constituted an identity for themselves which held the monopoly right to discuss such topics and an identity for the excluded which lacked this right, thus closing off any opportunity for inclusion. As before, they did not contain their discussions to political topics alone, despite claiming to do so.[53] Notably, it was at this meeting that the Four decided to exclude Australia from the G7.[54] Japan, the upcoming summit host and sponsor of Australia's inclusion, was entirely excluded from participating in the discussion. Excluding Italy and Canada from the discussion as well demonstrates that the Four were entirely acting as an executive directorate within the G7. Japan, Italy, and Canada may have been nominally equal members in the G7, but substantively they were anything. Guadeloupe was also significant as it was the first time that the Four were open about their exclusive meetings. With the cat out of the bag, the Four's coordination shifted from an emphasis on maintaining the secrecy of the meetings to protecting the sensitivities of those excluded. Furthermore, much effort went towards maintaining the secrecy of the content of their meetings, not wanting to alert Japan, Italy, and Canada to the extent to which the Four were colluding in advance of meetings of the Seven.

An exercise of deference on the part of Japan may be observed in their reaction to their exclusion. "Japan's feelings towards the Guadeloupe summit were ambivalent – a mixed reaction of taking exclusion for granted on the one hand, and a sense of humiliation on the other."[55] There was even the suggestion that this was felt by the Japanese population generally. As Shiro Saito relates, "it was almost a relief that the Japanese Prime Minister was not invited, for Japan did not have a leader of sufficient calibre to join in informal talks with these veteran politicians from the Western world."[56] In particular, it was suggested that the Four felt that Japan was not qualified to discuss international strategy.[57]

The Guadeloupe meeting was unlike the previous meetings of the Four as its existence was not kept secret, thus publically condemning Japan, Italy, and Canada to second-class status within the club. In reaction to being publically cast as not being suitable for the top stratum, Japan, Italy, and Canada had "a strong incentive to develop the economic summit into a more formal and visible vehicle of political discussion."[58] The Four's prohibiting of Japan, Italy, and Canada hosting a summit before the Four had themselves hosted, as a means of affirming their status as the core of group, provided the impetus for the integration of the second tier. Because these three ended up being successive hosts they were able to control the summit process over three successive years and thus had a greater ability to organise things in such a way that they were able to secure greater inclusion. As below, the Four's inability to hold an exclusive political meeting in Venice because of the hosts "susceptibilities" exemplifies this nicely.[59] The second tier were thus able to wrestle away one of the exclusive competences claimed by the Four.

The Four thus used Guadeloupe to cast others into subordinate positions. The meeting decided that Australia would be entirely excluded from the club, and Japan, Italy, and Canada's status as second-class members of the club was affirmed.[60] Conversely, the meeting publically affirmed the top strata of G-summitry which was particularly significant for West Germany as Giscard saw the country's inclusion at Guadeloupe as symbolising its return "to equal international status."[61]

For the 1980 Venice summit, the choreography involved in having a private meeting of the Four and managing the excluded was as much a concern for the Four as it was at the Downing Street summit. This was especially difficult as Italy was the summit host. The Four's Sherpas met in advance in Sardinia to plan the summit, one proposal for which was to have a "political day" at the summit, which would effectively make the previously secret meetings of the Four known publically, but would still exclude Canadian, Italy, and Japan. The UK Sherpa Robert Armstrong related that this would need to be explained "privately to the Canadian, Italian, and Japanese sherpas."[62] Armstrong questioned how to diplomatically "stage-manage" this arrangement, noting that "it will no doubt need to be pursued on a very discreet basis between the right people in the seven Governments nearer the time..."[63] The Sherpas, again affirming the principle of secrecy, "stressed the need to restrict to an absolute minimum the number of people who knew that the idea of a political discussion was even being considered."[64] They also "recognised that there would be a problem over the lesser allies, who would resent exclusion from political discussion even more than from a purely economic Summit [sic]."[65] Not only did "lesser allies" discursively cast the excluded into a subordinate position, this dimension was particularly problematic, given that it would eliminate the group's strictly economic remit as a justification for having their special status in the stratified order. The Sherpas recommended that the Four be open about the political discussions in the communiqué so as to quell suspicions of the excluded which "would simply be exacerbated if the communiqué referred only to economic subjects."[66] The French Sherpa, Bernard Clappier, objected bluntly to this arrangement, outright refusing to discuss anything but economic topics (though this protest did not hold).[67]

One British proposal suggested that the UK drafted a paper to be circulated amongst the Four on "Western foreign policy following Afghanistan" which would then be considered at a future meeting of the Four and then thereafter be shared with the Japanese, Italians, and Canadians.[68] This arrangement changed slightly over the next month such that each of the Four would prepare papers on different topics.[69] France suggested that Japan drafted a paper on China, to which the rest of the Four agreed.[70] As concerns Italy and Canada, "i[t] was not envisaged that the papers to be drafted by the Four would be distributed unchanged to the Seven."[71] The Sherpas agreed to decide at their next meeting whether Japan, Italy, and Canada would be required to undertake any preparation for the summit beyond "considering language for the communiqué."[72]

The Four's Sherpas continued to meet on political topics in the lead-up to the summit but did not conclusively agree on whether or not to make political discussions a formal part of the summit.[73] A month before the Venice summit, the Four's Sherpas met at the British Ambassador Lord Carrington's residence in Vienna to continue the debate. France argued strongly for keeping a political meeting to exclusively the Four.[74] The US' representative at the meeting remarked that "there was a problem about excluding countries from groups where they felt they belonged. Some cover was needed, and the cover was never adequate."[75] The "Berlin umbrella" was as good a cover as the Four would ever get. After a further meeting of the Four's Sherpas in Paris just before the summit, it was decided that they could not exclude the second-tier members "because of Italian susceptibilities."[76]

While the Four decided to include the second tier, they still sought to hide their "prior collusion particularly to the hyper-sensitive Italians."[77] It was agreed amongst the Four that France would propose, as a unilateral French document, the Four's draft communiqué.[78] Then, shortly before the meeting, the US would propose, as a unilateral American document, the Four's proposed agenda. The Permanent Secretary of the Foreign and Commonwealth

Office, Michael Palliser, wrote, "[w]hen we all meet in Rome, the British, French and Germans will of course support the 'American' annotated agenda, without revealing our part in drafting it."[79] Palliser continued, "Similarly, we, the Americans and the Germans will in principle support the 'French' draft of the communique passage: but we will, by agreement, subtlety suggest certain modifications designed to cover the French text at Annex B into the slightly preferable version at Annex C."[80] It was, in Palliser's words, "a rather complicated web."[81]

It is at this time that a code word, "Burning Bush," began appearing on British documents referring to meetings of the Four.[82] The first Burning Bush memorandum detailed how the Sherpas agreed to stage-manage the Four's meeting. They would sandwich the political discussion between two economic discussions. The idea was that the finance ministers would leave after the first discussion to draft text for the communiqué, allowing the leaders to discuss political matters in their absence. It was thought that this would be a good way of ensuring that EC's representative Roy Jenkins would not be present.[83] The Four particularly did not want the EC, as a non-state actor, in the room for the political discussions.

Japan too was marginalised by the Four. The near-total absence of communication with Tokyo about the summit is noteworthy. While included by virtue of their economic rank, the Japanese were not influential in shaping the summit. In addition, the Japanese proposed to host the third summit in 1977 but did not ultimately do so as the "core" countries each wanted to take a turn at hosting before the summit would move to Tokyo.[84] Japan thus did not get to host until 1979. For the 1979 Tokyo summit, the Japanese tried to use the host's privilege to have a greater say over invitations and include Australia at the summit, as they had intended to do if they had successfully won the bid to host in 1977.[85] They did not succeed. Japan's relatively marginal position to the Four is evidenced in a statement made by Ford that "I should like to stress that while we must, of course, conduct formal representations in a group of seven, this will not exclude continuing contact, when necessary, among Britain, France, Germany, and the United States, and with Japan where appropriate."[86] In all, while Japan was included as one of the initial G5, they were very much the fifth member.

Japan, though, was positioned relatively higher than Canada and Italy. The inferior positions of Canada and Italy is most apparent in advance of the 1976 Puerto Rico summit – the first to which both were invited. Indeed, the text for the announcement of the summit, proposed by France, went out of its way to draw a distinction between the Five and expanded Seven.[87] Ford suggested that the Five should meet secretly in advance of the Seven at Puerto Rico, and that the personal representatives of the Five should work together in Washington to decide on the summit's agenda and draft communiqué without Italian or Canadian representation.[88] The secrecy of their exclusion of Italy and Canada was threatened when at a Sherpa meeting the US "half let out of the bag some of the discussion which had taken place at a private meeting on the first day which had not been attended by Italy or Canada."[89] At the summit itself, the Four's leaders met secretly and even discussed Italy's domestic political situation, "but no mention of this was of course made to the other participants,"[90] not even Italy.[91] In the meetings to which Canada and Italy were included, their marginality was further apparent. For example, in a detailed note from Hunt to Callaghan reporting on a preparatory meeting in Bonn in 1978, Canada and Italy were not mentioned at all in the entire nine-page memorandum.[92] Two years previously, in advance of Puerto Rico, Hunt reported that the Italians, Canadians, and Japanese contributed little to the Carleton Group.[93]

In the 1990s, Russia, like Italy and Canada before it, was incorporated into the club and cast into a subordinate position within it. G7 finance ministries, the US Treasury chief among them, were opposed to Russia's inclusion. While the political case for Russia's incorporation was strong, the economic case was not. As the US Sherpa put it, Russia was an "economic basket case."[94] Despite its large GDP, it shrank throughout the decade, only beginning a recovery in 1999 and returning to its 1990 levels in 2007. Moreover, the country's economic and financial institutions were either weak or absent. The US Treasury thus argued fiercely against the White House and State Department in opposition to Russia's inclusion, stressing its unsuitability.[95] The Treasury's concerns were quashed by the overriding political imperative to bring the Russians in "to support their movement away from communism towards the world economy and give them an anchor in the West."[96] As a result, Russia was brought into the "political 8" but not the "economic 8." Like Japan, Italy, and Canada in the1970s, Russia was included in some meetings, but not all. Moreover, those from which it was excluded – the economics and finance discussions – were those that were of most important to the club and Russia's transition.[97]

In sum, those superiorly positioned at the Congress of Vienna and those superiorly positioned in G-summitry made the same types of moves to stratify their respective clubs, justifying doing so it terms of functional necessity when possible, and getting away with it through secrecy when not.

Functional incorporation

Great Powers

Russia wanted to control Poland so that it could be its proverbial foot in the European door as part of its overall strategy to rid itself from being ascribed as a semi-civilised state, and to increase its European power base so as to not be positioned at the margins of the Great Powers' club. Prussia wanted Saxony to likewise increase its own power. With their interests aligned, Russia and Prussia joined together to carve up Europe for their mutual aggrandisement. Britain and Austria opposed the Russo-Prussian plan on the grounds that it would make them too powerful, destabilising the balance of power that the Congress was meant to establish in the wake of Napoleon's conquests (and that the Concert of Europe was to then subsequently maintain). The Four were in deadlock over the issue. Prussia threatened war and Russia called for a formal conference to resolve the impasse.[98] Both acts had significant consequences for the establishment of order in the European system. Prussia's threat brought Britain, Austria, and France closer together, and Russia's move resulted in the Four for the first time formally and openly being constituted as the exclusive directorate of Europe.

Britain and France immediately called for France to be included in the conference, arguing that their inclusion was warranted given their interests in the Rhine.[99] Prussia objected strongly, knowing that French inclusion would almost necessarily mean they would not be able to annex Saxony.[100] Realising this, Prussian troops began organising and fortifying Dresden in an attempt to force a quick and favourable resolution before France could be included and Russia's position weakened.[101] In response, Britain, Austria, and France met secretly and formed a defensive alliance. While the move was a bluff, not least of all because Castlereagh had no mandate to commit Britain to war, it was never called.[102] Upon learning of the secret treaty Prussia backed down and agreed to France's inclusion in the group with the assurance that the Saxony settlement would be a genuine compromise. Russia likewise acquiesced the following day.[103]

What is significant about this is why France was incorporated into the group. As above, they were initially excluded owing to the Four's fear of France's power. This, by definition of how a concert works, makes the Four inappropriately constructed, as not all the great powers were included. France was incorporated to break a deadlock that threatened the survival of the club itself and the system which it had responsibility for maintaining. France's incorporation was thus a functionalist move. The in-group accepted the expansion of the club with the elevation of France in order to maintain the club's overall position as the managers of the stability and survival of international society.

While I primarily rely upon Webster's account of the Congress, I disagree with his analysis of France's incorporation, which he characterises as having "been less due to any effort or intrigue on [Talleyrand's] part then to the fact that the four Powers had been unable to agree, and had, in fact, come to the verge of war."[104] I agree with Webster insofar as the disagreement amongst the Four opened the opportunity for France's inclusion. However, France's inclusion would not have been possible if Talleyrand had not engaged in the entry strategy that he had. Spain was not dissimilarly positioned to France at the start of the Congress. Spain, however, made no comparable effort to gain entry into the top-tier group. Indeed, it is significant to note that France and Spain learned of the Four's designs for a stratified Congress wherein the Six were to be subordinate to the Four at the very same meeting. The proposal was no more acceptable to the Spanish plenipotentiary Labrador than it was to Talleyrand, who led the objection to the plan, with Labrador playing only a supporting role.[105] Moreover, Spain made no entry bid akin to France's banding strategy. While included alongside France in the Six, Spain did not manoeuvre itself to gain entry into the ranking club. Conversely, Talleyrand's moves positioned France to exploit the cleavage in the club at the right time in order to gain inclusion. In short, the proximate condition for France's inclusion may have been the Four's disagreement, but what ultimately made France's incorporation possible was twin effect of Talleyrand's entry strategy and the club's desire not to break apart. By looking at France's admission to the Great Powers' club, we may thus see both sides of the closure dynamic playing out via incorporation: the outsider seeking entry to increase its status and the insider(s) granting it to maintain their status.

G-summitry

The same functionalism motivated incorporation in G-summitry. Italy was the first addition to the G-summitry club. Against persistent objections from Giscard, Italy was included as doing so served the purpose of providing support for Italian democratic forces against a surging communist party. Despite Giscard including Italy in the original list of potential invitees to the summit, the country became the sole one that was explicitly named in the original interview whose inclusion was up for debate.[106] The US Ambassador to Italy John Volpe noted that Italy's exclusion would relegate the country to a "series B classification," which the Italian foreign ministry tried to avoid, principally by lobbying the US to give support for Italy's inclusion.[107] It was believed that the US would be more sympathetic to Italy's case for inclusion than its fellow Europeans. There were three reasons behind this: US support might (i) please Italian-American voters; (ii) dilute Franco-German pressure on the US at the summit by increasing the number of invitees to the summit; and (iii) counter social and economic problems affecting Europe, which could affect the Atlantic alliance, particularly by including the country – Italy – "in which social tensions appeared particularly grave."[108]

Italy was excluded from the Helsinki lunch at which the Four met and agreed to the summit. Italy's exclusion from the meeting was protested strongly by the Italian government. Prior to the lunch meeting, US Ambassador Volpe sent a telegram to Kissinger relating that Secretary General Raimondo Manzini, speaking on behalf of Italian Foreign Minister Mariano Rumor, was upset to learn about the meeting amongst the Four.[109] Manzini argued that Italy should be included because of its position as President of the European Commission and as the Italian Treasury Secretary Emilio Colombo was Chairman of the European finance ministers.[110] Manzini also argued that Italy's exclusion weakened Prime Minister Aldo Moro's domestic position, which was fragile as his "already shaky government" was under threat of being replaced by the Italian Communist Party, a concern which become a central point of discussion amongst the Four in their debates about Italy's inclusion.[111] Based on these arguments, Volpe recommended to Kissinger that Italy be included.

Kissinger met Rumor the morning prior to the Helsinki lunch meeting. Sticking to the Italian strategy, Rumor argued for Italy's inclusion at the meeting by evoking the threat of the Italian Communists, asserting that it provided a big boost to their popularity if the current Italian government was to be seen to not be a big player economically on the world stage.[112] Kissinger countered that the meeting was not to discuss economic matters and that the Four met solely to discuss Berlin, stressing that it is symbolically important for the Four to meet to underline their rights and responsibilities surrounding Berlin.[113] Kissinger further countered by stating that he would clarify publically that the meeting was to discuss Berlin, not economic matters.[114] The French account of the meeting, however, indicates that Kissinger was flat out lying to Rumor. The French account details four pages of discussion about the economy, how to coordinate a response, what the preparatory procedure for a summit might be, and the suggestion that the summit should happen in the autumn.[115]

Moro and Ford met at the Helsinki summit the day after the lunch.[116] They discussed the threat posed by the election of communist parties at length, both domestically within Italy and internationally. At the meeting Rumor raised the question of the four-power luncheon, which he had asked Kissinger about the previous day when the two had met.[117] Kissinger, with great diplomatic obfuscation, responded saying, "[t]hat has been denied by the British and by us." Rumor pressed him on the point, referring to rumours of a five-power meeting, about which Kissinger was again coy.[118] Rumor then related the consequences of Italy's exclusion in terms of it giving a "several percentage points" political boost to the Italian communists and very bluntly related the perception of deliberate exclusion, "You stopped many times on your trips in Bonn and we have a feeling we are on the outside."[119] The exchange continued, with Rumor pointedly asking why the US would not publically declare support for Italy's inclusion. He also noted that there would be a significant psychological impact on the Italian electorate if Italy were to be included and if there were to be more official visits between the US and Italy.[120] Kissinger concluded the argument, again denying that the US had agreed to the summit, relating that the US was willing to consult with Italy in its capacity as EC President, and asserting that the initiative for the summit was European-driven.[121] Kissinger's implication was that Moro should speak with his fellow Europeans.

Italian protestations over their exclusion continued after Helsinki. Volpe reported to Kissinger about press reports in which Colombo openly raised the question of Italy's exclusion. Volpe noted that the predominant fear of the Italians was that a new permanent economic directorate was being formed from which the Italians were either entirely excluded or, perhaps worse, "invited only as an apparent afterthought."[122] Italian anxieties over being cast in a subordinate status position outside of the "the Big Five or Big Six" were particularly palpable at this point.[123] The insecurities, in short, of exclusion were not articulated in terms of being upset about not being able to contribute to a solution to the world's economic problems or concerns over the size of a country's GDP, but rather were articulated in terms of status position.

The country's inclusion was characterised by Kissinger as "a matter of highest level consideration."[124] Kissinger wrote that the Italians had "mounted majo[r] [sic] pressure to be included" even adopting a mimicry move by having "unilaterally designated Dr Rinaoldo Ossala as their expert [Sherpa]."[125] An exchange of letters between Italy's UK Ambassador and the UK's Permanent Undersecretary of State at the Foreign Office and the chief UK diplomat Sir Thomas Brimelow indicated that the UK had agreed to Italian inclusion at the New York Sherpa meeting and for inclusion at the summit itself.[126] The move by the UK surprised the US; but, as a result, the US agreed in principle to Italian inclusion, suggesting that Italy should check with West Germany and France if indeed an invitation could be extended.[127] France and West Germany held out the longest, refusing approval of Italy's inclusion until "the last minute."[128] Following French and West German approval, Kissinger informed the Italian Ambassador on the 1st of October, 1975, just days before the New York meeting, that Italy would be included, transforming the G5 into the G6.

What is significant about Italy's arguments for inclusion is that the appeals were based on Italy's standing as President of the EC and based on an appeal to the threat of communism. Manzini did not argue Italy's right to inclusion based on the country's economic standing. Manzini's argument was not dissimilar from Talleyrand's at the Congress of Vienna, claiming that the country's inclusion would bring legitimacy to the group (as the EC President) and support the favoured principle governing domestic political organisation (as a democratic government).[129] Recall that Talleyrand argued that Restoration France's inclusion would bring legitimacy as a representative of the smaller, excluded European principalities and that its inclusion would reaffirm the principle of dynastic legitimacy against the destabilising force of revolutionism. On the other side of the closure coin, what is significant about the club's incorporation of Italy is that it was an entirely functionalist move. The club's interests were advanced by its incorporation, as Italy's inclusion bolstered legitimacy of the club in the eyes of the excluded, smaller European states; quieted (however momentarily) their objections to their exclusion; and helped prevent the communists taking control of the Italian government.

It is worthwhile to briefly consider the other case of incorporation, that of Canada, in the early days of G-summitry. Canada's bid for inclusion closely parallels that of Italy and for sake of brevity the same points about France's reluctance to grant membership and the US' push for it need not be explored in great detail. It is sufficient to note that both Canada and Italy adopted similar inclusion strategies. What is noteworthy is that the reason for Canada's incorporation is similar to the proximate reason for France's inclusion at Vienna. Canada's incorporation primarily served the particular interests of members within the club, rather than the interest of the club as a whole. Just as France's inclusion at Vienna was championed by Britain and France as doing so helped them secure a favourable resolution to the Polish-Saxony question, so was Canada's incorporation into G-summitry a move that served the American desire not to be "alone in the room with a bunch of Europeans."[130] For the US, Canada's incorporation was a balancing move.

The Outreach 5 (O5) and newly included G20 members were similarly incorporated into G-summitry for the functionalist reason to maintain the survival of the club, just as France's inclusion in the inner committee at Vienna rendered the great power concert built-for-purpose. As argued in Chapter 3, unevenly applied credentialism has served as a mobility dampener which prevents the loss of status for incumbent club members, despite an objective decline in their relative standing internationally. As was also previously argued, a reduction in the efficacy of the club to fulfil its international function creates an opportunity for new actors to be included or, from the perspective of the in-group, creates the necessity of revising the club's membership, or else risks the club becoming irrelevant. The imperative for the G8 to incorporate the rising/emerging powers was to protect its own status. This is exemplified well in the exchange detailed in Chapter 5 amongst the G8 leaders at the 2005 Gleneagles summit. With the O5's leaders waiting to be allowed into the meeting room to have lunch with the G8, the Canadian Prime Minister Paul Martin raised the possibility of usurpation by the O5.

Faced with usurpation, the club moved to incorporate those that posed a challenge. It was preferable to expand the club and have a relatively smaller loss of status for its members than to have the club to be eclipsed and entirely lose its status and function in the management of international society. This is further evidenced by the arguments made by Paul Martin to counter G8 members' objections to the G20's creation. The Germans were particularly opposed to the idea of the G20 out of concern for a loss of status resulting from the expansion of G-summitry.[131] Ian Bremmer misquotes and mischaracterises Martin in his work on the "G-Zero," asserting that "Martin believed that Canada could exchange its first-class seat on a sinking ship for a secure spot on a bigger boat."[132] This was not, however, Martin's motivation for including new actors; rather, it was the argument forwarded by Martin to counter German opposition to the inclusion of outsiders in a new G-summitry forum.[133] Indeed, the Germans were resistant to the expansion of the club when discussions of the incorporation of the O5 were being made, being especially reluctant to expand the G8 to a G13. Their private objection ran counter to their public position, having formally launched a dialogue process between the G8 and O5 at the Heiligendamm summit in 2007 to investigate the possibility of expansion.[134] The Germans were opposed to a larger group of twenty because they did not want to lose their status as a member of a more exclusive group of seven. Martin's counterargument was that it would be better to be part of a larger group that mattered than a smaller group that was becoming increasingly irrelevant, particularly in the face of the establishment of an "alternative global clique."[135]

Japan likewise resisted the G20's creation because of the perceived loss of status generally. Additionally, though, Japan also feared the elevation of regional neighbours' statuses.[136] Japan feared both a general loss of global status and a particular loss of regional status. Japan did not want to lose its exclusive position as the sole voice of East Asia in G-summitry,[137] feeling particularly threatened by the inclusion of Japan's main rival, China.[138]

Cultural stratification

The previous section detailed how outsiders justify the marginal incorporation of others in terms of functional necessity. Cultural stratification, on the other hand, likewise involves the incorporation of outsiders in unequal and subordinate ways, but instead involves stratification based on more collectivist attributes. Newly included actors are cast into lower strata within the club because they are unlike the club's incumbents. Incumbent members thus maintain their position through relatively greater collectivism.[139] What seems like a more just inclusion of new actors in a more just governance order is not quite as just as it appears: collectivist closure is still at work, but operating under the guise of inclusivity.

The closure rules that make up the Standard of Civilisation are predominantly functional-individualist in nature, with the exception of the criteria covering cultural dimensions and the Standard's implicit racism. In terms of broader cultural practices and institutions, the cultural dimension included the prohibition of suttee, polygamy, and slavery. It was, however, quotidian norms and practices, such as wearing particular styles of dress or listening to acceptable styles of music that made this dimension of the Standard amenable to subjective adjudication.[140] As a result, incumbent club members could use the mutability of particular rules to safeguard their status positions, picking and choosing which criteria to emphasise in their adjudication of the suitability of a particular entrant, exacting a higher standard from a particular actor relative to another. This was especially useful for safeguarding the status of insiders as it is almost entirely impossible for an outsider, particularly one coming from somewhere geographically and culturally outside of Europe, to satisfactorily meet all of the cultural criteria, not least of all because quite what constituted meeting the criteria could be changed subject to the whims of the club's incumbents. As Okagaki relates, "[s]ome of the criteria of the 'standard,' however, could be recognised more objectively than others."[141] If wanting to be more exclusionary, the club could raise a particular barrier to entry for any particular actor whom the club did not wish to admit as an equal. The cultural dimension of the Standard is thus what allowed for stratification within the club as the achievement of these criteria could be less objectively recognised by the in-group, allowing for the creation of the substrata of 'semi-civilised' actors.

The way that new entrants could be stratified within the club was a cause of much frustration. The Japanese charge d'affairs in France, Motono Ichiro, "was shocked to realise how much Japan was looked down on by the West" even after their victory over Russia in the Russo-Japanese War.[142] France even wanted to deny Japan the customary compensation owed to it by the defeated Russia as an Asian newcomer.[143] The denial of racial equality is the most well-documented dimension of Japan's frustration with the club's collectivist stratification, be it in their failure to secure a racial equality clause at Versailles or the racial discrimination faced by their American émigrés.[144] Indeed, Japan chose to exit Western international society in the 1930s in reaction to the way that the incumbent Europeans treated the country as Japan "perceived itself to have struggled hard to join them only to be denied a fair place after fulfilling the requirements set forth in their standard of 'civilization'."[145]

Similar frustrations were felt by states who believed that they had achieved entry into the Great Powers' club but who were likewise denied standing as an equal. Like the mutability of the cultural dimension of the Standard, the decision over who could be recognised as a great power was "vulnerable to manipulation (usually by the more powerful actors) and misperceptions. This does mean that for some states fulfilling the criteria need for entry can seem like chasing a floating target, and this only adds to their sense of annoyance."[146] Suzuki refers to such states as "frustrated powers" who "believe they have been refused social equality with other 'legitimate great powers' in the course of their interactions with their peers" and who are "not given privileges associated with 'legitimate great power status', and perceive a mismatch between their own expectations and the actual 'constitutive privileges' they are (or are not) accorded."[147]

Suzuki, following Ringmar, argues that a frustrated power needs to engage in recognition games in order to gain their denied status.[148] This involves identifying the norms and rules governing identity in the system and the persuading others that it fits the desired identity. Suzuki argues that being seen as a "good citizen" is especially important for recognition, particularly "in the post-Cold War international society under American unipolarity."[149] Principally, this involves demonstrating a "respect for human rights and liberal democratic governance as its core norms."[150] Moreover, quoting Reus-Smit, Suzuki gives a pride of place in the stratified order to liberal democracies whom "because of their distinctive qualities and historical standing... ought to have special rights in international society, both in international decision-making and with regard to domestic autonomy."[151] There are a few significant things to note here: first, the attributes that need to be signalled are almost exactly the same criteria that made up the Standard of Civilisation. Moreover, recalling considerations over Malaysia's, Indonesia's, and Nigeria's possible inclusions in the G20, it was according to these same criteria that their suitability for entry was adjudicated. Getting out of a frustrated position requires the adoption of Western norms and institutions. Conversely, stratifying ascendant others into subordinate positions can be achieved by the club ascribing those actors as being unsuitably dissimilar in terms of their values and institutions. Simplifying this into the language of identity, the club subordinately stratifies those who are otherwise objective equals by claiming that they are too dissimilar.

The Family of Civilised Nations used the cultural dimensions of the Standard and racial collectivism to stratify international society. The Great Powers' club likewise used hallmark criteria of the Standard to stratify, through at least ostensibly the Great Powers' club stratified based on more individualist dimensions than the Standard. Both clubs thus stratified according to the same norms, values, beliefs, and institutions of European international society, wherein incorporated actors ascribed as being dissimilar from incumbents were cast into inferior or marginal positions within the club. The absence – or, at least, lesser prevalence – of racial collectivism absent in stratifying the Great Powers' club marks it as being relatively more open.

G-summitry likewise culturally stratifies. Most significantly, it does so in such a way that those most similar in identity to incumbents are incorporated into relatively higher positions, while more dissimilar actors are positioned more marginally. The qualities justifying stratification are predominantly individualist in nature, marking G-summitry as being relatively open. However, the way that others' unsuitability is discussed is reminiscent of the more paternalist discourse through which the Family of Civilised Nations ascribed those it viewed as outsiders/inferiors.

Russia was incorporated as a stratified lesser, being welcomed into the G7's political discussions – to form the G8 – but excluded from the G7's finance and economics meetings.[152] As the US Sherpa at the time of Russia's incorporation related, "the scuttlebutt around the table was that it wasn't an industrial nation, wasn't a free market economy; why are we including them in the club?"[153] The debate over Russia's incorporation was fundamentally about their dissimilarity from the rest of the club. Russia was not just cast into a lower stratum because of its relatively weak economic position, but because its *identity* did not match those of the club's incumbents. While there was a functional reason for its stratified incorporation but that was not the only logic guiding Russia's marginalisation within the club.

What is necessary to add to the analysis of this case is that Russia's incorporation into G-summitry had the same significance as Japan's entry into international society in that Russia's inclusion demonstrated that the relatively homogenous, Western, liberal, and democratic club could expand to include actors that did not fit this description and that unalike actors were willing to join. Just as Japan's entry into international society served as a 'proof of concept' for the expansion of Western European international society, so too did Russia's entry into the G8 serve as a test case to

136 *Incorporation*

demonstrate the ability of the institution to expand, as it would relatively soon thereafter with the establishment of the much less homogenous G20. Moreover, that Russia could be incorporated ostensibly as a full member, but positioned into a lower stratum than the rest of the club, equally demonstrated that such stratified incorporation was possible in G-summitry. What sets the Russian case of stratification apart from that of Italy and Canada in the 1970s was that their marginalisations were entirely cases of functional stratification, whereas in the case of Russia cultural stratification is at play. What is significant about Russia's incorporation is that it set the precedence for the same sort of stratification that renders the G7 distinct from the G20 today.

G-summitry's further expansion meant further cultural stratification. The G20 did not replace or usurp the G7. Indeed, those involved in the summits stress that the G7 and G20 are separate groups with distinct identities.[154] Indeed, this is partially by design – Paul Martin related the importance of having the G20 as a distinct entity from the G7 as it allowed the G7 incumbents' concerns over a loss of status to the institution's expansion to be alleviated.[155] Conversely, having the groups stratified allowed for China to be able to accept membership. China could not have joined the G8 as doing so would have forced it to lose its ability to claim the status as being the head of the G77 group of developing countries. It would be seen as joining "the rich man's club."[156] China could, however, accept membership alongside other emerging/rising powers in the G20, thereby not forcing it to lose its status and identity as the developing countries' leader.

The G7's endurance has been met with animosity from those G20 members who are not included in the more exclusive club, though this has reduced in recent years as the G7's import has decreased. This animosity was particularly evident when Canada hosted the G8 and G20 back-to-back in 2010, conspicuously displaying what could be perceived as the marginalised G20 members having second-class status. The Canadians had intended for the sequencing of summits to signal that it was the G20 and not the G8 that had become the primary group for discussing macroeconomic issues.[157] The effect, however, was to make the G20 feel like a group that served only to legitimate decisions already made by the G8.[158]

What is most significant about the division between the G7 and G20 is that it is principally drawn along lines of cultural similarity. Whereas the G7 is a "community of values," the G20 is not so ideationally homogenous.[159] Much speculation about the future of the G20 revolves around whether or not the group will hold together in the face of the stress caused by the dissimilarity of the club's members.[160] Indeed, as one G7 Sherpa related during the wake of the Global Financial Crisis, "cleavages between actors will come to the fore. They're there, just suppressed because G20 is in crisis mode which forced people and countries to get along whereas they might have otherwise not."[161] The continuance of the G7 is justified by its members, despite its lack of representative legitimacy and the G20 having taken the status of being the "premier economic forum", on the grounds that the G7 works as a club of alike actors, whereas the G20 does not.[162] The club's incumbents often regarded the newly incorporated as inferiors. G7 Sherpas as well as international non-governmental organisations (INGO) representatives related how problematic they found working with some newly included actors in G-summitry. Civil society representatives were particularly frustrated with China's attempts to block any civil society outreach initiatives.[163] This was particularly problematic when China hosted the 2016 Hangzhou G20 summit. Indeed, the major INGOs who annually participate in the summit sat that year out. Prior to Russia's expulsion from the G8, one representative asserted that

> the G8 is a real cultural thing. Russia acts very European so it works. But with the G20 you have new cultures in and there is a shift in how you conduct business and diplomacy, they come to the table in different ways. Our people show up with a rough mandate and room for manoeuvre but they show no willingness to negotiate, have no room for manoeuvre, and are not willing to talk to the media. It's a new breed of players.[164]

This representative continued by asserting that "most of the intellectual ideas in the G20 were brought by the G8; and, of those, from five countries-not Japan, Russia, or Italy."[165] One Sherpa remarked that "Argentina is in its own world."[166] Another Sherpa, representing a newly included G20 country, related that invited guests at the summit "contribute very little at all. Ethiopia just sat there. They didn't do anything at all."[167] Another Sherpa related that "newcomers don't necessarily see that part of what confers legitimacy to a leader is compatibility with others. They don't have that level of maturity or level of domestic debate."[168] When an invitee bucked this trend, it was met with surprise, "Cambodia had a very good Sherpa – very good participation, very good contributions. We found this surprising."[169] Others, however, related that "I was very impressed with my Sherpa colleagues from China, India and Brazil, their behaviours were better than I would have expected."[170] The barely concealed paternalism is noteworthy.

Further evidence of cultural stratification can be observed in the relative positions of the newly included. Those most alike the G7 are superiorly positioned to the others. Most significantly, Korea, Mexico, and Turkey were the first of the newly incorporated members to be granted the honour of hosting the summit. As one G7 Sherpa admitted when asked about these three being the first of the new entrants to host, "They're closest to us [the G7]. We're most comfortable with them."[171] What marks them out as distinct from their cohort of entrants is that they are the only OECD members. Note that the G7's ranking members in the 1970s treated Japan, Italy, and Canada in the exact same way, preventing them from hosting the summits before they did.[172]

138 *Incorporation*

Despite what seems like "the systematically significant emerging countries [being] included as equals alongside the established G8 powers" in the G20, substantively they are not.[173] They are incorporated to provide both material and ideational benefits to the club such that G-summitry can maintain its role and position in the management of international society. However, the new members are not included as equals. Even in the contemporary context that calls for a more open, just governance order, stratification endures. Moreover, stratification endures in part through this relatively furtive cultural means.

Collectivist stratification

The stratification of international organisations (IOs) is included here as their relegation to marginal positions within the club is result of the legal-collectivism levelled against them. The nature of their stratification is slightly different from what is categorised here as cultural stratification in that what has so far been examined is a dissimilarity from incumbent members in terms of secondary closure criteria. In the case of IOs, their dissimilarity and exclusion is owing to the primary closure rule. This distinction aside, the nature of stratification remains the same: they are positioned marginally because of a dissimilarity with incumbents and not for functionalist reasons; moreover, they are so positioned in order to protect the status of incumbents. As non-sovereign actors, IOs' subordination within the club is a closure move that protects the primacy and exclusivity of states within international society. As state-like governmental entities, they are afforded a relatively greater degree of inclusion than other non-state actors, but they are nonetheless stratified according to a collectivist logic. As before, I am not claiming that IOs are less powerful than states. That is obviously not true. I am interested in their *status* in the international domain and how that plays out in terms of how they contribute to the management of international society.

The first non-state actor to be incorporated into the club was the European Community. As was detailed earlier, the club's motivation for incorporating the EC was to quell the smaller, European countries' objections to their exclusion. The prospect of EC inclusion was first discussed in terms of Italy's inclusion as, in 1975, Italy held the rotating presidency of the EC. Prior to the Rambouillet summit, one question that was circulating amongst the club when considering Italian participation was whether or not Italy could be included as a member in its own right or as President of the European Community. Italy's position on the matter was clear – if they were to be included it would be as a member country in its own right, thus putting them on par with the other members, and not because they happened to hold the EC presidency. The closest that Italy came to suggesting that inclusion should be based, in part, on its position as EC President came when Volpe informed Kissinger that Rumor wanted to be included at the Helsinki luncheon "especially when [Italy] is president of the EC and Treasury Minister Colombo is Chairman of the Finance Ministers."[174] Rumor's claim was still principally that Italy should be included because of its standing as a country, but claiming a right to inclusion because of holding the presidency was put forward as a way to bolster that claim. Aside from this one instance, all other arguments put forward by Italy for inclusion were solely articulated in terms of Italy's position as being one of the largest industrialised Western economies.[175] As President Moro stated when Italy finally was granted inclusion at Rambouillet, membership was granted because Italy was seen as "a first class power by the other larger industrialized nations."[176] Indeed, when the question of EC representation at the summit arose, Italy did not want its inclusion to be interpreted as being a result of its position as EC President to the extent that it outright refused to coordinate the positions of the EC members not invited to the summit.[177] As the UK Sherpa John Hunt later wrote, inviting the Italians because of the EC Presidency "could have created a potentially embarrassing precedent."[178] Having to invite a state only because it held the presidency would have meant that smaller, less powerful actors would be brought into the group, even if only temporarily. The UK held the EC presidency in 1977, the same year that the UK was to host third G7 summit. Callaghan asserted that he was hosting the summit solely as the UK prime minister and not in a dual capacity also as the EC President. He was careful to emphasise the UK's inclusion and role in the group in terms of its membership as a sovereign state rather than as the EC President, as any degree of inclusion on the grounds of the presidency "might set a precedent for others, such as Luxembourg, in future."[179]

After word about the Carleton Group's first meeting in 1975 leaked, smaller, industrialised EC states were particularly upset about their exclusion.[180] "The Benelux Ambassadors formally protested about the lack of prior consultation."[181] The excluded Europeans finally won their appeal for consultations in 1976, which Hunt characterised as something that "we... will have to live with."[182] Brussels' position was that there should be a discussion within the EC for how France, Germany, and the UK could represent the EC.[183] Belgium's Deputy Permanent Representative Hervé Robinet relayed to the US that what particularly upset smaller European states was the way in which their exclusion was decided – by *fiat*.[184] In the days leading up to Rambouillet, Commission officials took the line that the EC's exclusion from the summit would "have a negative impact on EC solidarity... exacerbating the small member states' concerns about being dominated by the large ones."[185] They also objected on grounds that their exclusion was unjustified as the issue of trade fell within the competency of the EC rather than the member states.[186] Their objections were exacerbated by the fact that Italy refused to coordinate EC views and represent them at the summit in an effort to not associate their inclusion with their position of EC President.[187] EC members continued to protest the exclusion of the EC and their own exclusion as industrialised countries in the lead-up to Puerto Rico.

Just prior to the summit, Callaghan's Private Secretary Patrick Wright wrote that Luxembourg sent a telegram protesting the summit; that the UK received ambassadorial representations from Belgium, Luxembourg, and Ireland; and that "further representations are expected from the Danes."[188] The Irish protested the lack of EC consultation and the Belgians protested the exclusion of the EC President. On the 3rd of June, 1976 Luxembourg went so far as to send a *demarché* to the White House and the State Department requesting the Luxembourgish Prime Minister Gaston Thorn be invited to attend the summit as the Head of the Government holding the EC presidency.[189]

The question of the EC's inclusion arose again in advance of the third summit in London in May 1977. The American President Jimmy Carter pushed hardest for the EC's incorporation.[190] The UK responded to Carter's position by asserting that Callaghan would consult EC members about the possibility of inclusion.[191] Callaghan personally phoned Giscard and Schmidt to discuss the fact that Carter was now pushing for EC inclusion.[192] Callaghan and Giscard raised the possibility of including the President of the European Commission Roy Jenkins as the representative of the EC. Giscard says it the decision ultimately rested with Callaghan in his role as current President of the Council.[193] Jenkins had become President in January 1977, having lost the race to succeed Wilson as Labour Leader and Prime Minister to Callaghan in March 1976. Callaghan and Jenkins by this point had become bitter political rivals,[194] though Callaghan did not articulate his opposition to the EC's representation in personal terms. In a phone call with Schmidt, Callaghan related, "I told him [Carter] privately I did not want to say anything against Roy Jenkins, as an old colleague, but privately my view was the Community would be adequately represented if you and Giscard and myself were there with [Italian Prime Minister] Andreotti."[195]

The topic remained highly contentious. Callaghan described a European Council dinner for Heads of Government and the President of the Commission at the Palazzo Barberini later that month, as a "long and ridiculous argument" with "the Belgian and Dutch Prime Ministers [taking] extreme positions," and indicated that "he was the only one present at the Dinner [*sic*] who did not lose his temper."[196] Giscard objected on the now familiar grounds that the inclusion of any additional actors would ruin the informality of the summits.[197] Significantly, he also raised the primary closure rule in objecting to the possibility of EC inclusion, stating that "[i]f the view was taken that the Commission had to attend, by right, he would not himself go."[198] Giscard took the position that the Council President (a state representative) could attend but not the Commission (a non-state representative), suggesting that Callaghan attended the summit in a double role as the UK Prime Minister and as the President of the Council.[199] To this, the Belgian Prime Minister Leo Tindemans exclaimed that he "could not possibly be represented at the Conference by Mr Callaghan!"[200] Giscard suggested that Callaghan could "be accompanied by the President of the Commission so that the latter could express an opinion on Community matters."[201] "Accompanied" is the operative word here, denoting a position for Commission President that is second tier to the state leaders. Callaghan retorted "that this would be an undignified role for Mr Jenkins."[202]

Jenkins was ultimately invited to participate at the third G7 summit held at Downing Street in May 1977. Like the others cast into second-tier positions, he was excluded from all political discussions.[203] At the press conference following the summit, he was not given a microphone. At later summits, when political discussions became part of the official agenda, the Sherpas agreed that it would be inappropriate for the EC representative to be part of any political discussions.[204] Giscard, speaking to Callaghan, mused that the inclusion of the Commission in any political meetings "would make it a very strange kind of meeting."[205]

In contemporary G-summitry, the EU has come closest to achieving equal standing to the state members of the club but still inhabits a secondary position. EU representatives characterise themselves as the twentieth member of the G20 to claim an equal status but acknowledge that as the only non-sovereign actor sitting at the table with the club of states they have to "behave accordingly."[206] In so doing they thus reveal deference to the prevailing order which holds that sovereign states – and sovereign states alone – are worthy of full membership.[207] That said, the EU is the sole non-sovereign entity that has near-equal standing to states. This is evident in both substantive and performative ways: EU Sherpas are included in the entire preparatory process, the EU is mentioned alongside states in communiqués, and the EU presidents are included in the "family photo" at the summits.

There are a number of important things to note about the EC/EU's stratified incorporation. First, the strength of the legal-collectivist closure rule is well exemplified, being used both to at first exclude the EC and then subsequently to justify its stratified incorporation. More than this, though, it is worthwhile to note how strongly state actors resisted being tarred by the collectivist brush, with Italy and the UK both strongly asserting that their inclusion in the club in no way was related to their status as EC President. The EC/EU is a near-perfect case for identifying legal-collectivism as a means of stratification. The EC/EU is alike the rest of the club members in all ways except that it is a non-sovereign actor. It is on these collectivist grounds alone that they are subjected to/through stratified incorporation.

Other IOs are also stratified in G-summitry, though with a relatively lesser degree of inclusion than the EU. Their position is explained by the fact that within G-summitry, IOs are characterised according to a functional institutionalist understanding. That is, they are simply the passive instruments of states.[208] They are included because they perform useful functions for the club, such as producing reports and providing impartial advice, which is especially helpful given that the club lacks a secretariat. Because their identity is ascribed in this way so as to stress their functionalist purpose, IOs are not threats to the prevailing order. They have agency in the system only insofar as states delegate it to them.[209] They are in an entirely responsive position, coming to the table with no agenda of their own. The added numbers of IOs in the process at the G20 speaks to this point. The increase is not due to a shift in the closure game wherein these non-state actors have greater standing, but due to a shift in the needs of the club. With the elevation of the G20 to the leaders' level in response to the Global Financial Crisis, the IOs that were granted greater inclusion were those with the technical/functional capacities to contribute to an effective solution. The list of included international financial institutions at the 2008 G20 summit which was first called at the leaders' level to address the Global Financial Crisis reveals this: the IMF, World Bank, and Financial Stability Forum (later, the Financial Stability Board). In short, the point is that the inclusion of IOs is entirely dependent on the priorities and functional needs of the state members in the management of international society.

IOs' swelled numbers do not mean that they are treated any differently in contemporary G-summitry. One Sherpa related that in the preparatory process he threw all the IO representatives out of the meeting, only then inviting them in when their relevant issues were being discussed. "They went mad, they hated it. But you have to kick some people out to make those in the room feel special."[210] This move firmly underlines the fact that IOs are included solely for functionalist reasons and that states recognise no universal, legitimist claim for their inclusion. Furthermore, IO representatives' exclusion is unambiguously relayed as being part of a status game.

Conclusion

The international domain is stratified; so too is international society within it. The most entrenched social division is between those sovereign actors inside international society and the non-sovereign actors outside in it, with there then being further gradations of positions within this broad division. Moreover, within international society's status groups there are social divisions, further adding layers to the stratified order. It is thus incorrect to describe membership in any group as a binary condition, wherein an actor is either inside or outside of a club. As Neumann observes, international society is a "layered phenomenon" – "joining it is not a digital question of being in or out, but an analogue question of the degree to which one is in."[211] To miss this is to miss a critical dimension of the international closure game. Groups are not just clubs with members, they are themselves stratified systems marked by unequal relations of power and status.

This chapter has also demonstrated that it is necessary to reformulate the way we theorise how clubs govern the inclusion of new members. It is not a simple process of bringing an outsider in. Incorporation *is* stratification. Outsiders are brought into a club in ways that protect, as best as is possible, the positions of insiders. This is achieved by casting new entrants into marginal or inferior positions. Thus, the dynamics of club membership are also more complex than we think, and to miss the way that clubs incorporate is to fail to grasp a key way that order is reproduced in international society.

This prompts three revisions of extant closure theory. It requires that closure theory changes the way it conceptualises groups so as to understand them as stratified entities rather than as clubs composed of members of equal standing. Related, it also requires closure theory to examine closure within groups, not just between them. Third, this chapter has demonstrated that relations between insiders and outsiders do not have to be antagonistic. Club composition can change through a more cooperative process of incorporation. Closure theory needs to reconceptualise how it understands the relations between insiders and outsiders and in so doing recognise that inclusion does not have to be the result of antagonism. This claim fits with that made in the previous chapter which argued for the reform of closure theory's conceptualisation of the possible types of strategies that outsiders may engage to seek entry into the club.

Finally, this chapter has argued that G-summitry stratifies by the same modes of closure as can be observed in the Family of Civilised Nations and the Great Powers' club. Critically, it does so not only through a functionalist logic but also through a persisting cultural logic. Despite the contemporary context requiring a more just, open, equal, inclusive, and representative governance order, stratified incorporation means that this is not entirely so. Greater and more diverse inclusion does not mean that new entrants are included as equals, nor does it necessarily mean that social mobility in the system is more fluid.

Notes

1 Bull, H. (1977). *The Anarchical Society: A Study of Order in World Politics* (4th edition). Basingstoke: Palgrave Macmillan.
2 Osiander, A. (1994). *The States System of Europe, 1640–1990: Peacemaking and the Conditions of International Stability.* Clarendon Press, 168.
3 Webster, S. C. (1950). *The Congress of Vienna 1814–1815* (Later edition). London: OUP, 74.
4 Ibid., 90.
5 Osiander, *The States System of Europe*, 1994, 168.
6 Webster, *The Congress of Vienna*, 1950, 97.
7 Ibid., 80.
8 Webster, *The Congress of Vienna*, 1950, 74.
9 Gooch, B. (1970). Europe in the 19th Century: A History. Retrieved 28 July 2014, from www.abebooks.co.uk/Europe-19th-Century-History-GOOCH-BRISON/19093649/bd, 57. There's an interesting parallel here with the informality of the Library Group.
10 See The Napoleon Series, 2008.
11 Webster (1950, pp. 79–80).
12 Simpson, G. (2004). *Great Powers and Outlaw States: Unequal Sovereigns in the International Legal Order.* Cambridge; New York: Cambridge University Press, 6; Webster (1950, p. 80).

144 *Incorporation*

13 Webster, *The Congress of Vienna*, 1950, 83–84.
14 Ibid., 84.
15 Ibid., 87–91.
16 Ibid., 80.
17 Ibid., 81.
18 Ibid., 88–92.
19 Ibid.
20 Ibid.
21 Ibid.
22 Ingersoll to US Embassy, 10 July 1975; UK Foreign and Commonwealth Office, 12 February 1976.
23 UK Foreign and Commonwealth Office, 12 February 1976.
24 Bayne to Fogarty, 11 July 1975, in *Giscard's Proposal for a Monetary Summit Conference*.
25 UK Foreign and Commonwealth Office, 12 February 1976.
26 Sauvagnargues Calinet, 31 September 1975, in *Sommet Monetaire*.
27 Schmidt, 31 July 1975, *Private Memorandum on International Concertation of Economic Action*.
28 Ibid.
29 Ibid.
30 Sauvagnargues Calinet, 31 September 1975, in *Sommet Monetaire*. This proposal, though, wasn't immediately adopted. Kissinger opposed it outright due to internal political problems that he and Ford had with William Simon, the Secretary of the Treasury (Morris to Kissinger, 7 August 1975, in *Proposed Five Power Economic Conference*).
31 This is not to contradict the argument advanced in Chapter 3 that G-summitry is *predominantly* underpinned by the diplomatic institution.
32 *EC Foreign Ministers Meeting in Lucca: Economic Topics*.
33 Hormats to Scowcroft, 2 December 1975, in *Memorandum of Conversation*.
34 Kissinger and Sonnenfeldt to Porter, 8 November 1975, in *Presidential Letter to Prime Minister Trudeau*; Rush to Kissinger, 18 December 1975, in *French-Canadian Relations: Ups and Down*; Sonnenfeldt and Ingersoll to US Ambassadors in London, Bonn, Rome, and Tokyo, 28 September 1975, in *Possible Economic Summit*; UK Foreign and Commonwealth Office, 12 February 1976, in *Rambouillet: The French View*.
35 Italy in 1975, Canada in 1976, and the EC in 1977.
36 Sauvagnargues Calinet, 31 September 1975, in *Sommet Monetaire*.; Shultz, G., Interview by Telephone, 5 September 2012. The Carleton Group was the name originally given to what has become known as the Sherpa group. It was so named after the Carleton Hotel in which they met.
37 Ingersoll to US Embassy, 10 July 1975.
38 Volpe to Kissinger, 29 July 1975, in *Possible Big Five Monetary Summit*; Volpe to Kissinger, 30 July 1975, in *Big Five Economic Directorate*; Volpe to Kissinger, 13 September 1975.
39 Callaghan and Giscard, 18 February 1977, in *Record of a Telephone Conversation Between the Prime Minister and President Giscard d'Estaing on Friday 18 February 1977*; Palliser, 6 June 1980, in *Political Discussion at the Venice Summit*.
40 "Puerto Rico Summit Meeting", 22 June 1976. The sentiment was reiterated in a note a month later.
41 Ibid.
42 Ibid.
43 "Economic Summit" 1976. Mondale also discussed the possibility with Callaghan & Mondale, 27 January 1976, in *Economic Summit*.

44 Carter to Callaghan, 12 February 1977.
45 Callaghan and Giscard, 18 February 1977, in *Record of a Telephone Conversation between the Prime Minister and President Giscard d'Estaing on Friday 18 February 1977.*
46 Callaghan and Giscard, 18 February 1977, in *Record of a Telephone Conversation between the Prime Minister and President Giscard d'Estaing on Friday 18 February 1977.* For a record of all that was discussed by the Four see:
47 21 February 1977, A phone call between Carter and Thatcher about the Four meeting in 1979 later parallels Giscard and Callaghan's conversation. 4 July 1979.
48 Callaghan, 9 May 1977; Carter and Callaghan, 25 February 1977.
49 Ibid.
50 Margaret Thatcher Foundation, 28 July 2014, in *Declassified G7 files.*
51 Volpe to Kissinger, 29 July 1975, in *Possible Big Five Monetary Summit.*
52 Margaret Thatcher Foundation, 28 July 2014, in *Declassified G7 files.*
53 Vile to Hunt, 15 January 1979, in *Guadeloupe Summit.*
54 Margaret Thatcher Foundation, 28 July 2014, in *Declassified G7 files.*
55 Saito, S. (1990). *Japan at the Summit: Its Role in the Western Alliance and in Asian Pacific Cooperation.* London: Routledge for the Royal Institute of International Affairs, 62.
56 Ibid.
57 Ibid.
58 Putnam, R. D., & Bayne, N. (1984). *Hanging Together: The Seven-Power Summits.* London: Heinemann for the Royal Institute of International Affairs, 112; Saito, *Japan at the Summit*, 1990, 641.
59 Archival documents: Palliser, 6 June 1980, in *Political Discussion at the Venice Summit*; see also: Thatcher and Trudeau, 25 June 1980, in *Venice Summit.*
60 Belgium, the Netherlands, and Denmark were also insulted by their exclusion (Saito, *Japan at the Summit*, 1990, 63).
61 Margaret Thatcher Foundation, 28 July 2014, in *Declassified G7 files.*
62 Armstrong and Wade-Gery, 16 May 1980, in *Quadripartite Meeting, Vienna.*
63 Ibid.
64 Ibid.
65 Ibid.
66 Ibid.
67 Ibid.
68 Ibid.
69 Armstrong and Wade-Gery, 16 May 1980, in *Quadripartite Meeting, Vienna.*
70 Ibid.
71 Ibid.
72 Ibid.
73 At a meeting on the 8th of February 1980, for example, they discussed Afghanistan, Iran, North Yemen, Saudi Arabia, Oman, Kenya, Somalia, and the Soviet Union, among other topics.
74 Armstrong to Palliser, 15 April 1980, in *Quadripartite Meeting*; Armstrong and Wade-Gery, 16 May 1980, in *Quadripartite Meeting, Vienna.*
75 Ibid.
76 Palliser, 6 June 1980, in *Political Discussion at the Venice Summit.* Though they would meet at Venice as a G7, they would meet at the at subsequent NATO meeting in Ankara as the Four under the "Berlin cover." The Four also did the same again a year later during Tokyo's summit. Dubbed "The Tokyo Guadeloupe," The Four held a night meeting excluding all others, including, as at Venice, their hosts. Funabashi, Y. (1980). *Samitto No Shiso (Philosophy of the Summits).* Tokyo: Asahi Shinbunsha., 26; Saito (1990).
77 Palliser, 6 June 1980, in *Political Discussion at the Venice Summit.*

146 Incorporation

78 Ibid.
79 Ibid.
80 Ibid.
81 Ibid.
82 Armstrong to Palliser, 15 April 1980, in *Quadripartite Meeting*; Armstrong and Wade-Gery, 16 May 1980, in *Quadripartite Meeting, Vienna*; Pallister, 6 June 1980, in *Political Discussion at the Venice Summit*.
83 Armstrong to Pallister, 15 April 1980, in *Quadripartite Meeting*; Armstrong and Wade-Gery, 16 May 1980, in *Quadripartite Meeting, Vienna*.
84 Government of Australia, 11 August 1976, in *Tokyo Economic Summit*; Bayne, N., Interview in Person, 9 October 2012.
85 Hunt, 29 May 1978, in *Bonn Summit*; Rose, 12 January 1979, in *Guadeloupe: Follow-Up Action*. On the proposed 1977 Tokyo summit, Menadue, in 11 August, in *Tokyo Economic Summit*, Government of Australia, 11 August 1976, in *Tokyo Economic Summit*; Enders to Kissinger, 26 November 1976, in *Canada and Next Economic Summit*.
86 Ford to Callaghan, 5 June 1976; see also: Hunt to Callaghan, 16 June 1976, in *Puerto Rico*.
87 Ford to Callaghan, 31 May 1976.
88 Ibid.
89 Hunt to Callaghan, 16 June 1976, in *Puerto Rico*.
90 Ibid.
91 Italy knew that their domestic situation was being discussed. Schmidt stated so publically (Rose, 12 January 1979, in *Guadeloupe: Follow-Up Action*)
92 Hunt, J. (1978, June 30). Bonn Summit. Memorandum. Retrieved from www.margaretthatcher.org/document/111462.
93 Hunt to Callaghan, 16 June 1976, in *Puerto Rico*.
94 Fauver, R., Interview by Skype, 16 July 2013.
95 Ibid.
96 Ibid.
97 It is interesting to note that there is a complete reversal here in terms of what meetings became exclusive. Japan, Italy, and Canada were included in economic discussions but not political ones; conversely, Russia was included in the latter but not the former.
98 Webster, *The Congress of Vienna*, 1950, 132
99 Only a few weeks before they had likewise called for the inclusion of France in the critically important Statistical Commission as doing so was a condition of France's continued support for Britain and Austria's position on the Polish-Saxony question (Webster, *The Congress of Vienna*, 1950, 92).
100 Webster, *The Congress of Vienna*, 1950, 132.
101 Ibid., 132–133.
102 Ibid., 126, 133.
103 Ibid., 135.
104 Ibid. 93.
105 Ibid., 84.
106 Volpe to Kissinger, 30 July 1975, in *Big Five Economic Directorate*.
107 Ibid.
108 Ibid.
109 Volpe to Kissinger, 29 July 1975, in *Possible Big Five Monetary Summit*.
110 Ibid.
111 Volpe to Kissinger, 29 July 1975, in *Possible Big Five Monetary Summit*.
112 Kissinger to Volpe, 30 September 1975, in *Secretary's Meeting with Italian Foreign Minister Rumor*.
113 Ibid.
114 Ibid.

115 Sauvagnargues Calinet, 31 September 1975, in *Sommet Monetaire*. Callaghan made the suggestion for an autumn meeting, echoing Giscard's original proposition.
116 Hormats to Scowcroft, 2 December1975, in *Memorandum of Conversation*. Also present are Kissinger, Sonnenfeldt, Hartman, Rumor, Manzini, and Valluri.
117 Scowcroft to Hormats, 2 December 1975, in *Memorandum of Conversation*.
118 Ibid.
119 Ibid.
120 Ibid.
121 Ibid.
122 Volpe to Kissinger, 13 September 1975. The feared permanence of the group was a particular concern of not just the Italians but other excluded countries, namely, Canada and smaller European states, that felt they had a right to be included (Volpe to Kissinger, 29 July 1975, in *Possible Big Five Monetary Summit*).
123 Volpe to Kissinger, 13 September 1975.
124 Kissinger, 10 October 1975, in *Economic Summit*;
125 Ibid.; Kissinger, 9 October 1975, in *Economic Summit*.
126 Sonnenfeldt and Ingersoll to US Ambassadors in Bonn, London, Paris, and Ottawa, 2 October 1975, in *Economic Summit*.
127 Ibid.
128 *EC Foreign Ministers Meeting in Lucca: Economic Topics*.
129 Volpe to Kissinger, 13 September 1975.
130 Bayne, N., Interview in Person, 9 October 2012. Japan's inclusion, it seems, was felt to be insufficient for the US to balance against the European bloc.
131 Martin, P., Interview in Person, 23 August 2012.
132 Bremmer, I. (2012). *Every Nation for Itself: Winners and Losers in a G-Zero World*. London: Portfolio, 2.
133 Martin, P., Interview in Person, 23 August 2012.
134 Interview: Anonymous subject 1.1
135 Martin, P., Interview in Person, 23 August 2012. It was not only due to status concerns that Germany objected to the G20. They were also concerned that the club would serve as a moral hazard, with members needing larger IMF bailouts should they default (Summers 2012).
136 Interview: Anonymous subject 4.4
137 Saito, *Japan at the Summit*, 1990.
138 The inclusion of South Korea likely also plays into this, though interview subjects only pointed to China as being seen as a threat by Japan.
139 To be clear, the argument is not that cultural stratification is purely collectivist, but rather that it is *relatively* collectivist.
140 Gong, G. W. (1984). *The Standard of Civilization in International Society*. Oxford: OUP.
141 Okagaki, T. T. (2013). *The Logic of Conformity: Japan's Entry into International Society*. Toronto: University of Toronto Press, 40.
142 Ibid., 117–118.
143 Ibid., 118.
144 Gong, *The Standard of Civilization in International Society*, 1984, 198.
145 Ibid., 165; Okagaki, *The Logic of Conformity*, 2013, 118.
146 Suzuki, S. (2008). Seeking 'Legitimate' Great Power Status in Post-Cold War International Society: China's and Japan's Participation in UNPKO. *International Relations*, 22 (1), 45–63, 49.
147 Ibid.
148 Ringmar, E. (2002). The Recognition Game Soviet Russia against the West. *Cooperation and Conflict*, 37 (2), 115–136. 121–122; Suzuki, Seeking 'Legitimate' Great Power Status, 2008, 50.
149 Ibid.

150 Clark, I. (2005). *Legitimacy in International Society*. Oxford: OUP, 157 and 275; Fidler, D. (2001), pp. 137–157. The Return of the Standard of Civilization. *Chicago Journal of International Law*, 2 (1), 137–157; Fukuyama, F. (1989). The End of History? *The National Interest*, (Summer 1989), 3–18; Morris, J. (2004). Normative Innovation and the Great Powers. In A. J. Bellamy (Ed.), *International Society and Its Critics* (pp. 265–282). OUP; Suzuki, Seeking 'Legitimate' Great Power Status, 2008, 50.
151 Reus-Smit, C. (2005). Liberal Hierarchy and the Licence to Use Force. *Review of International Studies*, *31* (Supplement S1), 71–92. 76.
152 Talbott, S. (2007). *The Russia Hand: A Memoir of Presidential Diplomacy*. Random House Publishing Group, 124–125.
153 Fauver, R., Interview by Skype, 16 July 2013.
154 Martin, P., Interview in Person, 23 August 2012.
155 Ibid.
156 Ibid.
157 Edwards, L., Interview by Telephone and Skype, 15 March 2012.
158 C.f. Kirton, J. J. (2010). The G20, the G8, the G5 and the Role of Ascending Powers. *Presented at the Ascending Powers and the International System*, Instituto Matias Romero, Secretaria de Relaciones Exteriores, Mexico City. Retrieved from www.g8.utoronto.ca/g20/biblio/index.html, 7.
159 Lesage, D. (2010). Introduction: The G8 and G20 in Flux, under the Skillful Presidency of Canada and Korea. *Studia Diplomatica*, *63* (2), 3–6, 3.
160 Cooper, A. F. (2012). The G20 as the Global Focus Group: Beyond the Crisis Committee/Steering Committee Framework. *G20 Research Group*. Retrieved from www.g20.utoronto.ca/analysis/120619-cooper-focusgroup.html; Cooper, A. F., & Bradford, C. (2010). The G20 and the Post-Crisis Economic Order. *CIGI G20 Papers*, (3). Retrieved from www.cigionline.org/publications/2010/6/g20-and-post-crisis-economic-order; Martin, P. (2013). The G20: From Global Crisis Responder to Steering Committee. In A. F. Cooper, J. Heine, & R. Thakur (Eds.), *Oxford Handbook of Modern Diplomacy* (1st edition, pp. 729–744). Oxford: OUP.
161 Edwards, L., Interview by Telephone and Skype, 15 March 2012.
162 Interviews: Martin, P., Interview in Person, 23 August 2012.
163 Rea, J., Interview in Person, 9 February 2012.
164 Interview: Anonymous subject 3.3.
165 Ibid.
166 Interview: Anonymous subject 4.4.
167 Interview: Anonymous subject 2.2.
168 Interview: Anonymous subject 3.3.
169 Interview: Anonymous subject 2.2.
170 Interview: Anonymous subject 4.4.
171 Interview: Anonymous subject 1.1.
172 Bayne, N., Interview in Person, 9 October 2012.
173 Kirton, J. J. (2013). *G20 Governance for a Globalized World*. Ashgate.
174 Volpe to Kissinger, 29 July 1975, in *Possible Big Five Monetary Summit*.
175 Greenwald to Kissinger, 30 October 1975 in *Reluctance of the Member States to Assume Community Budgetary Obligations Signals Setbacks in EC Solidarity*; Hodgson, 21 October 1975, in *Economic Summit*; Kissinger, 9 October 1975, in *Economic Summit*; Kissinger, 9 October 1975, in *Economic Summit*; Morris to Kissinger, 7 August 1975, in *Proposed Five Power Economic Conference*Morris to Kissinger, 7 August 1975, in *Proposed Five Power Economic Conference*; Volpe to Kissinger, 13 September 1975, in *Press Reports On Colombo-Giscard D'Estaing Talks*; Volpe to Kissinger,

13 September 1975; Volpe, 27 October 1975, in *Ambassador's Meeting with Prime Minster Moro.*
176 Volpe to Kissinger, 22 October 1975, in *EC Foreign Ministers Meeting in Lucca: Economic Topics.*
177 Greenwald to Kissinger, 30 October 1975, in *Reluctance of the Member States to Assume Community Budgetary Obligations Signals Setbacks in EC Solidarity.*
178 UK Foreign and Commonwealth Office, 12 February 1976.
179 "Economic Summit" 1976.
180 UK Foreign and Commonwealth Office, 12 February 1976.
181 Ibid.
182 Hunt, 19 January 1977, in *Preparations for an Economic Summit.*
183 Morris to Kissinger, 7 August 1975, in *Proposed Five Power Economic Conference*. At this time, Italy's inclusion had not been secured. The first occasion where a common EC position could be formed was at a meeting of EC finance ministers in Venice on the 24th of August, 1975.
184 Morris to Kissinger, 7 August 1975, in *Proposed Five Power Economic Conference.*
185 Greenwald to Kissinger, 30 October 1975 in *Reluctance of the Member States to Assume Community Budgetary Obligations Signals Setbacks in EC Solidarity.*
186 Ibid.
187 Ibid.
188 Wright to Callaghan, 4 June 1976.
189 Ibid.
190 Callaghan and Schmidt, 16 March 1977, *Record of a Telephone Conversation Between Chancellor Schmidt and the Prime Minister on Wednesday 16 March 1977.*
191 Callaghan, 9 May 1977.
192 Ibid.; Callaghan and Giscard, 18 February 1977, in *Record of a Telephone Conversation between the Prime Minister and President Giscard d'Estaing on Friday 18 February 1977*; Callaghan and Schmidt, 16 March 1977, *Record of a Telephone Conversation between Chancellor Schmidt and the Prime Minister on Wednesday 16 March 1977.*
193 Callaghan and Giscard, 18 February 1977, in *Record of a Telephone Conversation between the Prime Minister and President Giscard d'Estaing on Friday 18 February 1977*;
194 Bayne, N., Interview in Person, 9 October 2012.
195 Callaghan and Giscard, 18 February 1977, in *Record of a Telephone Conversation between the Prime Minister and President Giscard d'Estaing on Friday 18 February 1977*; Callaghan and Schmidt, 16 March 1977, *Record of a Telephone Conversation between Chancellor Schmidt and the Prime Minister on Wednesday 16 March 1977.*
196 UK Government 25 March 1977. Callaghan later noted that Liam Cosgrave, the Irish Taoiseach "had not been ill-tempered."
197 Ibid.
198 UK Government, 25 March 1977.
199 Ibid.
200 Ibid.
201 Ibid.
202 Ibid.
203 "Economic Summit" 1976. Callaghan related to American Vice-President Walter Mondale that the club had to be "careful" about political topics "because of possible trouble with the community."
204 Armstrong to Whitmore, 25 April 1980.

205 UK Foreign and Commonwealth Office, 12 February 1976.
206 Kobele, F., Interview by Telephone and Skype, 13 February 2012. The twentieth membership spot, however, is not the EU's, it is the place that was meant to be taken by Nigeria (Martin, P., Interview in Person, 23 August 2012).
207 Kobele, F., Interview by Telephone and Skype, 13 February 2012.
208 This characterisation of passivity was not shared by OECD Sherpa Gabriella Ramos, who characterised IOs more actively as "useful impartial advisors" (Ramos, J., Written Correspondence, 20 April–22 June 2012).
209 Ramos, J., Written Correspondence, 20 April–22 June 2012.
210 Interview: Anonymous subject 1.1.
211 Neumann, I. B. (2011). Entry into International Society Reconceptualised: The Case of Russia. *Review of International Studies*, *37* (2), 463–484, 466.

7 Conclusion

Closure theory

My main aim in this book has been to help produce a theory of international social closure so as to improve the English School's account of how order is reproduced in the international domain. Looking to answer questions about exclusion, inclusion, and stratification in and around international society, I have attempted to show that incorporation in status groups and participation in their management of international society is fundamentally a function of playing a 'closure game' with and against other actors.

Closure theory has not been introduced here unchanged from its neo-Weberian form. I have made a number of reforms of extant theory, rendering it suitable for studying international politics. First, I have stressed the need for understanding the institutional and normative context in which a closure game takes place. This is necessary for identifying what types of strategies, and means of closure other than strategies, are available to actors playing the closure game. This is also necessary for comparing closure systems across status groups and temporal periods. This allows us to see that while closure works differently across contexts, it operates nonetheless, even when it appears not to. Just because the status game today is played relatively more pacifically than in the past, it does not mean that closure is any less central in ordering the international domain.

Most notably, I have introduced the concept of mobility dampeners, rendering it possible to identify ways that insiders entrench status positions by subtler means than erecting exclusion barriers. Identifying and analysing mobility dampeners served as a first step towards identifying less obvious and more covert causes of stratification. This was particularly important for helping us to see how a system can be stratified despite a relative absence of collectivist barriers. By relying on the institutional underpinning of a status group, mobility dampeners can prevent or slow a loss of status while concurrently preventing or slowing the rise of others.

Second, I sought to improve extant closure theory's limited taxonomy of exclusion strategies and its understanding of the role they play in ordering the international domain. I categorised closure rules as being Achievable,

Unachievable, or Ostensibly Achievable. Doing so highlighted that it is necessary to know what type of rule is being levied in terms of whether it guards membership based on achieved for ascribed characteristics. As concerns achievable characteristics, this then also allowed us to analyse the relative ease or difficulty of fulfilling them. A functional-individualist criterion is characterised as a relatively open type of rule, but its requirements may be set so high that it is largely impossible for most actors in a system to achieve, thereby rending the system as seeming ostensibly open while being substantively closed. Even if the achievement of status seems like a fair contest, structurally it might not be.

Exclusion rules were also shown to be unable to entirely explain closure and stratification. I argued that closure rules in international society are predominantly functional-individualist, meaning that barriers to entry and mobility for state actors are relatively few and relatively open. Taking only this dimension into account, however, leaves us unable to fully explain stratification and provide a comprehensive account of how closure works, particularly in contemporary international society. In addition to adding mobility dampeners to our conceptual toolkit, I also amended the taxonomy of strategies available to those seeking to improve their positions, beyond the sole strategy of Usurpation, with which extant theory leaves us. These strategies – Banding, Differentiation, Legitimation, and Normalisation – were also classified as ranging from more assertive to more deferential. This allows us to see how entry strategies can also account for stratification, principally owing to the degree to which deference and mimicry are embedded in them. Outsiders also in part cause and reproduce the stratified social order. It also allows us to see that inferiorly positioned outsiders seek to improve their position within the status hierarchy, rather than only trying to overthrow it (as extant theory likewise leaves us).

Finally, I also demonstrated that international social closure need not be antagonistic. Entry strategies can be – and in significant instances and ways are – deferential in nature. Furthermore, incorporation strategies are also less antagonistic means of achieving stratification and preserving status. Taken together, the closure moves of outsiders and insiders alike are not necessarily conflictual.

Closure in international society

Broadly speaking, the international society of states has a relatively open closure system. This is owing to the predominance of functional-individualist closure rules in operation, with relatively few collectivist barriers guarding status groups and limiting the social mobility of sovereign actors. From the Standard of Civilisation to the requirements of the Great Powers' club to the criteria governing entry into G-summitry, the contest is relatively open, at least on the face of it.

Conclusion   153

However, a powerful legal-collectivism sits at the very heard of the international domain, outright excluding all non-sovereign actors from full membership in the clubs that manage international society, despite requiring their participation to maintain order in the contemporary context. Sovereignty is demanded as the system's primary closure rule; without it, an actor is necessarily subordinate and/or marginalised in the international domain. For states, closure barriers are relatively fair and open; non-state actors, in contrast, are necessarily subordinated as they face an insurmountable collectivist barrier. Moreover, international non-governmental organisations (INGOs) in particular face collectivist stereotypes, further enabling the entrenchment of their position, despite the functional contributions they offer to international society's management. That said, one type of collectivism does work against sovereign actors in contemporary international society – namely, Cultural Stratification. Collectivism thus stratifies both within international society and in the wider international domain.

By comparatively analysing status groups across time, I have argued that there is less social mobility in the contemporary international domain than in the past. Despite the appearance of contemporary global governance being more open, networked, and 'flat,' substantively it is not, owning to the way that social closure operates. As a status group, G-summitry is actually more closed, owing to the relative predominance of ostensibly achievable criteria guarding its membership. Moreover, in G-summitry, legal-collectivism is absolute, whereas with the Family of Civilised Nations the possession of sovereignty was not always a perfectly unachievable barrier to entry. Moreover, the Family of Civilised Nations had relatively more achievable, functional-individualist entry rules, though the cultural and racial elements were obviously not so. Additionally, entry into Western international society during its expansion and globalisation was largely governed according to an explicitly articulated Standard of Civilisation. While it lacks overt racism and cultural imperialism, G-summitry also lacks any sort of defined, explicit entry criteria. Inclusion is even more subject to the whims of those already superiorly positioned to decide who belongs and who does not.

G-summitry is also a relatively more closed status group, owing to the extent to which deference is required in entry strategies. Whereas more assertive strategies were possible – indeed, required – for gaining entry into the Great Powers' club, this is not so in G-summitry. In this same vein, there are fewer opportunities for entry into G-summitry. In this dimension too, the Family of Civilised Nations is actually more open than other clubs because of the greater number of opportunities for entry. For the Great Powers' club, entry and exits were largely limited to instances of major war. For G-summitry, entry is limited to instances in which the club cannot manage to achieve its aim of achieving international economic stability, and exits seem to be impossible other than in instances of a flagrant violation of international law.

Two broad normative changes in international society have also affected the closure game, rendering the contemporary context more closed: the shift in the institutional foundation of the ranking status group and a normative shift constituting what is held to be a just governance order. G-summitry is a construction predominantly of the diplomatic institution. The significance of this is that it places norms of precedence and pragmatism at the heart of the club's operation, broadening the ways that mobility dampening can guard and deny status positions. While uneven credentialism was a feature of the Standard of Civilisation's application, in G-summitry it endures alongside other dampeners, largely (though not entirely) preventing incumbent members' continued suitability for inclusion from being tested. This further renders exists from the club less likely.

The second shift changed what is required for a status group to be accepted by those excluded from it. The Great Powers' club could justify its exclusivity on purely functionalist grounds – its members were the most powerful actors capable of carrying out the club's managerial function in Western international society. The normative shift in international society that affects the composition of the G20 injects the requirement of representative legitimacy. Functional legitimacy is no longer sufficient for justifying the composition of a ranking status group. Having only the most powerful actors included can no longer solely determine club composition. Regional and cultural representation is required in order for the group to be accepted – or at least sufficiently tolerated – by those excluded from it. Closure endures and this shift obscures the ways that closure excludes those whom might otherwise be included. In the G20, those of a high economic rank but geographically alike to G-summitry's incumbents are thus excluded – Spain, the Netherlands, and Switzerland being key examples. This normative shift means that the mobility of some actors – namely, non-Western, rising economies – is increased while that of others is reduced.

Order and its reproduction

This book has detailed how international order is reproduced according to a twin dynamic of social closure: from above/within by insiders and from below/without by aspirant outsiders. Moreover, that functionalism features so heavily in the closure game ensures that incumbents and newer entrants alike commit to the maintenance and survival of international society. The perpetuation of the *status quo* is baked into the closure game itself.

I have demonstrated how incumbents attempt to secure their positions in the international social order. Nonetheless, losses of rank and status are still possible. Even in relatively closed systems, the closure game cannot be perfectly rigged in favour of insiders. That said, the game is arranged in such a way that even if insiders lose their rank in the international social hierarchy, the second, ideational – indeed, dispositional – way that we understand order is likely to survive. Particular actors may lose their

Conclusion   155

dominant positions, but their norms, values, ideas, beliefs, and practices are likely to endure. Deference, mimicry, and incorporation are the primary means by which this is accomplished. It is how hallmark features of Western European international society endure despite that society's globalisation. The particular actors who rank and manage international society may change, but the means by which they do so and the characteristics, values, and aims of that society largely persist. This is akin to an observation made by Parkin about a shift in domestic societies from collectivist to individualist closure systems. While bourgeois blood may no longer rank the status hierarchy because of the opening of the system, bourgeois values endure, owing to their reproduction being embedded in the closure process.[1] International society is no longer an exclusively Western European status group, but the Western European ideational underpinning of the club remains owing to the way that the international closure game works.

International society's relatively open closure barriers made its globalisation possible. The tandem structure of its closure system allowed for this while safeguarding the exclusive position of sovereign states in the international domain. A primary, legal-collectivist closure rule protects state actors vis-à-vis non-state actors, broadly stratifying the international domain so as to draw an absolute social division such that sovereign states have membership within international society while all other types of actors are necessarily cast into the marginal and subordinate 'world society' category. It is the secondary closure rules that made expansion relatively safe for incumbent states' status vis-à-vis newer entrants.

What is especially noteworthy about the structure of this closure game is that it allows us to explain how clubs survive in an ostensibly more open, flatter, networked governance order. This goes beyond the intuitive observation that sovereign states have obvious primacy as the core of international relations and that non-sovereign actors are peripherally positioned. What is significant is that the core club of states maintains its dominant centrality *because of* the network of non-state actors that surrounds it. Non-sovereign actors engaged in global governance are not challengers to the traditional club, they are its buttresses. Through the closure game the club is able to incorporate non-state actors to take advantage of the functional contributions that they can make towards the management of international society, but without threatening states' exclusive status as members of that society.

It is thus not accurate to say that the traditional, hierarchical club style of governance, typified by the Congress of Vienna, has been entirely superseded by a flatter, more open network style of governance, ostensibly typified by the G20. On the face of it, this appears to be the case, but as the pages that preceded have detailed, clubs endure, albeit with networks surrounding – indeed, supporting – them. International society survives as a club and clubs survive within international society through the operation of international social closure.

As we saw in the opening chapter, there are two competing narratives within the international diplomacy literature: one that continues to understand diplomacy as fundamentally a function of club-style governance; and the other, apparently more progressive account, that sees diplomacy as having evolved to having more of a network-style form. What the theory of international social closure produced here allows us to see is that these incongruous accounts are two partial images of a single system. They capture different elements of social closure in isolation of one another. The club account primarily captures legal-collectivist closure while the network account primarily captures functional-individualist inclusion. We are now equipped to overcome this standoff.

The network-focused literature is right to focus on the transformations in the international domain while the club-focused literature is right to focus on what endures despite these changes. It is not incorrect to say that international society is moving toward a more networked order, so long as the conception of that order recognises the enduring centrality of clubs. A theory of international social closure allows us to more accurately see that what is happening is that international society is moving towards a greater functionalist order that allows for the incorporation of new actors in that society's management, but one in which collectivism remains deeply embedded to maintain the privileged status of sovereign states. New states may be brought into a status group, but incumbents largely remain superiorly positioned within it; new non-state actors may also be incorporated, but in such a way that they are necessarily marginal to state actors. This is not to say that non-state actors have less *power* than state actors, but that they have less *status*. This is possible because the international closure system has a tandem structure in which there is a primary collectivist closure rule and secondary functionalist rules.

Social closure is neither necessarily a bad nor a good thing – it just is. What it is used for, by whom, and how can be normatively evaluated, but social closure as a process is in and of itself value free. A system can be relatively unfair to some actors and not others, it can be more open or more closed (and more open to some while more closed to others), and it can be governed according to certain criteria and not others. As much as possible, I have tried not to pass normative judgements in this book's production of a theory of international social closure and its analysis of how closure works in the international domain. That said, I have not bitten my tongue when it comes to the naked racism, brutal imperialism, and unrepentant ethnocentrism that features all too centrally in the history of international society. While I leave in-depth considerations of the normative dimension of international social closure for others, this book's analysis raises questions about the relative justness and fairness of the contemporary order that social closure produces. The normative shift requiring geographic and cultural representation in the G20 renders this status group closed off to actors who are geographically or culturally alike G-summitry's incumbents, despite such actors otherwise seeming suitable for admission. A state like the Netherlands would see this as unjust, while a state like South Africa would see it oppositely. One significance of this is that it undercuts the axiom that competition in the international domain can broadly be articulated as being the West versus the Rest. The story is not nearly so simple.

What's next?

The theory produced here is only a modest first step. It would be useful to empirically test the theory's extendibility. Especially useful would be an examination of entries into (and exits from, if possible) international societies other than that which developed in Western Europe to test whether this theory is limited to this single international society alone.

There is also further theoretical work to be done. While this book has answered open questions via international closure theory, in so doing other questions have presented themselves. Most significantly, I have claimed that moves made to improve status positions in international society are predominantly individualistic. With few exceptions, ascendant states do not work together to improve their collective lot. This is distinctly different from domestic societies wherein collective action may prevail; indeed, so much so that closure theory was originally formulated to look at how groups play the closure game rather than individuals. In short, the open question is as follows: why is there so little class struggle in international society?

One hint to the answer may be found in the fact that there is so much intra-group competition amongst outsiders, particularly via differentiation and abandonment. Ascendant actors are willing to sell-out alike others if it means a boost in their own status. Zarakol also identifies this, '[o]ne cannot but be struck by this fact – it is almost as if there was only one spot open for outsider states at the great powers' table. While there are of course perfectly reasonable geographical explanations for this development, we should also note that this pattern is well observed in the established-outsider stigmatisation dynamics in domestic society: for instance, the advances of younger women or people of colour in business settings often come at the expense of people from their own sub-group.'[2] The suggestion is that because there are so few high status spots available, collective action is not an appropriate way to improve position due to there being not enough 'rewards' of higher status to go around.

Another possibility is similarly about numbers. A brilliant conjecture of Edward Keene's is that the lack of collective action may not be due to the number of ranking status spots being limited, but rather might be due to the size of international society itself being so small in number.[3] An absolute increase in status for a group of alike actors amounts to a relative status increase vis-à-vis other groups, but does not amount to a relative status increase for those within the group vis-à-vis one another. In a large society, such collective action is acceptable because there are enough others against whom an actor can differentiate and compare status. In a small society, such action does not make sense (i) because collective action by an ascendant group does not leave enough others in lower status positions against whom status comparisons can be made and prestige can thereby be gained; and (ii) because it would leave an actor with still too many self-same actors in the same social strata against whom they socially compete in further status games. To answer this question, a comparative study of the ways the closure game is played in an international society with a larger number of actors would be useful. One possibility might be to examine closure in pre-Westphalian, Medieval Europe prior to the setting of the primary legal-collectivist closure rule.

We also need to consider whether we are presently observing a change in the means by which international society manages itself. If we are indeed witnessing a return of power politics and the ebbing of global governance, the institutions through which international society is managed and the criteria for inclusion in the club(s) responsible for its management will change. Whether this would mean the establishment of a great powers concert at the global level, a shift in emphasis to regional governance, or even a splintering of international society itself are speculative prospects for now, but any such scenario would see the closure game change. My conjecture is that the theoretical lens I have crafted here will continue to be useful, regardless of international society's trajectory.

For the time being, what a theory of international social closure allows us to see is that while contemporary international society seems more open, more just, and less hierarchical than its earlier iterations, in substantive ways it is not actually so. It allows us to detail precisely how it is not, who is disadvantaged by this, and what causes it to be so. All societies – domestic and international alike – have some form of order which means that there is some form of rank and some set of norms, values, ideas, beliefs, and practices underpinning that order. As such, in all societies there is a status game to be played, as well as a second game to be played over the rules governing that game. A theory of international social closure renders these games observable.

Notes

1 Parkin (1979, p. 63).
2 Zarakol (2010, p. 175). On stigmatisation, see Adler-Nissen (2014).
3 Keene relayed this idea in conversation some years ago. As far as I know he has not yet published this claim. I sincerely hope he does.

Annex
Methods

Introduction

How we do our work matters as much as what work we do. Indeed, a commitment to rigorous methods is a fundamental principle of academic scholarship. While relatively few readers will be interested in this research's underlying methodology, I nonetheless believe it necessary to be open about how I went about this project. The value of a piece of scholarship is not just in its conclusions, claims, and evidence, but how those elements of an argument were produced in the first place. I hope that readers will engage critically with this book, demonstrating the ways in which I am wrong and in so doing produce something better. This is how knowledge progresses. It is to the pursuit of knowledge that I am committed, not any particular argument that I have made in pursuing it. I hope that readers likewise critically engage with my methods. I have attempted a relatively novel approach in this project that I particularly hope might help lay foundations for new trajectories in examining contemporary international politics rooted in an English School perspective.

Cornelia Navari remarks that English School scholars "spend their time in archives getting their hands dirty. They come immersed in diplomatic archives, memoires, and newspapers. They spend time in international institutions, listening to what international civil servants say and observing what they are doing."[1] This is how I collected information and generated knowledge for this project. Most generally, I engaged in methodological 'triangulation,' complimenting textual sources with elite interviewers and ethnographic research. The most notable break from traditional scholarship was my use of interviews and ethnographic observation. This amounted to the collection of "different kinds of data from the field,"[2] making this research more than just "armchair analysis" and methodologically aligning it with the 'practice turn.'[3] This, in short, is how I accessed status groups and studied the closure games played within and around them.

What I looked for in were "the self-conceptions of actors who are participating in the processes that constitute international life."[4] Jackson and Navari alike assert that statespeople/agents/actors are the proper objects of English School scholarship,[5] a methodological commitment shared by early English School scholars including Manning, Wight, and Bull.[6] The participant actors in the international domain are the appropriate objects of research as it is they who (re)produce international society's common interests, values, rules, and institutions.[7] The aim in each of the empirical chapters was to access the micropolitics at play amongst the individuals who are playing the closure game on behalf of the actors they represent. Diplomats, for Bull, are the "visible expression" and "tangible evidence of international society."[8] Bull notes that diplomats serve as the "custodian[s] of the idea of international society, with a stake in preserving and strengthening it."[9] Their self-conceptions and intersubjective recognitions give international society expression, and they themselves serve as the closest thing to a physical embodiment of the abstract society as is possible to approximate.[10]

As I am concerned not just with international society, but the wider international domain, I broaden my approach beyond just statespeople and the sovereign actors they represent, incorporating the perspectives of representatives of non-state actors (chiefly international non-governmental organisations). It is for this reason that, as concerns the historical dimensions of this research, the recollections of individuals, via secondary sources and archival documents, form this work's empirical basis; as concerns the contemporary dimensions of this work, the accounts and records of Sherpas and their non-state interlocutors serve as primary empirical evidence. Be it from a history, a biography, an archival record, a research interview, or participant observation, what I looked for were (i) *statements* where these actors discuss instances of inclusion or exclusion from a club and (ii) *actions* that concern the inclusion or exclusion of actors from a club. From these it was then further possible to infer (iii) what ideas, beliefs, norms, values, and practices underpin and structure the closure system.

Interviews

The most significant means of generating new knowledge was via interviews. The most significant category of interviews was with G7/8 and G20 Sherpas. The Sherpas were the starting point for sampling as they are the most important individuals in the summitry process. I then 'built out' from the Sherpas to interview their interlocutors representing relevant INGOs and international organisations (IOs), as well as – when relevant and possible – their deputies and political masters. The technique by which I achieved access – often the most challenging dimension of doing elite interviewing – was through what the methodological literature refers to as 'snowballing.'[11] I prefer to refer to this practice as 'chain referral' for two reasons: first, as the snowball metaphor implies a cumulative addition of new knowledge with each subsequent interview, which is not borne out in practice once the 'saturation point' of information collection has been reached. At the saturation point the snowball, despite continuing to roll, stops collecting snow. The second reason is that searching for 'snowballing' on the internet produces results notably different from what the methodological literature has in mind.

Regardless of what it is called, this strategy involves asking a subject to recommend others to subsequently interview. Elite sampling is thus based in part on the subjective recommendations of other elites. This is an effective strategy for two reasons. First, it helped to overcome the challenge of gaining access. When requesting interviews, the approach had greater force when it was possible to say that a colleague or superior had suggested that they participate in this research. Moreover, subjects would often speak to their recommended contacts on my behalf, which gave an even higher success rate in securing interviews. To break into the Sherpa network in the first place, I sought out a Sherpa who had moved into academia after completing his public service career, as such an individual was more likely to be amenable to accepting to do a research interviews on the back of a cold call.[12] The snowball - so to speak - rolled from there.

Second, it helped map who was viewed intersubjectively as being important players in the field, thus aiding with the task of identifying the best sources from whom to glean information for process tracing.[13] Such an approach was especially appropriate for studying status, as it enables a charting of the relative positions of actors based on their appraisals of one another. Status as a fundamentally social, subjective, relational phenomenon must be methodologically approached as such. This approach thus selected sources less based on "positional" criteria and more on "representational" criteria.[14] That said, positional selection did feature in the method as certain actors in positions of significance were selected independently of recommendations based on the extant literature.[15] Notably, host Sherpas were particularly important by virtue of their position as being the *primus inter pares* among the Sherpa group during the year in which their country served as president of the club. Additionally, Paul Martin and Larry Summers were of critical importance as they were the two who established the membership list for the G20. George Shultz was singled out as the sole-surviving Sherpa who created the G7. Key Sherpas in the G20's elevation to the leaders' level were likewise identified as critical to the success of this research – Sir John Cunliffe, Lourdes Aranda, and Bernardino León Gross, being particularly noteworthy. As an empirical source, this book provides their only published accounts (as is likewise the case with other Sherpas and their civil society counterparts).

As concerns the representatives from different actor types whom I interviewed – be they representatives of IOs or civil society – I ensured that sources were diverse so as to not bias the picture of the G-summitry environment in a particular direction.[16] The risk, for example, of only interviewing Sherpas would be to skew the perspective unhelpfully towards state centricity and reproduce one of the problems in English School scholarship that this work is making an effort to correct.

The interviews themselves were carried out in a semi-structured form. Prior to starting, a set of themes were established and – within each theme – questions to ask subjects were set. Which questions asked were amended depending on the interview subject and the questions themselves evolved over the process of information collection, as my own understanding of the topic developed. Semi-structured interviews thus sit in the middle ground between the rigidity and formality of structured interviews and the fluidity and informality of unstructured interviews.

This technique was adopted for a number of reasons. First, it allowed subjects to "open up and express themselves in their own words" in a way that structured interviews do not.[17] Likewise, it was more amenable to a natural conversation flow which helped to keep subjects both relaxed and interested in the discussion. It allowed subjects to lead the general course of the discussion but equally allowed me to probe at the right moments and to choose when to shift themes or revisit points.[18] It was good for building rapport with subjects, particularly as the majority of this research's subjects were/are high-level officials and elite political figures, "people who are accustomed to efficient use of their time." Critical to establishing rapport was demonstrating that I was knowledgeable about the subject and in control of the interview.[19] Interviews started with simple and factual questions before moving, once rapport had been established, to questions of an interpretive character.[20]

Notes were taken to record information in lieu of using an audio recorder for most of the interviews. There is a trade-off involved in the use of recorders. While a recorder allows the researcher to review the interview and produce a transcript, this comes at the cost of the interview subject holding back on useful information because he/she does not want certain information to be of public record and/or attributable to him/herself. I have gleaned richer information from interviews which was only possible in the absence of recorder and in giving the promise of anonymity when requested. To bolster the validity and robustness of claims gathered in this way, multiple, independent sources for information were sought, and, when possible, were cross-checked against archival or textual sources. This approach was especially useful when dealing with contemporary events. Relevant interview subjects were elites whose information may be damaging to themselves, others, and/or the entities they represent. In addition to taking notes in the interviews, upon conclusion of each interview I would immediately review my notes and fill in any gaps from memory. In this review process, I also made note of initial summary observations about the information gathered.[21]

Research interviews stopped when no new information was being gleaned – the 'saturation point.'[22] This does not mean that there is no remaining information left unknown, only that the diminishing returns from each subsequent interview were such that it was no longer worth the investment of resources towards continuing with this dimension of the empirical research. Saturation also occurs with interview referrals, when "respondents begin repeating names to the extent that further rounds of nominations are unlikely to yield significant new information."[23]

Interviews are not without limitations. As Tansey points out, interview subjects can give distorted accounts in a number of ways. It is possible for subjects to inflate or minimise their roles in an event or the roles of others, a particular concern when dealing with political subjects.[24] George and Bennett warn of the "instant histories" produced immediately after an event as they tend to "portray a 'careful, multidimensional process of policy making' to the public" which does not match the reality of what occurred.[25] This was a particular concern when doing interviews and making observations at summits. To mitigate this, interviews at summits were subjected to greater scrutiny in analysis. On the other end of the timescale, if much time has elapsed since an event, a subject's memory of it is likely to be less than perfect. In interviewing former US Treasury Secretary George Shultz about the formation of the G7 and its precursor, the Library Group, it was especially important to be aware of this potential problem with the information conveyed. Archival sources were particularly important for mitigating this limitation. As is detailed below, they were useful for verifying interview subjects' claims and were critical for calibrating the level of confidence to have in any particular subject's accounts.

Textual sources

As concerns the use of textual sources, I adopted a comparative-historical approach. The closure strategies employed by actors were inferred from the reconstruction of historical events via historical and archival texts.[26] Following Zarakol, "the approach is neither purely indicative nor purely deductive, but should rather be thought of as layered, moving back and forth between various levels of abstraction, inference, and observability."[27]

Interviews were essential as a compliment to archival research, and *vice versa*. Holdings of the Thatcher Archive (which includes the papers of James Callaghan); the Carter, Ford, and Reagan Presidential Libraries; and the Australian National Archives were particularly valuable in reconstructing a history of the formation of the G7. As this research was conducted after the declassification of memoranda and diplomatic cables that circulated during the club's genesis and its early years, I was able to access source documents unavailable to those who have previously worked on the topic. This allowed me to identify key dimensions of the club's formation that had otherwise been unobserved by scholars. This book thus serves as a corrective to what has become an axiomatic and not entirely accurate history of the club's origins. I hope future scholars will improve on the account (and its mistakes, aberrations, and marginalisations) that I have provided here.

Interviews served as interpretive, corroborative, and additive compliments to textual sources. They are interpretive as they can help "decode" the language of official documents.[28] They do so in two ways. First, they were helpful with early G7 documents, as the diplomatic cables were classified as secret and some memoranda were code word classified. Interview subjects helped me to understand the significant of particular classifications; most notably, code word "Burning Bush" which concealed efforts by the US, the

UK, West Germany, and France – the Four – to exclude Japan, Italy, and Canada from substantive political discussions. Interviews also helped to decode specialist language and fill gaps in information, particularly if in correspondence certain facts were assumed as common knowledge between correspondents and so were left unstated or defined (and thus rendered unintelligible when reading these sources without the benefit of having the same contextual knowledge). Interviews with Sir Nicholas Bayne and George Shultz were especially helpful in this respect.

In this way interviews are also additive, filling the blanks that history has left us. Interviews may also be additive as they can help us access and understand debates and contestations that are often missing in official documents. Memoranda tend to only report what was agreed upon in meetings, not the details of debates which led to a decision.[29] This was especially so in the case of debates contesting the inclusion and exclusion of actors in the club. Two notable exceptions to this tendency are a fragment of the French account of the Helsinki meeting at which the Four's leaders first discussed the possibility of a summit and a British account of a Sherpa meeting in which Australia's possible inclusion was discussed.[30]

Finally, interviews are corroborative in that they help in understanding the validity of archival sources. It is erroneous to assume that textual documents are necessarily valid or accurate.[31] Conversely, archival sources can be corroborative of information from interviews.[32] This is particularly useful if there is only a single interview source for a piece of information, which was the case of much of the information gleaned from interviews concerning the formation of the club.[33] The two types of information can thus be used to corroborate one another and yield greater validity and robustness to the findings as a whole.

Ethnography

Ethnographic fieldwork was the third method employed in this research to produce new knowledge, drawing from participant observation at the 2012 (Los Cabos, Mexico), 2013 (Saint Petersburg, Russia), 2015 (Antalya, Turkey), 2016 (Hangzhou, China), and 2017 (Hamburg, Germany) G20 summits.

The largest challenge to this approach was gaining access to the summits, a kind of problem that "looms large" in ethnography more generally.[34] As Hammersley and Atkinson assert, overcoming this obstacle is often a "thoroughly practical matter."[35] Indeed it was. Through the network of contacts I developed over the course of my research, I became affiliated with the G7 and G20 Research Groups at the Munk School of Global Affairs based at the University of Toronto. Through my affiliation with the group I was able to obtain credentials to the summits as a journalist.

Additionally, for the Los Cabos summit I was able to concurrently get accreditation as a member of civil society via the network of civil society contacts I developed through my interviews. This dual accreditation allowed me to observe and compare if – and, if so, how – inclusion was differently granted to civil society representatives than it was to the international media. Civil society accreditation was more difficult to secure, with their accreditation was only finally granted a few days prior to the summit, as the Mexican president's office got worried that accredited civil society representatives would cause trouble.[36] It was only after one of the lead civil society representatives who coordinated their advocacy efforts wrote a letter endorsing all of the UK NGO representatives that accreditation was granted.[37] This points to one of the significant means of collectivist exclusion which INGOs seek to overcome and the need for INGOs to socially differentiate themselves from civil society protest groups in order to gain inclusion.

Participant observation contributed significant information to this research. It allowed for multiple types of data to be included as a complement to that produced from interviews and archival sources. This information is observational in nature; for example, observing who interacted with whom and how; who was allowed into which parts of the summit; what different actors used the summits and preparatory processes to achieve; and how different categories of actors were treated at the summits. This method also reduced the problem of "reactivity," wherein an actor under observation changes his/her behaviour because he/she knows that he/she is being observed, such as in an interview. The two further benefits of this approach were that it helped to contribute to an intuitive understanding of the object of study. This allowed for greater confidence in findings and claims, as well as help with conceptual refinement during the course of research (which, in turn, aided the refinement of interview questions). Finally, it helped to gain access to elites for interviews as it afforded me the chance to interact with them. Moreover, attending summits helped build my credibility as a researcher and, consequently, rapport with interview subjects.

List of interviews

1. Alexander, Nancy
   Director, Economic Governance Program, Heinrich Boell Foundation
   Participant, Think20
   a   Interview conducted 8 June 2012; 14:15–15:15 GMT (Skype)

2. Allan, Sir Alex KCB
   Sherpa, 1994–1997
   Private Secretary to the Prime Minister, 1992–1997
   Undersecretary, HM Treasury, 1989–1992
   a   Interview conducted 31 July 2012; 14:00–15:00 GMT (Skype)

3. Aranda Bezaury, Ambassador Lourdes
   Vice Minister of Foreign Affairs, Mexico
   Sherpa, Mexico, 2008–2012
   Host G20 Sherpa, 2012
   a   Interview conducted 21 August 2012; 20:00–21:00 GMT (Skype)

4. Arturo Gómez, Edgar Cubero
   Deputy Director General, CSO Liaison Office, Mexican Ministry of Foreign Affairs
   a   Interview conducted 19 June 2012; 15:30–16:00 PST (In-Person, Los Cabos, Mexico)

5. Bayne, Sir Nicholas KCMG
   British Diplomat
   Economic Director, Foreign and Commonwealth Office, UK, 1988–1992
   a   Interview conducted 9 October 2012; 13:00–15:00 GMT (In-person, The Travellers' Club, London)

6. Boehm, Peter
   Deputy Minister of International Development, Global Affairs Canada
   Host G7 Sherpa, 2018
   a   Interview conducted 13 February 2018; 12:00–13:00 EST (In-person, Wendake Reserve, Quebec, Canada)

7. Burnley, Jasmine
   G8/G20 Policy Adviser, Oxfam GB
   a   Interview conducted 30 January 2012; 16:00–17:15 GMT (In-person, Oxfam International, Oxford, UK)
   b   On-going correspondence after initial interview including discussions at Los Cabos G20 Summit, 17–19 June 2012

8. Carin, Barry
   Assistant Deputy Minister, Foreign Affairs, Canada, 1992–1996
   Sous-sherpa, Canada 1992–1996
   Organiser, Think20
   a   Interview conducted 8 March 2012; 16:30–17:30 GMT (Skype)

9 Colloff, Nicholas
   Director, Strategy and Innovation, Oxfam GB
   Country Director, Oxfam Russia, 2005–2009
   a   Interview conducted 14 August 2012; 11:30–12:15 CET (Skype)

10 Cunliffe, Sir John CB
   Deputy Director of the Bank of England,
   Managing Director, HM Treasury, 2001–2007
   Head, European and Global Issues Secretariat, Prime Minister's Office, 2007–2012
   Sherpa 2008–2011
   Host Sherpa 2009
   a   Interview conducted 2 March 2013; 13:00–14:00 GMT (In-person, Patisserie Valerie, Oxford, UK)

11 Currah, Kel
   Senior Program Officer, Bill and Melinda Gates Foundation, 2012–2013
   Associate Director, Policy and Advocacy, World Vision International, 2000–2008
   a   Interview conducted 20 August 2012; 18:00–19:00 GMT (Skype)
   b   Interview conducted in-person, 26 May 2017; 12:00–12:30 CET (In-person, Taormina, Sicily)

12 Edwards, Leonard
   Sherpa 2008–2010
   Host Sherpa 2010
   Deputy Minister of Foreign Affairs, Canada 2007–2010
   a   Interview conducted 15 March 2012; 16:00–17:00 GMT (Skype)

13 Evans, John
   General Secretary, Trade Union Advisory Committee
   a   Interview conducted 2 April 2012; 14:00–15:00 GMT (Skype)

14 Fauver, Robert
   Sherpa 1993–1994
   National Intelligence Officer for Economics, National Intelligence Council
   Undersecretary for International Affairs, US Treasury
   Special Assistant to the President, National Security Affairs and Economic Policy
   a   Interview conducted 16 July 2013; 19:00–20:00 GMT (Skype)

15 Flaherty, James
   Minister of Finance, Canada, 2006–2014
   a   Interview conducted 6 September 2013; 17:00–17:10 MSK (In-person, Constantine Palace, Saint Petersburg, Russia)

168 *Annex*

16 Fowler, Robert
    Host Sherpa 2002
    African Personal Representative 2003–2006
    Canadian Diplomat
    a   Interview conducted 9 February 2012; 14:00–15:15 GMT (Skype)

17 Fues, Thomas
    Economist, German Development Institute
    Participant, Think20
    a   Interview conducted 8 May 2012; 16:30–17:30 GMT (Skype)

18 González Laya, Arancha
    Chief of Staff to the Director General, World Trade Organisation, 2005–2013
    a   Interview conducted 30 March 2012 (Skype)

19 Grey, Jean-Christophe
    Spokesperson, Chancellor of the Exchequer
    Deputy Director, General Expenditure Policy, HM Treasury, UK
    a   Interview conducted 23 January 2012; 12:45–14:30 GMT (In-person, HM Treasury, London)

20 Harder, V. Peter
    Sherpa, 2005–2006
    Deputy Minister of Foreign Affairs, Canada 2003–2007
    a   Interview conducted 25 January 2012; 16–17:00 GMT (Skype)

21 Harper, Prime Minister Stephen
    Prime Minister of Canada 2006–Present
    a   Interview conducted 6 September 2013; 17:00–17:10 MSK (In-person, Constantine Palace, Saint Petersburg, Russia)

22 Howard, James
    Director, Economic and Social Policy, International Trade Union Confederation, 1986–Present
    a   Interview conducted 2 April 2012; 15:30–16:30 GMT (In-person, University College, Oxford, UK)

23 Khatchadourian, Rouben
    Host Sous-Sherpa Assistant for G8 and G20, 2010
    Head of G8 Policy Unit 2008–2010
    Canadian Diplomat
    a   Interview conducted 8 February 2012; 14:00–15:30 GMT (In-person, Canadian High Commission, London, UK)

24 Kitajima, Ambassador Shinichi
    Deputy Vice Minister, Foreign Ministry, Japan, 2002–2005
    Think20 Participant
    a   Interview conducted 16 May 2012; 8:30–9:30 GMT (Skype)

Annex 169

25 Kobele, Florian
    Sous-Sherpa, European Union, 2010–Present
    a   Interview conducted 13 February 2012; 9:00–10:00 GMT (Phone)

26 Leo, Ben
    Global Policy Director, ONE, 2001
    a   Interview conducted 15 May, 2012; 14:30–15:30 GMT (Skype)

27 León Gross, Bernardino
    Spanish Sherpa, 2009–2011
    Secretary General, Office of the Prime Minister, 2008–2011
    Secretary of State for Foreign Affairs, 2004–2008
    a   Interview conducted 18 May 2018; 16:00–18:00, GMT (In-person, The Espresso Room, Holborn, London)

28 Lévêque, Alexandre
    G7 and G20 Sous-Sherpa, Canada, 2016–2018
    Executive Director, Global Affairs Canada
    a   Interview conducted 15 February 2018; 11:00–12:00 EST (In-person, Lester B. Pearson Building, Ottawa, Canada)

29 Martin, Prime Minister Paul
    Prime Minister of Canada, 2003–2006
    Finance Minister, Canada, 1993–2002
    Founding Chair of G20, 1999–2001
    a   Interview conducted 23 August 2012; 14:30–16:30 EST (In-person, Martin Residence, Cowansville, Quebec, Canada)

30 Martinez, Raphael
    Sous-Sherpa, European Commission, 2010–2012
    a   Interview conducted 16 March 2012; 14:00–14:45 GMT (Phone)

31 Price-Thomas, Stephen
    International Director of Advocacy and Campaigns Manager, Oxfam
    G20/BRICSAM Strategy Manager, Oxfam International, 2010–2014
    a   Interview conducted 1 August 2012; 10:00–11:00 GMT (Skype)
    b   Ongoing correspondence 2012–2018

32 Pursey, Stephen
    Senior Adviser to the Director-General, International Labour Organization, 1999–Present
    a   Interview conducted 16 March 2012; 13:30–14:30 GMT (Skype)
    b   Second interview conducted 30 July 2012; 15:00–15:30 GMT (via Skype)

33 Ramirez, Leticia Lara
    Civil Society Liaison Officer, Mexican Ministry of Foreign Affairs
    a   Interview conducted 19 June 2012; 15:00–15:30 PST (In-person)
    b   Ongoing correspondence, 2012

170 *Annex*

34 Ramos, Gabriela
    Sherpa and Chief of Staff, OECD
    a   Interview conducted via written correspondence, 20 April 2012–2022; June, 2012

35 Rea, Joanna
    Head of Policy and Public Affairs, Bond UK
    a   Interview conducted 9 February 2012; 11:30–12:30 (In-person, Costa Coffee, King's Cross, London)
    b   Ongoing correspondence 2012–2013

36 Reynoso, Don Miguel Díaz
    Director General, CSO Liaison Office, Mexican Ministry of Foreign Affairs
    a   Interview conducted 19 June 2012; 16:00–17:00 PST (In-person, Los Cabos, Mexico; Translator Present)

37 Ruthrauff, John
    Director, International Advocacy, InterAction, 2005–Present
    a   Interview conducted 2 August 2012; 15:00–16:00 GMT (Phone)
    b   Ongoing correspondence, 2012–2013

38 Shorr, David
    Program Officer, Stanley Foundation, 2000–2014
    Participant, Think20
    a   Interview conducted 25 May 2012, 15:00–16:30 GMT (Skype)
    b   Further discussions at Los Cabos G20 Summit, 17–19 June 2012

39 Shultz, Secretary George
    Secretary of Labour, United States, 1969–1970
    Secretary of the Treasury, United States, 1972–1974
    Secretary of State, United States, 1982–1989
    Sherpa, United States, 1975–1976
    a   Interview conducted 5 September 2012; 13:00–14:00 EST (Skype)

40 Smith, Dr Gordon
    Sherpa, 1995–1997
    Host Sherpa, 1995
    Deputy Minister of Foreign Affairs, Canada 1994–1997
    a   Interview conducted 19 December 2011; 11:00–12:00 PST (In-person, University of Victoria, Victoria, Canada)
    b   Ongoing correspondence, 2012–2013.

41 Sobreira, Rogério
    Associate Professor, Brazilian School of Public and Business Administration
    Getulio Vargas Foundation
    Participant, Think20
    a   Interview conducted 30 May 2012; 21:00–21:30 GMT (Skype)

42 Summers, Secretary Lawrence
    Secretary of Treasury, United States, 1999–2001
    Deputy Secretary of the Treasury, United States, 1995–1999
    Chief Economist of the World Bank, 1991–1993
    a   Interview conducted 23 October 2012; 14:30–15:30 GMT (Skype)

43 Zaldivar, Adriana
    Summit Accommodation and Transportation Logistics Coordinator
    a   Interview conducted 17 June 2012; 14:30–15:00 PST (In-person, Los Cabos, Mexico)

Notes

1 Navari, C. (2009). *Theorising International Society: English School Methods.* Basingstoke; New York: Palgrave Macmillan, 12.
2 Hansen (2006, p. 107).
3 Neumann (2002, p. 628). See also Adler (2008); Jackson (2000); Navari (2011); Neumann (2012, p. 16); Pouliot (2008, p. 265).
4 Navari, *Theorizing International Society*, 2009, 12.
5 Jackson (2000); Navari, C. (2009). What the Classical English School Was Trying to Explain, and Why Its Members Were Not Interested in Causal Explanation. In C. Navari (Ed.), *Theorising International Society: English School Methods* (pp. 39–57). Basingstoke; New York: Palgrave Macmillan, Print, 42.
6 Bull, H. (1977). *The Anarchical Society: A Study of Order in World Politics* (4th edition). Basingstoke: Palgrave Macmillan, 13; Manning, C. (1962). *The Nature of International Society*. London: London School of Economics and Political Science; Wight, M. (1977). *Systems of States*. Leicester University Press [for] the London School of Economics and Political Science, 36; see also: Navari, What the Classical English School Was Trying to Explain, 2009, 41.
7 C.f. Bull, *Anarchical Society*, 1977, 36.
8 Ibid., 166; see also 176–177; Sharp and Wiseman (2007), *The Diplomatic Corps as an Institution of International Society*, Palgrave Macmillan.
9 Bull, *Anarchical Society*, 1977, 176.
10 Hurrell, A. (2002). Hedley Bull and Diplomacy. *Presented at the International Studies Association*, New Orleans.
11 Babbie, E. (1995). *The Practice of Social Research* (7th edition). Cengage Learning; Tansey, O. (2007). Process Tracing and Elite Interviewing: A Case for Non-probability Sampling. *PS: Political Science & Politics*, 40 (4), 765–772, 775.
12 Peabody, R. L., Hammond, S. W., Torcom, J., Brown, L. P., Thompson, C., & Kolodny, R. (1990). Interviewing Political Elites. *PS: Political Science & Politics*, 23 (3), 451–455. Thus, former-sherpa Gordon Smith (a four time sherpa and host sherpa) served as my entry point.
13 George, A. L., & Bennett, A. (2005). *Case Studies and Theory Development in the Social Sciences*. Cambridge, MA: MIT Press.
14 Tansey, Process Tracing and Elite Interviewing, 2007, 770.
15 Ibid.
16 Ibid.
17 Bernard, H. R. (2006). *Research Methods in Anthropology: Qualitative and Quantitative Approaches*. Lanham, MD: Rowman Altamira, 211.
18 Ibid., 215.
19 Ibid., 212.
20 Peabody et al., Interviewing Political Elites, 1990, 453.
21 C.f. ibid., 454.

22 Guest, G., Bunce, A., & Johnson, L. (2006). How Many Interviews Are Enough? An Experiment with Data Saturation and Variability. *Field Methods, 18* (1), 59–82. Mason, M. (2010). Sample Size and Saturation in PhD Studies Using Qualitative Interviews. *Forum Qualitative Sozialforschung / Forum: Qualitative Social Research, 11* (3). Retrieved from www.qualitative-research.net/index.php/fqs/article/view/1428; Ragin, C. C., & Becker, H. S. (1992). *What Is a Case?: Exploring the Foundations of Social Inquiry.* Cambridge: Cambridge University Press.
23 Tansey, Process Tracing and Elite Interviewing, 2007, 770.
24 Ibid.
25 George and Bennett, *Case Studies and Theory Development*, 2005, 99; Tansey, Process Tracing and Elite Interviewing, 2007, 10.
26 On the use of historical narratives to reconstruct causal processes, see Abbott, A. (2001). *Time Matters: On Theory and Method.* Chicago, IL: University of Chicago Press; Brady, H. E., & Collier, D. (Eds.). (2010). *Rethinking Social Inquiry: Diverse Tools, Shared Standards* (2nd edition). Lanham, MD: Rowman & Littlefield Publishers; Glass, L., & Mackey, M. C. (1988). *From Clocks to Chaos.* Princeton, NJ: Princeton University Press; Griffin, L. J. (1993). Narrative, Event-Structure Analysis, and Causal Interpretation in Historical Sociology. *American Journal of Sociology, 98* (5), 1094–1133. Mahoney, J. (2004). Comparative-Historical Methodology. *Annual Review of Sociology,* (30), 81–101; Reisch, G. A. (1991). Chaos, History, and Narrative. *History and Theory, 30* (1), 1–20; Sewell, W. H. (1990). *Three Temporalities: Toward a Sociology of the Event.* Ann Arbor: University of Michigan; Shermer, M. (1995). Exorcising Laplace's Demon: Chaos and Antichaos, History and Metahistory. *History and Theory, 34* (1), 59. Stryker, R. (1996). Beyond History versus Theory: Strategic Narrative and Sociological Explanation. *Sociological Methods & Research, 24* (3), 304–352.
27 Zarakol, A. (2010). *After Defeat: How the East Learned to Live with the West.* Cambridge; New York: Cambridge University Press, 24.
28 Davies, P. H. J. (2001). Spies as Informants: Triangulation and the Interpretation of Elite Interview Data in the Study of the Intelligence and Security Services. *Politics, 21* (1), 73–80.
29 Ibid., 75; George and Bennett, *Case Studies and Theory Development*, 2005, 103; Tansey, Process Tracing and Elite Interviewing, 2007, 767.
30 Hunt to John, 30 June 1978, in Bonn Summit; Sauvagnargues, 8 August 1975, in Sommet Monetaire.
31 Booth, A., & Glynn, S. (1979). The Public Records and Recent British Economic Historiography. *The Economic History Review, 32* (3), 303–315. Davies, P. H. J. (2001). Spies as Informants: Triangulation and the Interpretation of Elite Interview Data in the Study of the Intelligence and Security Services. *Politics, 21* (1), 73–80.
32 Tansey, Process Tracing and Elite Interviewing, 2007, 766.
33 Davies, P. H. J. (2001). Spies as Informants: Triangulation and the Interpretation of Elite Interview Data in the Study of the Intelligence and Security Services. *Politics, 21* (1), 73–80. Eftimiades, N. (1994). *Chinese Intelligence Operations.* Nicholas Eftimiades, 11; Webb, E. J., Campbell, D. T., & Schwartz, R. D. (1966). *Unobtrusive Measures: Nonreactive Research in the Social Sciences.* Oxford: Rand McNally.
34 Hammersley, M., & Atkinson, P. (2007). *Ethnography: Principles in Practice.* London; New York: Taylor & Francis, 41.
35 Ibid.
36 Rea, J., Interview in Person, 9 February 2012.
37 Ibid.

Bibliography

Aalberts, T., 2014. Rethinking the Principle of (Sovereign) Equality as a Standard of Civilisation. *Millennium: Journal of International Studies* 42, 767–789.
Abbott, A., 2001. *Time Matters: On Theory and Method.* University of Chicago Press, Chicago, IL.
Aberbach, J.D., Rockman, B.A., 2002. Conducting and Coding Elite Interviews. *PS: Political Science & Politics* 35, 673–676.
Adler, E., 2008. The Spread of Security Communities: Communities of Practice, Self-Restraint, and NATO's Post—Cold War Transformation. *European Journal of International Relations* 14, 195–230.
Adler-Nissen, R., 2014. Stigma Management in International Relations: Transgressive Identities, Norms, and Order in International Society. *International Organization* 68, 143–176.
Adomeit, H., 1995. Russia as a "Great Power" in World Affairs: Images and Reality. *International Affairs (Royal Institute of International Affairs 1944–)* 71, 35–68.
Akerlof, G.A., Kranton, R.E., 2000. Economics and Identity. *The Quarterly Journal of Economics* 115, 715–753.
Alagh, Y., 2004. *On Sherpas and Coolies: The G20 and Non-Brahmanical Futures.* University of Victoria, Victoria.
Albert, M., Buzan, B., Zürn, M. (Eds.), 2013. *Bringing Sociology to International Relations: World Politics as Differentiation Theory.* Cambridge University Press, Cambridge.
Alderson, K., Hurrell, A. (Eds.), 2000a. *Hedley Bull on International Society.* Macmillan, Basingstoke, p. 279.
Alderson, K., Hurrell, A. (Eds.), 2000b. The Continuing Relevance of International Society, in: *Hedley Bull on International Society.* Macmillan, Basingstoke, pp. 54–76.
Alexandroff, A., G-8? G-20? G-x?. The Stanley Foundation. www.stanleyfoundation.org//articles.cfm?id=580 (accessed 10.29.12).
Alexandrowicz, C.H., 1967. *An Introduction to the History of the Law of Nations in the East Indies: (16th, 17th and 18th centuries).* Clarendon Press.
America Latina en Movimiento, 2012. Statement of the Peoples Summit against G20. Agencia Latinoamericana de Informacion. http://alainet.org/active/55800 (accessed 4.16.13).
Amnesty International, 2008. *Anwar Ibrahim Continues Campaign Despite Questionable Charges* Amnesty International. www.amnesty.org/en/news-and-updates/news/anwar-ibrahim-continues-campaign-despite-questionable-charges-20080808 (accessed 7.27.14).

Anderson, B., 1991. *Imagined Communities: Reflections on the Origin and Spread of Nationalism*. Verso, NY; London.

Anderson, M.S., 2003. *The Ascendancy of Europe, 1815–1914*, 3rd ed. Pearson Longman, Harlow.Anderson, M.S., 1993. *The Rise of Modern Diplomacy 1450–1919*. Longman, London.

Anghie, A., 1999. Finding the Peripheries: Sovereignty and Colonialism in Nineteenth-Century International Law. *Harvard International Law Journal* 40, 1–80.

Anthony Pella, John, 2014. Expanding the Expansion of International Society: A New Approach with Empirical Illustrations from West African and European Interaction, 1400–1883. *Journal of International Relations and Development* 17, 89–111.

Antkiewicz, A., Cooper, A.F., 2008. *Emerging Powers in Global Governance: Lessons from the Heiligendamm Process*. Wilfrid Laurier University Press, Waterloo.

Ariga, N., 1896. *La Guerre Sino-Japonaise Au Point De Vue Du Droit International*. Nabu Press A. Pedone, Paris.

Armstrong, R., 1991. *Summits: A Sherpa's Eye View*. University of Leeds Review, Leeds.

Babbie, E., 1995. *The Practice of Social Research*, 7th ed. Cengage Learning, Belmont.

Bain, W., 2009. The English School and the Activity of Being an Historian, in: Navari, C. (Ed.), *Theorising International Society*. Palgrave, Basingstoke, pp. 148–166.

Bain, W., 2007. Are There Any Lessons of History? The English School and the Activity of Being an Historian. *International Politics* 44, 513–530.

Barnett, M., Duvall, R., 2005. Power in International Politics. *International Organization* 59, 39–75.

Barnett, M.N., 2004. *Rules for the World: International Organizations in Global Politics*. Cornell University Press, Ithaca, NY; London.

Barry, T., 2005. *G8/G7 and Global Governance*, Foreign Policy in Focus.

Barston, R., 2006. *Modern Diplomacy*. Pearson, Harlow.

Bayne, N., 2007. G8 Process and Performance: Past, Present, and Future, in: Fratianni, M., Savona, P., Kirton, J.J. (Eds.), *Corporate, Public and Global Governance: The G8 Contribution*. Ashgate, Aldershot.

Bayne, N., 2005. *Staying Together: The G8 Summit Confronts the 21st Century*, 1st ed. Ashgate, Aldershot; Burlington, VT.

Bayne, N., 2000. *Hanging in There: The G7 and G8 Summit in Maturity and Renewal*. Ashgate, Aldershot.

Bayne, N., Putnam, R.D., 2000. *Hanging in There: The G7 and G8 Summit in Maturity and Renewal*. Ashgate, Aldershot; Brookfield, CT.

Bayne, N., Woolcock, S. (Eds.), 2011. *The New Economic Diplomacy*, 3rd ed. Ashgate, Farnham; Burlington, VT.

BBC News, 1998a. Malaysia's Deputy Prime Minister Fired. BBC.

BBC News, 1998b. Sodomy Charges Turn up Heat on Anwar. BBC.

BBC News, 1998c. Anwar Arrested Amid Kuala Lumpur protests. BBC.

Beeson, M., Bell, S., 2017. The Impact of Economic Structures on Institutions and States, in: Dunne, T., Reus-Smit, C. (Eds.), *The Globalization of International Society*. Oxford University Press, Oxford, pp. 284–303.

Bellamy, A.J. (Ed.), 2004. *International Society and its Critics*. Oxford University Press, Oxford; New York.

Bernard, H.R., 2006. *Research Methods in Anthropology: Qualitative and Quantitative Approaches*. Rowman Altamira, Oxford.

Berridge, G., 2005. *Diplomacy: Theory and Practice*. Palgrave Macmillan, Basingstoke.
Berridge, G.R., 2005. *Diplomacy: Theory and Practice*, 3rd ed. Palgrave Macmillan.
Berridge, G.R., Keens-Soper, M., Otte, T. (Eds.), 2001. *Diplomatic Theory from Machiavelli to Kissinger*. Palgrave Macmillan, Basingstoke; Hampshire; New York.
Berry, J.M., 2002. Validity and Reliability Issues in Elite Interviewing. *PS: Political Science & Politics* 35, 679–682.
Bhabha, H., 1984. Of Mimicry and Man: The Ambivalence of Colonial Discourse. *Discipleship: A Special Issue on Psychoanalysis* 28, 125–133.
Bisley, N., 2012. *Great Powers in the Changing International Order*, 1st ed. Lynne Rienner Publishers, Boulder, CO.
Black, L., Hwang, Y.-J., 2012. China and Japan's Quest for Great Power Status: Norm Entrepreneurship in Anti-Piracy Responses. *International Relations* 26, 431–451.
Bolewski, W., 2007. *Diplomacy and International Law in Globalized Relations*. Springer, Berlin; New York.
Bond, 2013. About us | Bond. www.bond.org.uk/about-us (accessed 4.17.13).
Booth, A., Glynn, S., 1979. The Public Records and Recent British Economic Historiography. *The Economic History Review* 32, 303–315.
Borger, J., 2009. Calls Grow Within G8 to Expel Italy as Summit Plans Descend into Chaos. The Guardian available online: https://www.theguardian.com/world/2009/jul/06/g8-considers-expelling-italy.
Bornschier, V., Trezzini, B., 1997. Social Stratification and Mobility in the World System: Different Approaches and Recent Research. *International Sociology* 12, 429–455.
Bottero, W., 2005. *Stratification: Social Division and Inequality*. Routledge, London.
Bourdieu, P., 1990. *The Logic of Practice*. Stanford University Press, Stanford, CA.
Bourdieu, P., 1985. The Social Space and the Gensis of Groups. *Theory and Society* 14, 723–744.
Bowden, B., 2014. To Rethink Standards of Civilisation, Start with the End. *Millennium* 42, 614–631.
Bowden, B., 2009. *The Empire of Civilization: The Evolution of an Imperial Idea*. University of Chicago Press, Chicago, IL.
Bowden, B., Seabrooke, L., 2006. *Global Standards of Market Civilization*. Routledge, Abingdon.
Bradford, C., Lim, W. (Eds.), 2011a. *Global Leadership in Transition: Making the G20 More Effective and Responsive*. Brookings Institution Press, Washington, DC.
Bradford, C., Lim, W. (Eds.), 2011b. The G8 and G20: What Relationship Now? in: *Global Leadership in Transition: Making the G20 More Effective and Responsive*. Brookings Institution Press, Washington, DC, pp. 48–54.
Brady, H.E., Collier, D. (Eds.), 2010. *Rethinking Social Inquiry: Diverse Tools, Shared Standards*, 2nd ed. Rowman & Littlefield Publishers, Lanham, MD.
Bravely-Wagner, J.A., 2009. The Diplomacy of Caribbean Community States: Searching for Resilience, in: Cooper, A.F., Shaw, T.M. (Eds.), *Diplomacies of Small States*. Palgrave Macmillan, Basingstoke; New York, pp. 96–115.
Bremmer, I., 2012. *Every Nation for Itself: Winners and Losers in a G-Zero World*. Portfolio, London.
Bridge, F.R., Bullen, R., 2005. *The Great Powers and the European States System 1814–1914*. Pearson Education, London.

Bibliography

Brown, C., 2001. World Society and the English School: An 'International Society' Perspective on World Society. *European Journal of International Relations* 7, 421–441.

Brown, G., 2010. *Beyond the Crash: Overcoming the First Crisis of Globalization.* Simon & Schuster, London.

Bull, H., 2000. The European International Order, in: Alderson, K., Hurrell, A. (Eds.), *Hedley Bull on International Society.* Macmillan, Basingstoke, pp. 170–187.

Bull, H., 1984a. The Emergence of a Universal International Society, in: Bull, H., Watson, A. (Eds.), *The Expansion of International Society.* Oxford University Press, Oxford, pp. 117–126.

Bull, H., 1984b. The Emergency of a Universal International Society, in: Bull, H., Watson, A. (Eds.), *The Expansion of International Society.* Clarendon Press, Oxford, pp. 117–126.

Bull, H., 1977. *The Anarchical Society: A Study of Order in World Politics*, 4th ed. Palgrave Macmillan, Basingstoke.

Bull, H., 1972. International Relations as an Academic Pursuit. *Australian Outlook* 26, 251–265.

Bull, H., 1966a. Society and Anarchy in International Relations, in: Butterfield, H., Wight, M. (Eds.), *Diplomatic Investigations.* Allen & Unwin, London, pp. 35–50.

Bull, H., 1966b. The Grotian Concept of International Society, in: Butterfield, H., Wight, M. (Eds.), *Diplomatic Investigations.* Allen & Unwin, London, pp. 50–73.

Bull, H., 1966c. International Theory: The Case for a Classical Approach. *World Politics* 18, 361–377.

Bull, H., Watson, A. (Eds.), 1984a. *The Expansion of International Society.* Oxford University Press, Oxford.

Bull, H., Watson, A., 1984b. Conclusion, in: Bull, H., Watson, A. (Eds.), *The Expansion of International Society.* Oxford University Press, Oxford, pp. 425–436.

Bull, H., Watson, A., 1984c. Introduction, in: Bull, H., Watson, A. (Eds.), *The Expansion of International Society.* Oxford University Press, Oxford, pp. 1–12.

Bureau of Democracy, Human Rights, and Labor, US Department of State, 1999. Indonesia Country Report on Human Rights Practices for 1998. Indonesia Country Report on Human Rights Practices. http://fas.org/irp/world/indonesia/indonesia-1998.htm (accessed 7.27.14).

Burton, J.W., 1972. World Society. Cambridge University Press, Cambridge.

Butterfield, H., 1962. *Christianity, Diplomacy and War*, 3rd ed. Epworth Press, London.

Butterfield, H., Wight, M., 1966. *Diplomatic Investigations: Essays in the Theory of International Politics.* Allen & Unwin, London.

Buzan, B., 2018. Revisiting World Society. International Politics 55, 125–140.

Buzan, B., 2014a. *An Introduction to the English School of International Relations.* Polity Press, Cambridge.

Buzan, B., 2014b. *An Introduction to the English School of International Relations: The Societal Approach.* John Wiley & Sons.

Buzan, B., 2014c. The 'Standard of Civilisation' as an English School Concept. *Millennium* 42, 576–594.

Buzan, B., 2004a. *From International to World Society? English School Theory and the Social Structure of Globalisation.* Cambridge University Press, Cambridge.

Buzan, B., 2004b. *The United States and the Great Powers: World Politics in the Twenty-First Century*, 1st ed. Polity, Cambridge; Malden, MA.

Buzan, B., 2004c. Primary Institutions in International Society, in: From International to World Society? English School Theory and the Social Structure of Globalisation. Cambridge University Press, pp. 161–204.
Buzan, B., Albert, M., 2010. Differentiation: A Sociological Approach to International Relations Theory. European Journal of International Relations 16, 315–337.
Buzan, B., Foot, R. (Eds.), 2004. Does China Matter? A Reassessment: Essays in Memory of Gerald Segal, New ed. Routledge, London; New York.
Buzan, B., Lawson, G., 2015. The Global Transformation. Cambridge University Press, Cambridge.
Buzan, B., Little, R., 2013. The Historical Expansion of International Society, in: Navari, C., Green, D.M. (Eds.), Guide to the English School in International Studies. John Wiley & Sons, pp. 59–75.
Calendar |G20 Argentina, www.g20.org/en/calendar?agenda=afinidad (accessed 12.1.17).
Caliari, A., 2011. Multiple Multilateralisms in the Post-Crisis Response: UN vs. G20. The Academic Council on the United Nations System, available online: https://acuns.org/wp-content/uploads/2012/06/MultipleMultilaterisms.pdf
Caliari, A., 2011 Multiple Multilateralisms in the Post-Crisis Response: UN vs. G20, The Academic Council on the United Nations System, available online: https://acuns.org/wp-content/uploads/2012/06/MultipleMultilaterisms.pdf.
Callaghan, M., Grenville, S., Sharman, J., Thirlwell, M., 2013. G20: Rebutting Some Misconceptions. Lowy Institute G20 Monitor, available online: https://www.lowyinstitute.org/publications/g20-rebutting-some-misconceptions
Cameron, D., 2010. Summits Must Deliver More than Big Talk. The Globe and Mail, available online: https://www.theglobeandmail.com/news/world/summits-must-deliver-more-than-big-talk/article1373831/.
Campbell, D., 1992. Writing Security: United States Foreign Policy and the Politics of Identity. University of Minnesota Press, Minneapolis.
Canadian and Associated Press, 2014. Stephen Harper Calls for Russia to be Booted from G8 as U.S. Warns Vladimir Putin likely Prepping for Invasion. National Post.
Carin, B., 2010. The Future of the G20 Process, CIGI G20 Papers. CIGI.
Carin, B., Smith, G., 2004. Making Change Happen at the Global Level.
Carin, B., Smith, G., Heinbecker, P., 2010. Making the G20 Summit Process Work: Some Proposals for Impriving Effectiveness and Legitimacy. CIGI G20 Papers 16.
Cheng, S., 2004. Gauging China's Capabilities and Intentions under Deng and Mao Cheng, in: Nolan, C.J. (Ed.), Power and Responsibility in World Affairs: Reformation Versus Transformation. Praeger, Westport, CT, pp. 103–126.
Chin, G., 2010. The Emerging Countries and China in the G20: Reshaping Global Economic Governance. Studia Diplomatica 63, 105–124.
Civil20, 2013a. G8/G20 Sherpa List. Civil20 Russia. www.g20civil.com/sherpateam/sherpa-list.php
Civil20, 2013b. G8/G20/BRICS Calendar and CSO Events. Civil20 Russia. www.g20civil.com/calendar/
Clark, I., 2011. Hegemony in International Society. Oxford University Press, Oxford; New York.
Clark, I., 2009. Democracy in International Society: Promotion or Exclusion? Millennium 37, 563–581.

Clark, I., 2007. *International Legitimacy and World Society*. Oxford University Press, Oxford.
Clark, I., 2005. *Legitimacy in International Society*. Oxford University Press, Oxford.
Clark, I., 1989. *The Hierarchy of States: Reform and Resistance in the International Order*. Cambridge University Press, Cambridge; New York.
Cohen, R., 1998. Putting Diplomatic Studies on the Map. Diplomatic Studies Programme Newsletter, Leicester University, Leicester.
Coicaud, J.-M., Heiskanen, V.A., 2001. *The Legitimacy of International Organizations*. United Nations University Press.
Collingwood, V., 2006. Non-Governmental Organisations, Power and Legitimacy in International Society. *Review of International Studies* 32, 439–454.
Collins, R., 1979. *Credential Society: An Historical Sociology of Education and Stratification*. Academic Press Inc., New York.
Committee on Human Rights, The National Academy, Case Information: Anwar Ibrahim. Committee on Human Rights. www7.nationalacademies.org/humanrights/Cases/CHR_068423.htm (accessed 7.27.14).
Constantinou, C.M., 1998. Before the Summit: Representations of Sovereignty on the Himalayas. *Millennium* 27, 23–53.
Constantinou, C.M., 1996. *On the Way to Diplomacy*. University of Minnesota Press.
Constantinou, C.M., Der Derian, J., 2010a. *Sustainable Diplomacies*. Palgrave Macmillan, Basingstoke.
Constantinou, C.M., Der Derian, J., 2010b. Sustaining Global Hope: Sovereignty, Power and the Transformation of Diplomacy, in: *Sustainable Diplomacies*. Palgrave Macmillan, Basingstoke, pp. 12–22.
Cooley, A., 2005. *Logics of Hierarchy: The Organization of Empires, States, and Military Occupations*. Cornell University Press, Ithaca, NY.
Cooper, A.F., 2012a. The Death and Return of Middle Power Influence in Global Governance, The Global Summitry Project, University of Toronto, available online: http://globalsummitryproject.com.s197331.gridserver.com/blog/policy-experts-reports/the-death-and-return-of-middle-power-influence-in-global-governance/.
Cooper, A.F., 2012b. The G20 as Global Focus Group, G20 Information Centre, University of Toronto, available online: http://www.g20.utoronto.ca/analysis/120619-cooper-focusgroup.html.
Cooper, A.F., 2013a. The Changing Nature of Diploamcy, in: Cooper, A.F., Heine, J., Thakur, R. (Eds.), *Oxford Handbook of Modern Diplomacy*. Oxford University Press, Oxford, pp. 35–53.
Cooper, A.F., 2013b. Civil Society Relationships with the G20: An Extension of the G8 Template or Distinctive Pattern of Engagement? *Global Society* 27, 179–200.
Cooper, A.F., 2012. The G20 as the Global Focus Group: Beyond the Crisis Committee/Steering Committee Framework.
Cooper, A.F., 2011. The G20 and Its Regional Critics: The Search for Inclusion. *Global Policy* 2, 203–209.
Cooper, A.F., 2008a. *Celebrity Diplomacy*. Paradigm Publishers, Boulder, CO.
Cooper, A.F., 2008b. Introduction: Diplomacy and Global Governance: Locating Patterns of (Dis)Connection, in: Cooper, A.F., Hocking, B., Maley, W. (Eds.), *Global Governance and Diplomacy: Worlds Apart?* Palgrave Macmillan, Basingstoke, pp. 1–14.
Cooper, A.F., 2007. Celebrity Diplomacy and the G8: Bono and Bob as Legitimate International Actors, CIGI Working Papers. CIGI.

Cooper, A.F., Antkiewicz, A., 2010. G20 for Global Governance: Lessons from G8 Outreach. *Studia Diplomatica* 33, 91–104.
Cooper, A.F., Bradford, C., 2010. The G20 and the Post-Crisis Economic Order. CIGI G20 Papers, available online: Cooper, A.F., Bradford, C., 2010. The G20 and the Post-Crisis Economic Order.
Cooper, A.F., Heine, J., Thakur, R. (Eds.), 2013a. *Oxford Handbook of Modern Diplomacy*, 1st ed. Oxford University Press, Oxford.
Cooper, A.F., Heine, J., Thakur, R., 2013b. Introduction: The Challenges of 21st Century Diplomacy, in: Cooper, A.F., Heine, J., Thakur, R. (Eds.), *Oxford Handbook of Modern Diplomacy*. Oxford University Press, Oxford, pp. 1–34.
Cooper, A.F., Hocking, B., Maley, W., 2008a. *Global Governance and Diplomacy: Worlds Apart?* Palgrave Macmillan, Basingstoke, New York. Print.
Cooper, A.F, Hocking, B., Maley, W., 2008b. Introduction: Diplomacy and Global Governance: Locating Patterns of (Dis)Connection, in: Cooper, A.F., Hocking, B., Maley, W. (Eds.), *Global Governance and Diplomacy: Worlds Apart?* Palgrave Macmillan, Basingstoke, Print, New York, pp. 1–14.
Cooper, A.F., Shaw, T.M. (Eds.), 2009. *The Diplomacies of Small States: Between Vulnerability and Resilience*. Palgrave Macmillan, Basingstoke; New York.
Cooper, A.F., Shaw, T.M., Braveboy-Wagner, J. (Eds.), 2009. The Diplomacy of Caribbean Community States: Searching for Resilience, in: *The Diplomacies of Small States: Between Vulnerability and Resilience*. Palgrave Macmillan, Basingstoke; New York, pp. 96–115.
Cooper, Andrew F, Thakur, R., 2013. *The Group of Twenty*. Routledge, Abingdon, New York.
Cooper, D., 2001. *Talleyrand*. Grove Press.
Cornago, N., 2010. Perforated Sovereignties, Agnostic Pluralism and the Duability of (Para)diplomacy, in: Constantinou, C.M., Der Derian, J. (Eds.), *Sustainable Diplomacies*. Palgrave Macmillan, Basingstoke, pp. 89–108.
Cox, R.W., 1981. Social Forces, States and World Orders: Beyond International Relations Theory. *Millennium* 10, 126–155.
Craib, I., 1992. *Modern Social Theory: From Parsons to Habermas*, 2nd ed. Harvester Wheatsheaf, New York; London.
Crawford, N., 2017. Native Americans and the Making of International Society, in: Dunne, T., Reus-Smit, C. (Eds.), *The Globalization of International Society*. Oxford University Press, Oxford, pp. 102–124.
Crawford, N.C., 2002. *Argument and Change in World Politics: Ethics, Decolonization, and Humanitarian Intervention*. Cambridge University Press, Cambridge; New York.
Cross, M.K.D., 2007. *The European Diplomatic Corps: Diplomats and International Cooperation from Westphalia to* Maastricht. Palgrave Macmillan, Basingstoke.
Cross, M.K.D., 2006. *The European Diplomatic Corps: Diplomats and International Cooperation from Westphalia to Maastricht*. Palgrave Macmillan, Houndmills; Basingstoke; New York. Print.
Crow, G., 2004. Social Networks and Social Exclusion: An Overview of the Debate, in: Phillipson, C., Allan, G., Morgan, D.H.J. (Eds.), *Social Networks and Social Exclusion: Sociological and Policy Perspectives*. Ashgate, Aldershot, pp. 7–20.
Dafoe, J., Lin, M., 2007. 'The Choreography of Resistance' Civil Society Action at the 2007 G8 Summit.

Dahl, R.A., 1999. Can International Organizations Be Democratic? A Skeptic's View, in: Shapiro, I., Hacker-Cordón, C. (Eds.), *Democracy's Edges, Contemporary Political Theory*. Cambridge University Press, Cambridge.
Daniels, J.P., Kaiser, K., Kirton, J.J. (Eds.), 2000. *Shaping a New International Financial System : Challenges of Governance in a Globalizing World*. Ashgate, Aldershot.
Davies, C.A., 2012. *Reflexive Ethnography: A Guide to Researching Selves and Others*. Routledge, Abingdon.
Davies, P.H.J., 2001. Spies as Informants: Triangulation and the Interpretation of Elite Interview Data in the Study of the Intelligence and Security Services. *Politics* 21, 73–80.
De Clercq, G., 2014. *Russia's Lavrov Says No Problem if G8 Does Not Meet*. Reuters.
Death, C., 2010. *Governing Sustainable Development: Partnerships, Protests and Power at the World Summit*. Routledge, London.
Der Derian, J., 1987. *On Diplomacy: A Genealogy of Western Estrangement*. Basil Blackwell, Oxford; New York.
Der Derian, J., 1983. *A Genealogy of Western Diplomacy: From States of Alienation to the Alienation of States*. Thesis DPhil, University of Oxford.
Dezalay, Y., 1996. *Dealing in Virtue: International Commercial Arbitration and the Construction of a Transnational Legal Order*. University of Chicago Press, Chicago, IL.
DiCicco, J.M., Levy, J., 2003. The Power Transition Research Program, in: Elman, C., Fendius, M. (Eds.), *Progress in International Relations Theory: Appraising the Field*. MIT Press, Cambridge, pp. 109–158.
Dieter, H., Kumar, R., 2008. The Downside of Celebrity Diplomacy: The Neglected Complexity of Development. *Lynne Rienner Publishers* 14, 259–264.
Dobson, H., 2007. *The Group of 7/8*. Routledge, London.
Donnelly, J., 2011. The Differentiation of International Societies: An Approach to Structural International Theory. *European Journal of International Relations*.
Donnelly, J., 2009. Rethinking Political Structures: From "Ordering Principles" to "Vertical Differentiation" – and Beyond. *International Theory* 1, 49–86.
Donnelly, J., 2006. Sovereign Inequalities and Hierarchy in Anarchy: American Power and International Society. *European Journal of International Relations* 12, 139–170.
Donnelly, J., 1998. Human Rights: A New Standard of Civilization? *International Affairs (Royal Institute of International Affairs 1944–)* 74, 1–23.
Doran, C.F., 1991. *Systems in Crisis: New Imperatives of High Politics at Century's End*. Cambridge University Press, New York.
Doty, R.L., 1996. *Imperial Encounters: The Politics of Representation in North-South Relations*. University of Minnesota Press, Minneapolis.
Doty, R.L., 1993. Foreign Policy as Social Construction: A Post-Positivist Analysis of U.S. Counterinsurgency Policy in the Philippines. *International Studies Quarterly* 37, 297.
Dudden, A., 1999. Japan's Engagement with International Terms, in: Liu, L.H. (Ed.), *Tokens of Exchange: The Problem of Translation in Global Circulations*. Duke University Press, Durham, pp. 165–191.
Dunn, D.H., 2007. Summit Diplomacy: High-Level Meeting or Courtesy Call? A Response to John Young. *The Hague Journal of Diplomacy* 2, 147–160.
Dunn, D.H., 1996a. *Diplomacy at the Highest Level: The Evolution of International Summitry*. Macmillan, Basingstoke.

Dunn, D.H., 1996b. *The Lure of Summitry: International Dialogue at the Highest Level*. Leicester University, Centre for the Study of Diplomacy, Leicester.

Dunne, T., 2008. The English School, in: Reus-Smit, C., Snidal, D. (Eds.), *The Oxford Handbook of International Relations*. Oxford University Press, Oxford, pp. 267–285.

Dunne, T., 2003. Society and Hierarchy in International Relations. *International Relations* 17, 303–320.

Dunne, T., 1998. *Inventing International Society: A History of the English School*. Macmillan, London.

Dunne, T., 1995a. International Society: Theoretical Promises Fulfilled? *Cooperation and Conflict* 30, 125–154.

Dunne, T., 1995b. The Social Construction of International Society. *European Journal of International Relations* 1, 367–389.

Dunne, T., Reus-Smit, C. (Eds.), 2017a. *The Globalization of International Society*. Oxford University Press, Oxford.

Dunne, T., Reus-Smit, C., 2017b. The Globalization of International Society, in: *The Globalization of International Society*. Oxford University Press, Oxford, pp. 18–40.

Eftimiades, N., 1994. Chinese Intelligence Operations. Nicholas Eftimiades.

Elman, C., Fendius, M. (Eds.), 2003. *Progress in International Relations Theory: Appraising the Field*. MIT Press, Cambridge, MA.

Emmott, B., Since when has G-anything run the world? Reuters Blogs – The Great Debate.

Erlanger, S., 1998. The Fall of Suharto: The Legacy. The New York Times.

Ertel, M., 2010. Norway Takes Aim at G-20: "One of the Greatest Setbacks Since World War II." Spiegel Online.

Esteri, M. degli A., 2009. *G8 Summit 2009*. www.g8italia2009.it/G8/Home/G8-G8_Layout_locale-1199882089535_Home.htm

Fabry, M., 2010. *Recognizing States: International Society and the Establishment of New States since 1776*. Oxford University Press, Oxford.

Falkner, R., 2012. Global Environmentalism and the Greening of International Society. *International Affairs* 88, 503–522.

Falkner, R., Buzan, B., 2017. The Emergence of Environmental Stewardship as a Primary Institution of Global International Society. *European Journal of International Relations*, 1–25. doi:10.1177/1354066117741948.

Fazal, T.M., 2007. *State Death: The Politics and Geography of Conquest, Occupation, and Annexation*. Princeton University Press, Princeton, NJ.

Feinberg, R.E., Rosenberg, R.L., 1999. *Civil society and the Summit of the Americas: The 1998 Santiago Summit*. North-South Center Press, University of Miami; Boulder, CO, Coral Gables, FL.

Ferguson, T., 2012 G20: Boot Argentina, Include Poland. Forbes. www.forbes.com/sites/timferguson/2012/04/09/g20-boot-argentina-include-poland/ (accessed 4.17.13).

Fidler, D., 2001. The Return of the Standard of Civilization. *Chicago Journal of International Law* 2(1), 137–157.

Fidler, D., 2000. A Kinder, Gentler System of Capitulations? International Law, Structural Adjustment Policies, and the Standard of Liberal, Globalized Civilization. *Texas International Law Journal* 35, 387–413.

Finnemore, M., 1996. *National Interests in International Society*. Cornell University Press, Ithaca, NY; London.

Bibliography

Finnemore, M., Toope, S.J., 2001. Alternatives to "Legalization": Richer Views of Law and Politics. *International Organization* 55, 743–758.

Flint, C., 2005. *The Geography of War and Peace: From Death Camps to Diplomats*. Oxford University Press, New York; Oxford.

Fortner, R.S., 1994. Public *Diplomacy and International Politics: The Symbolic Constructs of Summits and International Radio News*. Praeger, Westport, CT; London.

Foucault, M., 1984. Of Other Spaces, Heterotopias. *Architecture, Mouvement, Continuité* 5, 46–49.

Foucault, M., 1967. Of Other Spaces. Foucault.info. http://foucault.info/documents/heteroTopia/foucault.heteroTopia.en.html (accessed 4.16.13).

Frankel, J., 2010. South Korea in the G-20 Spotlight. Project Syndicate.

Fratianni, M., 2005. *New Perspectives on Global Governance: Why America Needs the G8*. Ashgate, Aldershot.

Fratianni, M., Savona, P., Kirton, J.J. (Eds.), 2003. *Sustaining Global Growth and Development: G7 and IMF Governance*. Ashgate, Aldershot; Burlington, VT.

Fratianni, M., Savona, P., Kirton, J.J., 2007. *Corporate, Public and Global Governance: The G8 Contribution*. Ashgate, Aldershot.Frey, L., Frey, M., 1999. *The History of Diplomatic Immunity*. Ohio State University Press, Columbus.

Freytag, A., 2011. *Securing the Global Economy: G8 Global Governance for a Postcrisis World*. Ashgate, Farnham.

Fry, M., Goldstein, E., Langhorne, R., 2004. *Guide to International Relations and Diplomacy*, New ed. Continuum International Publishing Group Ltd., New York; London.

Fukuzawa, Y., 1875. *An Outline of a Theory of Civilization*. Columbia University Press, New York.

Fukayama, F., 1989. The End of History? *The National Interest* 16, 3–18.

Funabashi, Y., 1980. *Samitto No Shiso (Philosophy of the Summits)*. Asahi Shinbunsha.

G6, 1975. The Declaration of Rambouillet. G8 Research Group. www.g8.utoronto.ca/summit/1975rambouillet/communique.html (accessed 7.27.14).

G8, 2012. The Camp David Declaration. G8 Research Group. www.g8.utoronto.ca/summit/2012campdavid/g8-declaration.html (accessed 7.27.14).

G8, 2010. 2009 L'Aquila Summit – Official Documents. G8 Information Centre. www.g8.utoronto.ca/summit/2009laquila/ (accessed 7.28.14).

G8 Information Centre, 2013. Group of Five. www.g8.utoronto.ca/g5/index.html

G8 Research Group, 2012. Group of Five. G8 Information Centre. www.g8.utoronto.ca/g5/index.html (accessed 7.27.14).

G20, 2011. G20 2011 Summit Communique. G20 Research Group. www.g20.utoronto.ca/2011/2011-cannes-communique-111104-en.html (accessed 7.27.14).

G20, 2010. The Seoul Summit Document. G20 Research Group. www.g20.utoronto.ca/summits/2010seoul.htm (accessed 7.27.14).

G20 Information Centre, 2008. G20 Leaders summit on Financial Markets and the World Economy: Delegations. G20 Research Group. www.g20.utoronto.ca/2008/2008delegations1115.html (accessed 7.27.14).

Gates, B., 2011. Innovation with Impact: Financing 21st Century Development. GatesNotes.

Gaubatz, K.T., MacArthur, M., 2000. How International Is International Law. *Michigan Journal of International Law* 22, 239.

Gaventa, J., McGee, R., 2010. *Citizen Action and National Policy Reform: Making Change Happen*. Zed, London.
Geertz, C., 1980. *Negara: The Theatre State in Nineteenth-century Bali*. Princeton University Press, Princeton, NJ.
George, A.L., Bennett, A., 2005. *Case Studies and Theory Development in the Social Sciences*. MIT Press, Cambridge, MA.
Gerring, J., 2007. Is There a (Viable) Crucial-Case Method? *Comparative Political Studies* 40, 231–253.
Gilpin, R., 1983. *War and Change in World Politics*. Cambridge University Press, Cambridge.
Glass, L., Mackey, M.C., 1988. *From Clocks to Chaos*. Princeton University Press, Princeton, NJ.
Gnath, K., Mildner, S.-A., Schmucker, C., 2012. G20, IMF, and WTO in Turbulent Times: Legitimacy and Effectiveness Put to the Test. German Institute for International and Security Affairs Working Paper 37.
Goldstein, K., 2002. Getting in the Door: Sampling and Completing Elite Interviews. *PS: Political Science & Politics* 35, 669–672
Gong, G., 2002. Standards of Civilization Today, in: Mozaffair, M. (Ed.), *Globalization and Civilization*. Routledge, New York, pp. 77–96.
Gong, G., 1984. *The Standard of Civilization in International Society*. Oxford University Press, Oxford.
Gooch, B., 1970. Europe in the 19th Century: A History. www.abebooks.co.uk/Europe-19th-Century-History-GOOCH-BRISON/19093649/bd (accessed 7.28.14).
Goodman, L.-A., 2014. Harper Ready to Urge G7 to Go Tougher on Vladimir Putin. Global News.
Government of Canada, 2011. Chapter 1—Expenditures for the 2010 G8 and G20 Summits www.oag-bvg.gc.ca/internet/english/parl_oag_201104_01_e_35220.html (accessed 7.27.14).
Green, D., 2012. *How Change Happens*. Oxford: Oxford University Press..
Grewal, D.S., 2008. *Network Power: The Social Dynamics of Globalization*. Yale University Press, New Haven, CT; London.
Griffin, L.J., 1993. Narrative, Event-Structure Analysis, and Causal Interpretation in Historical Sociology. *American Journal of Sociology* 98, 1094–1133.
Guebert, J., 2010. The G8, G20 and Multilateral Organizations: Cooperating and Collaborating. *Studia Diplomatica* 33, 53–70.
Guest, G., Bunce, A., Johnson, L., 2006. How Many Interviews Are Enough? An Experiment with Data Saturation and Variability. *Field Methods* 18, 59–82.
Gulick, E., 1967. *Europe's Classical Balance of Power: A Case History of the Theory and Practice of One of the Great Concepts of European Statecraft*. W. W. Norton & Company, New York.
Gurria, A., 2004. *The G20 at the Leaders' Level?* University of Victoria, Victoria. https://www.uvic.ca/research/centres/globalstudies/assets/docs/publications/TheG20attheLeadersLevel.pdf.
Guzzini, S., 2006. Applying Bourdieu's Framework of Power Analysis to IR: Opportunities and Limits. Paper prepared for the 47th Annual convention of the International Studies Association in Chicago (22–25 March 2006).
Guzzini, S., 2005. The Concept of Power: A Constructivist Analysis. *Millennium – Journal of International Studies* 33, 495–521.

Bibliography

Haas, M., 1975. *International Conflict*. Bobbs-Merrill Co Inc., Indianapolis, IN.
Haas, P.M., 1992. Introduction: Epistemic Communities and International Policy Coordination. *International Organization* 46, 1–35.
Hafner-Burton, E.M., Kahler, M., Montgomery, A.H., 2009. Network Analysis for International Relations. *International Organization* 63, 559–92.
Hajnal, P.I., 1999. *The G7/G8 System: Evolution, Role and Documentation*. Ashgate, Aldershot; Brookfield, CT.
Hajnal, P.I., 2007a. Summitry from G5 to L20: A Review of Reform Initiatives.
Hajnal, P.I., 2007b. Can Civil Society Influence G8 Accountability? CSGR Working Paper Series 7 University of Warwick, available online: https://warwick.ac.uk/fac/soc/pais/research/researchcentres/csgr/research/abstracts/235/.
Hajnal, P.I., 2007c. The G8 System and the G20: Evolution, Role and Documentation. Ashgate, Aldershot.
Hajnal, P.I., 2013. *The G8 System and the G20: Evolution, Role and Documentation*, 2nd Rev ed. Ashgate, Aldershot.
Hajnal, P.I., 2014. *The G20: Evolution, Interrelationship, Documentation*, New ed. Ashgate, Burlington
Haldén, P., 2013. Republican Continuities in the Vienna Order and the German Confederation (1815–66). *European Journal of International Relations* 19, 281–304.
Hall, R.B., 2003. The Discursive Demolition of the Asian Development Model. *International Studies Quarterly* 47, 71–99.
Halton, D., 1975a. G6 Summit Excludes Canada in 1975, CBC – Sunday Magazine. CBC – Sunday Magazine.
Halton, D., 1975b. G6 Summit Excludes Canada in 1975. CBC Digital Archives. www.cbc.ca/archives/categories/politics/international-politics/at-the-summit-canada-welcomes-the-g8/1975-first-g6.html (accessed 4.17.13).
Hamilton, K., Langhorne, R., 1995. *The Practice of Diplomacy: Its Evolution, Theory and Administration*. Routledge, London.
Hammersley, M., 2007. *Ethnography: Principles in Practice*, 3rd ed. Routledge, London.
Hammersley, M., Atkinson, P., 2007. *Ethnography: Principles in Practice*. Taylor & Francis, London.
Hansen, L., 2006. *Security as Practice: Discourse Analysis and the Bosnian War*. Routledge, London.
Hartcher, P., 2010. Outdated Political Thuggery Embarrasses Malaysia. The Sydney Morning Herald.
Headlam, J.W., 1930. *Studies in Diplomatic History*. Methuen, London.
Hedley, B., 2000. The European International Order, in: Alderson, K., Hurrell, A. (Eds.), *Hedley Bull On International Society*. Palgrave Macmillan, London, pp. 170–187.
Heinbecker, P., 2011. The Future of the G20 and Its Place in Global Governance. CIGI G20 Papers 20.
Heine, J., 2013. From Club to Network Diplomacy, in: Cooper, A.F., Heine, J., Thakur, R. (Eds.), *Oxford Handbook of Modern Diplomacy*. Oxford University Press, Oxford, pp. 54–69.
Heine, J., 2008. On the Manner of Practicing the New Diplomacy, in: Cooper, A.F., Hocking, B., Maley, W. (Eds.), *Global Governance and Diplomacy: Worlds Apart?* Palgrave Macmillan, Print, Basingstoke; New York, pp. 271–287.

Held, D., 1995. *Democracy and the Global Order: From the Modern State to Cosmopolitan Governance*. Stanford University Press, Stanford, CA.

Hobson, C., "Democracy as Civilisation", *Global Society* 22(1), 75–95.

Hobson, C., 2008. Democracy as Civilisation. *Global Society* 22, 75–95.

Hobson, J.M., 2014. The Twin Self-Delusions of IR: Why 'Hierarchy' and Not 'Anarchy' is the Core Concept of IR. *Millennium* 42, 557–575.

Hobson, J.M., Sharman, J.C., 2005. The Enduring Place of Hierarchy in World Politics: Tracing the Social Logics of Hierarchy and Political Change. *European Journal of International Relations* 11, 63–98.

Hocking, B., 1999. Catalytic Diplomacy: Beyond 'Newness' and 'Decline', in: Melissen, J. (Ed.), *Innovation in Diplomatic Practice*. Palgrave Macmillan, New York, pp. 21–42.

Hocking, B., Spence, D., 2003. *Foreign Ministries in the European Union: Integrating Diplomats*. Palgrave Macmillan, Basingstoke; Hampshire; New York.

Hodges, M., Kirton, J.J., Daniels, J.P. (Eds.), 1999. *The G8's Role in the New Millennium*. Ashgate, Aldershot; Brookfield, VT.

Hodgson, G., 2010. Can the G20 Survive? Financial Post.

Hoffmann, S., 1965. *The State of War: Essays on the Theory and Practice of International Politics*. Praeger, New York.

Holbraad, C., 1984. *Middle Powers in International Politics*. Palgrave Macmillan, London. Holbraad, C., 1970. *Concert of Europe: German and British International Theory, 1815–1914*. Prentice Hall Press, Harlow.

Holsti, K.J., 2004. *Taming the Sovereigns: Institutional Change in International Politics*. Cambridge University Press, Cambridge; New York.

Hopf, T., 1998. The Promise of Constructivism in International Relations Theory. *International Security* 23, 171.

Hopgood, S., 2006. *Keepers of the Flame: Understanding Amnesty International*, 1st ed., Cornell University Press, Ithaca, NY.

How does the G20 work? 2017. www.g20.org/en/g20/how-it-works (accessed 7.19.18).

Howard, M., 1976. *War in European History*, Updated ed. Oxford University Press, Oxford; New York.

Howard, M.E., 1971. *Studies in War and Peace*. Viking Press.

Hu, W., 2000. Escaping the Periphery, in: *China's International Relations in the 21st Century: Dynamics of Paradigm Shifts*. University Press of America, Lanham, MD, pp. 40–70.

Huang, X., Patman, R.G. (Eds.), 2013. *China and the International System: Becoming a World Power*. Routledge, New York.

Huang, X., Patman, R.G., Zhao, S. (Eds.), 2013. Core Interests and Great Power Responsibilities: The Evolving Pattern of China's Foreign Policy, in: *China and the International System: Becoming a World Power*. Routledge, New York, pp. 32–56.

Huigens, J., Niemann, A., 2011. The G8 1/2: the EU's Contested and Ambiguous Actorness in the G8. *Cambridge Review of International Affairs* 24, 629–658.

Hurd, I., 1999. Legitimacy and Authority in International Politics. *International Organization* 53, 379–408.

Hurrell, A., 2008. *On Global Order: Power, Values, and the Constitution of International Society*, 1st ed. Oxford University Press, Oxford; New York.

Hurrell, A., 2006. Hegemony, Liberalism and Global Order: What Space for Would-be Great Powers? *International Affairs* 82, 1–19.

Hurrell, A., 2002. Hedley Bull and Diplomacy, in: *The English School and Diplomacy.* Presented at the International Studies Association, New Orleans, LA.
Hurrell, A., 2000. The Continuing Relevance of International Society. In Hedley Bull on International Society, in: Bull, H., Alderson, K. (Eds.), *Hedley Bull On International Society.* Palgrave Macmillan, Basingstoke.
Ikenberry, G.J., 2009. *After Victory: Institutions, Strategic Restraint, and the Rebuilding of Order after Major Wars.* Princeton University Press, Princeton, NJ.
Inayatullah, N., Blaney, D.L., 2004. *International Relations and the Problem of Difference.* Routledge, New York.
InterAction, 2013. About InterAction. www.interaction.org/about (accessed 7.27.14).
ITAR-TASS News Agency, 2014 Italy Calls for Preserving Present G8 format. ITAR-TASS.
Jackson, P., 2008. Pierre Bourdieu, the 'Cultural Turn' and the Practice of International History. *Review of International Studies* 34, 155–181.
Jackson, P.T., Nexon, D.H., 1999. Relations before States: Substance, Process and the Study of World Politics. *European Journal of International Relations* 5, 291–332.
Jackson, R., 2000. *The Global Covenant: Human Conduct in a World of States.* Oxford University Press, New York; Oxford.
Jackson, R., 1992. Pluralism in International Political Theory. *Review of International Studies* 18, 271–281.
Jackson, R.H., 1993. *Quasi-States: Sovereignty, International Relations and the Third World.* Cambridge University Press.
Jansen, M.B., 1974. Modernization and foreign policy in Meiji Japan, in: Ward, R.E. (Ed.), *Political Development in Modern Japan: Studies in the Modernization of Japan.* Princeton University Press, Princeton, NJ.
Jayasuriya, K., 2004. Breaking the "Westphalian" Frame: Regulatory State, Fragmentation, and Diplomacy, Discussion Papers in Diplomacy, Netherlands Institute of International Relations 'Clingendael'.
Jenkins, R., 2006. *A Life at the Centre.* Politico's, London.
Johnston, A.I., 2008. *Social States: China in International Institutions, 1980–2000.* Princeton University Press, Princeton, NJ.
Jönsson, C., 2008. Global Governance: Challenges to Diplomatic Communication, Representation, and Recognition, in: Cooper, A.F., Hocking, B., Maley, W. (Eds.), *Global Governance and Diplomacy: Worlds Apart?* Palgrave Macmillan, Basingstoke; New York, pp. 29–38. Print.
Jönsson, C., Hall, M., 2005. *Essence of Diplomacy.* Palgrave Macmillan, Basingstoke; Hampshire; New York. Print.
Jönsson, C., Tallberg, J. (Eds.), 2010. *Transnational Actors in Global Governance: Patterns, Explanations and Implications.* Palgrave Macmillan, Basingstoke.
Jordan, P.A., 2010. Russia's Managed Democracy and the Civil G8 in 2006. *The Journal of Communist Studies and Transition Politics* 26, 101–125.
Kahler, M., 2013. Rising Powers and Global Governance: Negotiating Change in a Resilient Status Quo. *International Affairs* 89, 711–729.
Kahler, M., Lake, D.A. (Eds.), 2003. *Governance in a Global Economy: Political Authority in Transition.* Princeton University Press, Princeton, NJ.
Kaiser, K., Kirton, J.J., Daniels, J.P. (Eds.), 2000. *Shaping a New International Financial System: Challenges of Governance in a Globalizing World.* Ashgate, Aldershot; Burlington, VT.

Kaufman, R.R., 1974a. The Patron-Client Concept and Macro-Politics: Prospects and Problems. *Comparative Studies in Society and History* 16, 284–308.

Kaufman, R.R., 1974b. The Patron-Client Concept and Macro-Politics: Prospects and Problems. *Comparative Studies in Society and History* 16, 284–308.

Kayaoglu, T., 2010. Westphalian Eurocentrism in International Relations Theory. *International Studies Review* 12, 193–217.

Keal, P., 2003. *European Conquest and the Rights of Indigenous Peoples: The Moral Backwardness of International Society*. Cambridge University Press.

Keal, P., 2000. An "International Society"?, in: Fry, G., O'Hagan, J. (Eds.), *Contending Images of World Politics*. Macmillan, Basingstoke.

Keene, E., 2014. The Standard of "Civilisation" the Expansion Thesis and the 19th-century International Social Space. *Millennium* 42, 1–23.

Keene, E., 2012a. The Treaty-Making Revolution of the Nineteenth Century. *The International History Review* 34, 475–500.

Keene, E., 2012b. Social Status, Social Closure and the Idea of Europe as a "Normative Power." *European Journal of International Relations* 19(4), 1–18.

Keene, E., 2010. New Histories and International Relations: Social Closure and the Rise of the New Diplomac, in: *IR Theory and International History in Dialogue*. Presented at the International Relations in Dialogue, London.

Keene, E., 2009. International Society as an Ideal Type, in: Navari, C. (Ed.), *Theorising International Society: English School Methods*. Palgrave Macmillan, Basingstoke; New York, pp. 104–124.

Keene, E., 2008a. The English School and British Historians. *Millennium* 37, 381–93.

Keene, E., 2008b. *Mapping the Boundaries of International Society: A Comparative Analysis of European and Non-European Diplomacy in the Nineteenth Century*.

Keene, E., 2007a. *Hierarchy and Stratification in International Society: A Comparison of the Old and New Diplomacies*. Presented at the International Studies Association, Chicago, IL.

Keene, E., 2007b. *Stratification, Hierarchy and Closure in International Relations*. Presented at the International Studies Association, Chicago, IL.

Keene, E., 2007c. A Case Study of the Construction of International Hierarchy: British Treaty-Making against the Slave Trade in the Early Nineteenth Century. *International Organization* 61, 311–339.

Keene, E., 2002. *Beyond the Anarchical Society: Grotius, Colonialism, and World Order*. Cambridge University Press.

Keohane, R., Nye, J., 2003. Redefining Accountability for Global Governance, in: *Governance in a Global Economy: Political Authority in Transition*. Kahler, M., Lake, D.A. (Eds.), Princeton University Press, Princeton, NJ, pp. 386–411.

Keohane, R.O., Nye, J., 1977. *Power & Interdependence*, 4th ed. Pearson, Boston, MA.

Keukeleire, S., 2003. The European Union as a Diplomatic Actor: Internal, Traditional, and Structural Diplomacy. *Diplomacy & Statecraft* 14, 31–56.

King, G., Keohane, R.O., Verba, S., 1994. *Designing Social Inquiry: Scientific Inference in Qualitative Research*. Princeton University Press, Princeton, NJ.

Kingsbury, B., 1999. Soveregnty and Inequality, in: Hurrell, A., Woods, N. (Eds.), *Inequality, Globalization, and World Politics*. Oxford University Press, Oxford, pp. 66–94.

Kirton, J., 2012. Contemporary Concert Diplomacy G8 Information Centre. www.g8.utoronto.ca/scholar/kirton198901/index.html (accessed 9.23.12).

Bibliography

Kirton, J., 2001. The G7/8 and China: Toward a Closer Association, in: Kirton, J.J., Daniels, J.P., Freytag, A. (Eds.), *Guiding Global Order: G8 Governance in the Twenty-First Century, Global Governance Series*. Ashgate, Aldershot, pp. 189–222.

Kirton, J., 1995. The Diplomacy of Concert: Canada, the G-7 and the Halifax Summit. G8 Information Centre. www.g8.utoronto.ca/scholar/kirton199501/cfp95glo.htm (accessed 9.23.12).

Kirton, J.J., Guebert, J., Tanna, S., 2010. G8 and G20 Summit Costs.

Kirton, J.J., 2013. G20 Governance for a Globalized World. Ashgate.

Kirton, J.J., 2010a. *The G20, the G8, the G5 and the Role of Ascending Powers*. Presented at the Ascending Powers and the International System, Instituto Matias Romero, Secretaria de Relaciones Exteriores, Mexico City.

Kirton, J.J., 2010b. The G8-G20 Partnership. *Studia Diplomatica* 33, 7–22.

Kirton, J.J., 1989. Contemporary Concert Diplomacy, in: *G8 Information Centre*. Presented at the Meeting of the International Studies Association and the British International Studies Association, London.

Kirton, J.J., Daniels, J.P., Freytag, A. (Eds.), 2001. *Guiding Global Order: G8 Governance in the Twenty-first Century*. Ashgate.

Kirton, J.J., Fratianni, M., Savona, P. (Eds.), 2013a. *Corporate, Public and Global Governance: The G8 Contribution*. Ashgate, Aldershot; Burlington, VT.

Kirton, J.J., Fratianni, M., Savona, P. (Eds.), 2013b. G8 Process and Performance: Past, Present, and Future, in *Corporate, Public and Global Governance: The G8 Contribution*. Ashgate, Aldershot; Burlington, VT.

Kirton, J.J., Fratianni, M., Savona, P. (Eds.), 2002. *Governing Global Finance: New Challenges, G7 and IMF Contributions*. Ashgate, Aldershot; Burlington, VT.

Kirton, J.J., Hajnal, P.I. (Eds.), 2006. *Sustainability, Civil Society and International Governance: Local, North American and Global Contributions*. Ashgate, Aldershot; Burlington, VT.

Kirton, J.J., Takase, J., 2002. *New Directions in Global Political Governance: The G8 and International Order in the Twenty-First Century*. Ashgate, Aldershot; Burlington, VT.

Kirton, J.J., Von Furstenberg, G.M., 2001. *New Directions in Global Economic Governance: Managing Globalisation in the Twenty-First Century*. Ashgate, Aldershot.

Kleiner, J., 2009. *Diplomatic Practice: Between Tradition and Innovation. World Scientific Publishing*, Singapore; Hackensack, NJ.

Knoema, 2015. World GDP Ranking 2015 | Data and Charts. Knoema. http://knoema.com/nwnfkne/world-gdp-ranking-2015-data-and-charts (accessed 8.19.15).

Knudsen, T.B., 2013. *Master Institutions of International Society: Theorizing Continuity and Change*. Presented at the 8th Pan-European Conference on International Relations, Warsaw.

Krasner, S.D., 1999. *Sovereignty: Organized Hypocrisy*. Princeton University Press, Princeton, NJ; Chichester.

Kuntz, F., Urrestarazu, U.S., Weber, J.P., 2012. The Emergence and Transformation of Foreign Politics. Conceptual Issues.

Lake, D., 2011. Hierarchy in International Relation, in: Larionova, M. (Ed.), *The European Union in the G8: Promoting Consensus and Concerted Actions for Global Public Goods*. Ashgate, Farnham.

Lake, D., 2003. The New Sovereignty in International Relations. International *Studies Review* 5, 303–323.

Lake, D., 1996. Anarchy, Hierarchy and the Variety of International Relations. *International Organization* 50, 1–33.

Lake, D.A., 2009. *Hierarchy in International Relations*. Cornell University Press, Ithaca, NY; London.
Lake, D.A., 2003. The New Sovereignty in International Relations. *International Studies Review* 5, 303–323.
Landé, C.H., 1973. Networks and Groups in Southeast Asia: Some Observations on the Group Theory of Politics. *The American Political Science Review* 67, 103–127.
Larionova, M. (Ed.), 2012. *The European Union in the G8: Promoting Consensus and Concerted Actions for Global Public Goods*. Ashgate, Farnham; Burlington, VT.
Larionova, M., 2010. Is it G8 or G20? For Russia, Of Course, It's Both. *Studia Diplomatica* 63, 81–90.
Larson, D.W., Shevchenko, A., 2010. Status Seekers: Chinese and Russian Responses to U.S. Primacy. *International Security* 34, 63–95.
Lawson, M., Green, D., 2005. *Gleneagles: What Really Happened at the G8 Summit?* Oxfam International, Oxford. https://policy-practice.oxfam.org.uk/publications/gleneagles-what-really-happened-at-the-g8-summit-114465.
Lawson-Remer, T., 2012. *Does the G20 Matter?* Reuters Blogs–The Great Debate.
Leander, A., 2011. The Promises, Problems, and Potentials of a Bourdieu-Inspired Staging of International Relations. *International Political Sociology* 5, 294–313.
Leander, A., 2010. Staging International Relations Practicing Bourdieu's Sociology. 51st ISA Annual Convention: International Studies Association Conference 2010, New Orleans, 17–20.
Lebow, R.N., 2008. *A Cultural Theory of International Relations*, 1st ed. Cambridge University Press, Cambridge; New York.
Lee, D.-H., 2010. From Toronto to Seoul: Evolution of the G20 Process. *Studia Diplomatica* 63, 35–52.
Leech, B.L., 2002. Asking Questions: Techniques for Semistructured Interviews. *PS: Political Science & Politics* 35, 665–668.
Legitimacy and Democratic Quality: The European Union, the G7/8 Summit Regime, and the United Nations in Western Legitimation Discourses, 2009, ISA-ABRI Joint International Meeting, Pontifical Catholic University, Rio de Janeiro Campus (PUC-Rio), Rio de Janeiro, Brazil, Jul 22, 2009.
Leguey-Feilleux, J.-R., 2009. *The Dynamics of Diplomacy*. Lynne Rienner Publishers, Boulder, CO.
Leifso, D., 2011. Inclusion vs. Exclusion: Addresing the Problem of Legitimacy. www.cigionline.org/publications/2011/10/inclusion-vs-exclusion-addressing-problem-legitimacy.
Leigh, C., 2007. *The Struggle for Legitimacy: Gleneagles 2005 and the Limits of Transnational Activism*. Thesis MPhil, University of Oxford, Oxford.
Lemarchand, R., 1972. Political Clientelism and Ethnicity in Tropical Africa: Competing Solidarities in Nation-Building. *The American Political Science Review* 66, 68–90.
Lesage, D., 2010. Introduction: The G8 and G20 in Flux, under the Skillful Presidency of Canada and Korea. *Studia Diplomatica* 63, 3–6.
Lesage, D., Kacar, Y., 2010. Turkey's Profile in the G20: Emerging Economy, Middle Power and Bridge-Builder. *Studia Diplomatica* 63, 125–140.
Levy, J.S., 1984. *War in the Modern Great Power System: 1495–1975*. The University Press of Kentucky, Kentucky.
Lieven, D.C.B., 1983. *Russia and the Origins of the First World War*. St. Martin's Press, New York.

Lilleker, D.G., 2003. Interviewing the Political Elite: Navigating a Potential Minefield. *Politics* 23, 207–214.

Linklater, A., 2009. The English School, in: Burchill, S., Linklater, A. (Eds.), *Theories of International Relations*. Palgrave Macmillan, Basingstoke, pp. 86–110.

Linklater, A., Suganami, H., 2006. *The English School of International Relations: A Contemporary Reassessment*. Cambridge University Press, Cambridge.

Linsenmaier, T., 2018. World Society as Collective Identity: World Society, International Society, and Inclusion/Exclusion from Europe. *International Politics* 55, 91–107.

Little, R., 2009. History, Theory and Methodological Pluralism in the English School, in: Navari, C. (Ed.), *Theorising International Society: English School Methods*. Palgrave Macmillan, Basingstok; New York, pp. 78–103. Print.

Little, R., 2000. The English School's Contribution to the Study of International Relations. *European Journal of International Relations* 6, 395–422.

Little, R., 1995. Neorealism and the English School: A Methodological Ontological and Theoretical Reassessment. *European Journal of International Relations* 1, 9–34.

Lunn, S., 2014. Ukraine Crisis: G7 Leaders to Hold Summit in Brussels without Russia. CBC News.

Mahoney, J., 2004. Comparative-Historical Methodology. *Annual Review of Sociology* 81–101.

Mahoney, J., Rueschemeyer, D., 2003. *Comparative Historical Analysis in the Social Sciences*. Cambridge University Press, Cambridge.

Manning, C., 1962. *The Nature of International Society*. London School of Economics and Political Science, Richard Clay and Company, Bungay, Suffolk.

Maoz, Z., Kuperman, R.D., Terris, L.G., Talmud, I., 2003. International Relations: A Network Approach, Gilman Conference on New Directions in International Relations, Yale University February 21-23, 2003. Available online: https://www.researchgate.net/profile/Ranan_Kuperman/publication/228567895_International_relations_A_network_approach/links/0c96052139b08a0778000000/International-relations-A-network-approach.pdf.

Marks, S., 2002. *The Ebbing of European Ascendancy: An International History of the World 1914–1945*. Hodder Arnold, London: New York.

Martin, P., 2013. The G20: From Global Crisis Responder to Steering Committee, in: Cooper, A.F., Heine, J., Thakur, R. (Eds.), *Oxford Handbook of Modern Diplomacy*. Oxford University Press, Oxford, pp. 729–744.

Martinez-Diaz, L., 2009. The G20 after Eight Years: How Effective a Vehicle for Developing-country Influence? in: Martinez-Diaz, L., Woods, N. (Eds.), *Networks of Influence? Developing Countries in a Networked Global Order*. Oxford University Press, Oxford, New York, pp. 39–62.

Martinez-Diaz, L., Woods, N. (Eds.), 2009a. *Networks of Influence? Developing Countries in a Networked Global Order: Developing Countries in a Networked Global Order*. Oxford University Press.

Martinez-Diaz, L., Woods, N., 2009b. *The G20- The Perils and Opportunities of Network Governance for Developing Countries*. Global Economic Governance Programme Briefing Paper, University of Oxford, available online: https://www.odi.org/sites/odi.org.uk/files/odi-assets/events-documents/3714.pdf.

Mason, M., 2010. Sample Size and Saturation in PhD Studies Using Qualitative Interviews. Forum Qualitative Sozialforschung / *Forum: Qualitative Social Research* 11(3). http://www.qualitative-research.net/index.php/fqs/article/view/1428.

Mattern, J.B., Zarakol, A., 2016. Hierarchies in World Politics. *International Organization* 70, 623–654.
Mayall, J., 2008. Introduction, in: Sharp, P., Wiseman, G. (Eds.), *The Diplomatic Corps as an Institution of International Society*. Palgrave Macmillan, Basingstoke; New York, pp. 1–12. Print.
Mayall, J., 2000. *World Politics: Progress and its Limits*. Polity Press, Cambridge.
McCormack, G., 2000. The Okinawa Summit seen from below Japan Policy Research Institute, available online: www.jpri.org/publications/workingpapers/wp71.html.
McCormick, D., 2005. *When the G8 Came to My Town: A Big Event in a Small Town in the Big Country*. NorthernSky, Stirling.
McGregor, R., Fontanella-Khan, J., 2014. Russia Suspended from G8, But Not Expelled. Financial Times.
MercoPress, 25 April 2012, available online: https://www.google.com/search?q= G-20Membership+Attracts+Chile%2C+but+not+prepared+to+replace+ dissident+Argentina+merco&ie=utf-8&oe=utf-8&client=firefox-b-ab
Medina, L.K., 2004. *Negotiating Economic Development: Identity Formation and Collective Action in Belize*. University of Arizona Press, Tucson.
Melissen, J., 2005. *The New Public Diplomacy: Soft Power in International Relations*. Palgrave Macmillan, Basingstoke.
Melissen, J. (Ed.), 1999. *Innovation in Diplomatic Practice*. Palgrave Macmillan Ltd, New York.
Melissen, J., 1995. *Summit Diplomacy and Alliance Politics: The Road to Nassau, December 1962*. Leicester University, Centre for the Study of Diplomacy, Leicester.
Milliken, J., 1999. The Study of Discourse in International Relations: A Critique of Research and Methods. *European Journal of International Relations* 5, 225–254.
Mitzen, J., 2013. *Power in Concert: The Nineteenth-Century Origins of Global Governance*. University of Chicago Press, Chicago, IL.
Modelski, G., 1972. *Principles of World Politics*. Free Press, New York.
Modelski, G., Thompson, W. R., (1981). *Testing cobweb models of the long cycle of world leadership*. Delivered at the annual meeting of the Peace Science Society (International), Philadelphia, Pennsylvania.
Morris, J., 2004. Normative Innovation and the Great Powers, in: Bellamy, A.J. (Ed.), *International Society and Its Critics*. Oxford University Press, Oxford; New York, pp. 265–282.
Mösslang, M., Riotte, T., German Historical Institute in London, 2008. In: *The Diplomats' World: A Cultural History of Diplomacy, 1815–1914*. Oxford University Press, Oxford.
Mozaffari, M., 2001. The Transformationalist Perspective and the Rise of a Global Standard of Civilization. *International Relations of the Asia-Pacific* 1, 247–264.
Murphy, R., 1988. *Social Closure: The Theory of Monopolization and Exclusion*. Clarendon Press, Oxford.
Navari, C., 2013. Liberalism, Democracy, and International Law — An English School Approach, in: Friedman, R., Oskanian, K., Pach, R. (Eds.), *After Liberalism?* Palgrave Studies in International Relations Series. Palgrave Macmillan, London, pp. 33–50.
Navari, C., 2011. The Concept of Practice in the English School. *European Journal of International Relations* 17, 611–630.
Navari, C. (Ed.), 2009a. *Theorising International Society: English School Methods*. Palgrave Macmillan School, Basingstoke; New York. Print.

Navari, C., 2009b. Introduction: Methods and Methodology in The English School, in: Navari, C. (Ed.), *Theorising International Society: English School Methods*. Palgrave Macmillan, Print, Basingstoke; New York, pp. 1–20.

Navari, C., 2009c. What the Classical English School was Trying to Explain, and Why its Members Were not Interested in Causal Explanation, in: Navari, C. (Ed.), *Theorising International Society: English School Methods*. Palgrave Macmillan, Basingstoke; New York, pp. 39–57. Print.

Navari, C., Green, D., 2013. Guide to the English School in International Studies. John Wiley & Sons, Oxford.

Naylor, T., 2012a. Civil Society Inclusion at Los Cabos 2012. G20 Information Centre.

Naylor, T. 2012b. 'Social Closure in Diplomacy: Inclusion and Exclusion in the G8 and G20', Presented at European Consortium for Political Research Joint Sessions, 10-15 April, 2012, Antwerp. Available online: https://ecpr.eu/Events/PaperDetails.aspx?PaperID=6032&EventID=6.

Naylor, T., 2011. Deconstructing Development: The Use of Power and Pity in the International Development Discourse. *International Studies Quarterly* 55, 177–197.

Neumann, I.B., 2014. Status is Cultural: Durkheimian Poles and Weberian Russians Seek Great-Power Status, in: Paul, T.V., Welch Larson, D., Wohlforth, W.C. (Eds.), *Status in World Politics*. Cambridge University Press, New York, pp. 85–114.

Neumann, I.B., 2012. *At Home with the Diplomats: Inside a European Foreign Ministry*, 1st ed. Cornell University Press, Ithica.

Neumann, I.B., 2011. Entry into International Society Reconceptualised: The Case of Russia. *Review of International Studies* 37, 463–484.

Neumann, I.B., 2008a. Globalisation and Diplomacy, in: Cooper, A.F., Hocking, B., Maley, W. (Eds.), *Global Governance and Diplomacy: Worlds Apart?* Palgrave Macmillan, Basingstoke; New York, pp. 15–28.

Neumann, I.B., 2008b. Russia as a Great Power, 1815–2007. *Journal of International Relations and Development* 11, 128–151.

Neumann, I.B., 2008c. The Body of the Diplomat. *European Journal of International Relations* 14, 671–695.

Neumann, I.B., 2007. "A Speech That the Entire Ministry May Stand for," Or: Why Diplomats Never Produce Anything New. *International Political Sociology* 1, 183–200.

Neumann, I.B., 2006. Sublime Diplomacy: Byzantine, Early Modern, Contemporary. *Millennium – Journal of International Studies* 34, 865–888.

Neumann, I.B., 2003. The English School on Diplomacy: Scholarly Promise Unfulfilled. *International Relations* 17, 341–369.

Neumann, I.B., 2002. Returning Practice to the Linguistic Turn: The Case of Diplomacy. *Millennium – Journal of International Studies* 31, 627–651.

Neumann, I.B., 2001a. The English School and the Practices of World Society. *Review of International Studies* 27, 503–507.

Neumann, I.B., 2001b. 'Grab a Phaser, Ambassador': Diplomacy in Star Trek. *Millennium* 30, 603–624.

Neumann, I.B., 1999. *Uses of the Other: "The East" in European Identity Formation*. Manchester University Press, Manchester.

Neumann, I.B., 1996. Self and Other in International Relations. *European Journal of International Relations* 2, 139–174.

Neumann, I.B., 1995. *Russia and the Idea of Europe: A Study in Identity and International Relations*. Routledge, London; New York.

Neumann, I.B., Welsh, J.M., 1991. The Other in European Self-Definition: An Addendum to the Literature on International Society. *Review of International Studies* 17, 327–348.
Nexon, D.H., 2009. *The Struggle for Power in Early Modern Europe: Religious Conflict, Dynastic Empires, and International Change.* Princeton University Press, Princeton, NJ.
Nicolaidis, K., Vergerio, C., Onar, L.F., Viehoff, J., 2014. From Metropolis to Microcosmos: The EU's New Standards of Civilisation. *Millennium* 42, 718–745.
Nicolson, H., 1988. *Diplomacy.* Institute for the Study of Diplomacy, Washington, DC.
Nicolson, H., 1963. *Diplomacy*, 3d ed. Oxford University Press, London.
Nicolson, H., 1946. *The Congress of Vienna: A Study in Allied Unity, 1812–1822.* Viking Press, New York.
Nish, I., 1977. *Japanese Foreign Policy, 1869–1942: Kasumigaseki to Miyakezaka.* Routledge, London.
Noortmann, M., Reinisch, A., Ryngaert, C. (Eds.), 2015. *Non-State Actors in International Law*, UK ed. Bloomsbury Publishing, Oxford; Portland, OR.
Nye, J., 2012. 'What is Ethical Foreign Policy Leadership?' Presented at Department of Politics and International Relations, University of Oxford, 24 May 2012.
Okagaki, T.T., 2013. *The Logic of Conformity: Japan's Entry into International Society.* University of Toronto Press, Toronto.
Olson, D.J., 2012. In Management of G8, G20 Summits, Mexican Performance Was Vastly Superior to U.S. The Huffington Post.
ONE, 2009. About www.one.org/international/about/ (accessed 3.14.18).
ONE, 2011. Annual Report. ONE. one.org.s3.amazonaws.com/pdfs/oneannualreport2011.pdf (accessed 7.27.14).
ONE, 2011. ONE History. ONE. www.one.org/c/international/about/944/ (accessed 7.27.14).
ONE, 2013. Frequently Asked Questions. ONE.org. www.one.org/c/international/faq/ (accessed 4.17.13).
ONE, 2018. About www.one.org/international/about/ (accessed 3.19.18).
Onea, T.A., 2014. Between Dominance and Decline: Status Anxiety and Great Power Rivalry. *Review of International Studies* 40, 125–152.
Onuf, Nicholas G., 1989. *World of Our Making: Rules and Rule in Social Theory and International Relations.* University of South Carolina Press.
Osiander, A., 1994. *The States System of Europe, 1640–1990: Peacemaking and the Conditions of International Stability.* Clarendon Press, Oxford.
Otte, T., 2001. Satow, in: Berridge, G.R., Keens-Soper, M., Otte, T. (Eds.), *Diplomatic Theory from Machiavelli to Kissinger.* Palgrave Macmillan, Basingstoke; Hampshire; New York.
Otte, T.G., 1998. *Harold Nicolson and Diplomatic Theory : Between Old Diplomacy and New. Centre for the Study of Diplomacy.* Leicester University, Leicester.
Oxenstierna, R.F., 1993. *The 1992 Group of Seven Summit and Its Impact on the Middle East.* Gulf Centre for Strategic Studies Limited, London.
Paige, J.M., 1999. Conjuncture, Comparison, and Conditional Theory in Macrosocial Inquiry. *American Journal of Sociology* 105, 781–800.
Pallain, G., 1881. Correspondance inédite du prince de Talleyrand et du roi Louis XVIII pendant le Congrès de Vienne. E. Plon et Cie, Paris.
Palmujoki, E., 2013. Fragmentation and Diversification of Climate Change Governance in International Society. *International Relations* 27, 180–201.

Parkin, F., 1979. *Marxism and Class Theory: A Bourgeois Critique*. Taylor & Francis, New York.
Parkin, F. (Ed.), 1974. *The Social Analysis of Class Structure*. Tavistock Press, London.
Parris, M., 2012. *The Spanish Ambassador's Suitcase: Stories from the Diplomatic Bag*. Penguin, London.
Parris, M., 2011. *Parting Shots*. Viking, London.
Parry, T., 2014. Stephen Harper Says he'll Push for Russia's Expulsion from the G8. CBC News.
Paul, T.V., Shankar, M., 2014. Status Accomodation through Institutional Means: India's Rise and the Global Order, in: Paul, T.V., Welch Larson, D., Wohlforth, W.C. (Eds.), *Status in World Politics*. Cambridge University Press, New York, pp. 165–191.
Paul, T.V., Welch Larson, D., Wohlforth, W.C. (Eds.), 2014. *Status in World Politics*. Cambridge University Press, New York.
Payne, G. (Ed.), 2006. *Social Divisions*, 2nd ed. Palgrave Macmillan, Basingstoke; New York.
Payne, G., 2000a. *Social Divisions*. Macmillan, Basingstoke.
Payne, G., 2000b. An Introduction to Social Divisions, in: *Social Divisions*. Macmillan, Basingstoke, pp. 1–19.
Payne, G., 2000c. Social Divisions and Social Cohesion, in: *Social Divisions*. Macmillan, Basingstoke, pp. 242–253.
Peabody, R.L., Hammond, S.W., Torcom, J., Brown, L.P., Thompson, C., Kolodny, R., 1990a. Interviewing Political Elites. *PS: Political Science & Politics* 23, 451–455.
Peabody, R.L., Hammond, S.W., Torcom, J., Brown, L.P., Thompson, C., Kolodny, R., 1990b. Interview Political Elites. *Political Science and Politics* 23, 451–455.
Penttilä, R., 2013. *The Role of the G8 in International Peace and Security*. Routledge, Abingdon.
Penttilä, R.E.J., 2003. *The Role of the G8 in International Peace and Security*. Oxford University Press for the International Institute for Strategic Studies, Oxford.
Peryshkina, A., Alexander, N., Chernigov, V., Haoliang, X., Malkin, J.-E., McCabe, A., Ramos, G., 2012. *Russia's Presidency in G20: The Role of Civil Society in Forming the Agenda*, Panel Presentation, available online: http://www.g20civil.com/documents/197/814/.
Peterson, M.J., 1997. *Recognition of Governments: Legal Doctrine and State Practice, 1815–1995*. Macmillan Publishers Limited, Basingstoke.
Petrie, S.C., 1949. *Earlier diplomatic history, 1492–1713*. Hollis and Carter, London.
Pflantze, O., 1990. *Bismark and the Development of Germany, Vol. 1, The Period of Unification*. Princeton University Press, Princeton, NJ.
Phillipson, C., Allan, G., Morgan, D.H.J., 2004a. *Social Networks and Social Exclusion : Sociological and Policy Perspectives*. Ashgate, Aldershot.
Phillipson, C., Allan, G., Morgan, D.H.J., 2004b. Introduction, in: Phillipson, C., Allan, G., Morgan, D.H.J. (Eds.), *Social Networks and Social Exclusion : Sociological and Policy Perspectives*. Ashgate, Aldershot, pp. 1–6.
Pigman, G.A., Kotsopoulos, J., 2007. "Do This One for Me, George": Blair, Brown, Bono, Bush and the "Actor-ness" of the G8. *The Hague Journal of Diplomacy* 2, 127–145.
Pouliot, V., 2016. *International Pecking Orders: The Politics and Practice of Multilateral Diplomacy*. Cambridge University Press, Cambridge.

Pouliot, V., 2008. The Logic of Practicality: A Theory of Practice of Security Communities. *International Organization* 62, 257–288.
Powell, J.D., 1970. Peasant Society and Clientelist Politics. *The American Political Science Review* 64, 411–425.
President, European Council, 1975. The Hague Declaration G7. G8 Research Group. www.g8.utoronto.ca/summit/1975rambouillet/communique.html (accessed 7.27.14).
Putnam, R.D., Bayne, N., 1987. *Hanging Together: Cooperation and Conflict in the Seven-power Summits*. Harvard University Press, Cambridge.
Putnam, R.D., Bayne, N., 1984. *Hanging Together: The Seven-Power Summits*. Heinemann for the Royal Institute of International Affairs, London.
Qin, Y., 2010. Why is there no Chinese International Relations Theory? in: Acharya, A., Buzan, B. (Eds.), *Non-Western International Relations Theory Perspectives on and beyond Asia*. Routledge, New York, pp. 26–50.
Ragin, C.C., Becker, H.S., 1992. *What Is a Case?: Exploring the Foundations of Social Inquiry*. Cambridge University Press, Cambridge.
Ramirez, A., 2012. Gratitude Message. www.b20.org/gratitude.aspx (accessed 4.17.13).
Rana, P.B., 2011. A Proposal to Enhance the G20's "Input" Legitimacy. VoxEU.org.
Rani, R.S., 2016. The Management Set. BRIGHT Magazine.
Ranke, L. von, 1973. *The Theory and Practice of History*. Bobbs-Merrill, Indianapolis.
Reisch, G.A., 1991. Chaos, History, and Narrative. *History and Theory* 30, 1–20.
Renard, T., 2010. G20: Towards a New World Order. *Studia Diplomatica* 33, 7–22.
Reus-Smit, C., 2009. Constructivism and The English School, in: Navari, C. (Ed.), *Theorising International Society: English School Methods*. Palgrave, Basingstoke, pp. 58–77.
Reus-Smit, C., 2005. Liberal Hierarchy and the Licence to Use Force. *Review of International Studies* 31, 71–92.
Reus-Smit, C., 2004. The Constructivist Challenge after September 11, in: Bellamy, A.J. (Ed.), *International Society and Its Critics*. Oxford University Press, Oxford, pp. 81–96.
Reus-Smit, C., 1999. *The Moral Purpose of the State: Culture, Social Identity, and Institutional Rationality in International Relations*. Princeton University Press, Princeton, NJ.
Reus-Smit, C., 1996. The Normative Structure of International Society, in: Hampson, F.O., Reppy, J. (Eds.), *Earthly Goods: Environmental Change and Social Justice*. Cornell University Press, Ithaca, NY, pp. 96–121.
Reynolds, D., 2007. *Summits: Six Meetings that Shaped the Twentieth Century*. Allen Lane, London.
Richards, D., 1996. Elite Interviewing: Approaches and Pitfalls. *Politics* 16, 199–204.
Ringmar, E., 2002. The Recognition Game Soviet Russia against the West. *Cooperation and Conflict* 37, 115–136.
Riordan, S., 2008. The New International Security Agenda and the Practice of Diplomacy, in: Cooper, A.F., Hocking, B., Maley, W. (Eds.), *Global Governance and Diplomacy: Worlds Apart?* Palgrave Macmillan, Basingstoke; New York, pp. 135–144. Print.
Riordan, S., 2003. *The New Diplomacy*. Polity, Cambridge.
Risse, T., 2007. Transnational Actors and World Politics, in: Zimmerli, W., Richter, K., Holzinger, M., (Eds.), *Corporate Ethics and Corporate Governance*. Springer, Berlin; Heidelberg, pp. 251–286.

Roberts, I. (Ed.), 2009. *Satow's Diplomatic Practice*, 6th ed. Oxford University press, Oxford.
Rosenau, J.N., 1990a. *Turbulence in World Politics: A Theory of Change and Continuity*. Harvester Wheatsheaf, New York; London.
Rosenau, J.N., 1990b. *Turbulence in World Politics*. Princeton University Press, Princeton, NJ.
Ross, C., 2007. *Independent Diplomat: Dispatches from an Unaccountable Elite*. Cornell University Press, Ithaca, NY.
Ross, G., 1983. *The Great Powers and the Decline Of The European States System 1914–1945*. Longman, London; New York.
Rothstein, F., 1979. The Class Basis of Patron-Client Relations. *Latin American Perspectives* 6, 25–35.
Rothstein, R.L., 1968. *Alliances and Small Powers*. Columbia University Press, New York.
Rubio-Marquez, V., 2009. The G20: A Practitioner's Perspective, in: Martinez-Diaz, L., Woods, N. (Eds.), *Networks of Influence?: Developing Countries in a Networked Global Order*. Oxford University Press, Oxford New York, pp. 19–38.
Russian International Affairs Council, 2012. G20, G8, BRICS development momentum and interests of Russia. http://russiancouncil.ru/en/inner/?id_4=677#top (accessed 7.27.14).
Sabel, R., 1998. *The Relevance of Procedure at International Conferences*. Centre for the Study of Diplomacy, Leicester.
Said, A.M., 2004. The G20 and Restructing of the International Economis Order: An Egyptian Perspective. African Portal. Available online: https://www.africa portal.org/publications/the-g20-and-the-restructuring-of-the-international-economic-order-an-egypt-perspective/.
Said, E.W., 1978. *Orientalism*. Penguin Books, London.
Saito, S., 1990. *Japan at the summit: Its Role in the Western Alliance and in Asian Pacific Cooperation*. Routledge for the Royal Institute of International Affairs, London.
Salter, M.B., 2002. *Barbarians and Civilization in International Relations*. Pluto Press, London; Sterling, VA.
Sarkozy, N., 2007. *Testimony: France, Europe, and the World in the Twenty-First Century*. Harper Perennial, New York.
Satow, E.M., 2009. *Satow's Diplomatic Practice*. 6th ed. Sir Roberts, I. (Ed.). Oxford University Press, Oxford.
Save the Children, 2012. Save the Children Says Pregnancy Kills or Injures One Million Girls a Year. www.interaction.org/document/save-children-says-pregnancy-kills-or-injures-one-million-girls-year (accessed 7.27.14).
Savona, P., 2005. *New Perspectives on Global Governance: Why America Needs the G8*, illustrated ed. Ashgate, Aldershot; Burlington, VT.
Schachter, O., 1977. Invisible College of International Lawyers. *Northwestern University Law Review* 72, 217.
Scharpf, F.W., 1999. *Governing in Europe: Effective and Democratic?* Oxford University Press, Oxford.
Schaumber-Muller, S., 2010. The Concept of Law and International Society, Paper presented at SGIR 7th Pan-European International Relations Conference, Stockholm..
Schneider, S., Gronau, J., Krell-Laluhova, Z., Nonhoff, M., Nullmeier, F., 2008. *The G8 as a Newly Emerging Legitimation Object in Global Politics*. Presented at the Annual Conference of the Canadian Political Science Association, Vancouver.

Scholte, J.A., 2011. *Building Global Democracy?: Civil Society and Accountable Global Governance.* Cambridge University Press, Cambridge.

Scholte, J.A., 2008. From Government to Governance: Transition to a New Diplomacy, in: Cooper, A.F., Hocking, B., Maley, W. (Eds.), *Global Governance and Diplomacy: Worlds Apart?* Palgrave Macmillan, Basingstoke; New York, pp. 39–62. Print.

Schouenborg, L., 2011. A New Institutionalism? The English School as International Sociological Theory. *International Relations* 25, 26–44.

Schulz, C.-A., 2014. Civilisation, Barbarism and the Making of Latin America's Place in 19th-Century International Society. *Millennium* 42, 837–859.

Scott, H.M., 2006. *The Birth of a Great Power System: 1740–1815.* Longman Publishing Group, Harlow.

Scott, J., 2000. *Social Network Analysis: A Handbook*, 2nd ed. Sage, London.

Scott, J.C., 1972. Patron-Client Politics and Political Change in Southeast Asia. *The American Political Science Review* 66, 91–113.

Searle, J.R., 1995. *The Construction of Social Reality.* Simon and Schuster, New York.

Sen, A., 2000. Social Exclusion: Concept, Application, and Scrutiny. Office of Environment and Social Development, Asian Development Bank, Social Development Papers 1–60.

Sewell, W.H., 1990. *Three Temporalities: Toward a Sociology of the Event.* University of Michigan, Ann Arbor.

Sharp, P., 2009. *Diplomatic Theory of International Relations.* Cambridge University Press, Cambridge; New York.

Sharp, P., 2003. Herbert Butterfield, the English School and the Civilizing Virtues of Diplomacy. *International Affairs* 79, 855–878.

Sharp, P., Wiseman, G. (Eds.), 2008. The Diplomatic Corps as an Institution of International Society, 1st ed. Palgrave Macmillan, Print, Basingstoke; New York.

Sharp, P., Wiseman, G., 2007. *The Diplomatic Corps as an Institution of International Society.* Palgrave Macmillan, Basingstoke.

Shermer, M., 1995. Exorcising Laplace's Demon: Chaos and Antichaos, History and Metahistory. *History and Theory* 34, 59.

Shifrinson, J.R.I., 2018. *Rising Titans, Falling Giants: How Great Powers Exploit Power Shifts.* Cornell University Press, Ithaca, NY.

Simmons, B.A., 2011. International Studies in the Global Information Age. *International Studies Quarterly* 55, 589–599.

Simpson, G., 2004. *Great Powers and Outlaw States: Unequal Sovereigns in the International Legal Order.* Cambridge University Press, Cambridge; New York.

Sinha, S.P., 1965. Perspective of the Newly Independent States on the Binding Quality of International Law. *International & Comparative Law Quarterly* 14, 121–131.

Slaughter, A., 2005. *A New World Order.* Princeton University Press, Princeton, NJ.

Slaughter, A., 2004a. *A New World Order.* Princeton University Press, Princeton, NJ; Oxford.

Slaughter, A., 2004b. *Government Networks, World Order, and the G20.* Presented at the The G20 at Leaders' Level? IDRC, Ottawa.

Slaughter, S., 2013. The Prospects of Deliberative Global Governance in the G20: Legitimacy, Accountability, and Public Contestation. *Review of International Studies* 39, 71–90.

Slaughter, S., 2012. Debating the International Legitimacy of the G20: Global Policymaking and Contemporary International Society. *Global Policy* 4, 43–52.

Smith, G., 2012a. The Evolving Role of the G20. Perspective on the G20: The Los Cabos Summit.
Smith, G., 2012b. The Evolving Role of the G20, CIGI G20 Papers. CIGI.
Smith, G., 2011. G7 to G8 to G20: Evolution in Global Governance. CIGI G20 Papers, CIGI G20 Papers.
Smith, G., Heap, P., 2010. Canada, the G8, and the G20: A Canadian Approach to Shaping Global Governance in a Shifting International Environment. *School of Public Policy Research Papers* 3, 1–27.
Spruyt, H., 1994. *The Sovereign State and Its Competitors: An Analysis of Systems Change.* Princeton University Press, Princeton, NJ.
Stanley Foundation, 2011. How Are Key 21st-Century Power Arranging Themselves? For Competition, Coexistence, or Cooperation? Policy Dialogue Brief, Muscatine, Iowa, 6-8 June.
Stark, D., 2011. Heterarchy: Exploiting Ambiguity and Organizing Diversity. *Brazilian Journal of Political Economy* 21, 21–39.
Steffek, J., 2003. The Legitimation of International Governance: A Discourse Approach. *European Journal of International Relations* 9, 249–275.
Stivachtis, Y.A., 2006. Democracy: The Highest Stage of 'Civilized' Statehood. *Global Dialogue* 8, 87–99.
Stivachtis, Y.A., 2018. 'International Society' versus 'World Society': Europe and the Greek War of Independence. *International Politics* 55, 108–124.
Stivachtis, Y.A., 1998. *The Enlargement of International Society: Culture Versus Anarchy and Greece's Entry into International Society.* Palgrave Macmillan, Basingstoke; Hampshire; New York.
Stivachtis, Y.A., McKeil, A., 2018. Conceptualizing World Society. *International Politics* 55, 1–10.
Stroikos, D., 2014. Introduction: Rethinking the Standard(s) of Civilisation(s) in International Relations. *Millennium* 42, 546–556.
Stryker, R., 1996. Beyond History Versus Theory: Strategic Narrative and Sociological Explanation. *Sociological Methods & Research* 24, 304–352.
Subacchi, P., Pickford, S., 2011. Legitimacy vs Effectiveness for the G20: A Dynamic Approach to Global Economic Governance. Chatham House Briefing Paper. Available online: https://www.chathamhouse.org/sites/default/files/1011bp_subacchi_pickford.pdf.
Suganami, H., 1989. *The Domestic Analogy and World Order Proposals.* Cambridge University Press, Cambridge.
Suganami, H., 1984. Japan's Entry in International Society, in: Bull, H., Watson, A. (Eds.), *The Expansion of International Society.* Oxford University Press, Oxford, pp. 185–199.
Suzuki, S., 2014. Journey to the West: China Debates Its 'Great Power' Identity. *Millennium* 42, 632–650.
Suzuki, S., 2013. *Civilization and Empire: China and Japan's Encounter with European International Society.* Routledge, London.
Suzuki, S., 2009. *Civilization and Empire: China and Japan's Encounter with European International Society.* Routledge, Abingdon.
Suzuki, S., 2008. Seeking 'Legitimate' Great Power Status in Post-Cold War International Society: China's and Japan's Participation in UNPKO. *International Relations* 22, 45–63.

Takahashi, S., 1908. *International Law Applied to the Russo-Japanese War*. New York.
Takahashi, S., 1899. *Cases on International Law during the Chino-Japanese War*. Cambridge University Press, Cambridge.
Talbott, S., 2007. *The Russia Hand: A Memoir of Presidential Diplomacy*. Random House Publishing Group, New York.
Talbott, S., 2003. *The Russia Hand: A Memoir of Presidential Diplomacy*, Random House trade paperback ed. Random House, New York.
Tansey, O., 2007. Process Tracing and Elite Interviewing: A Case for Non-probability Sampling. *PS: Political Science & Politics* 40, 765–772.
Tareen, A., 2010. The UN and the G20: Efficiency vs. Legitimacy? CIGI Blogs.
Tashakkori, A., Teddlie, C., 2010. *SAGE Handbook of Mixed Methods in Social & Behavioral Research*. SAGE, New York.
Taylor, A.J.P., 1971. *The Struggle for Mastery in Europe, 1848–1918*, New ed. Oxford Paperbacks, London; New York.
Teschke, B., 2003. *The Myth of 1648: Class, Geopolitics, and the Making of Modern International Relations*. Verso, London.
Thakur, R., 2013. A Balance of Interests, in: Cooper, A.F., Heine, J., Thakur, R. (Eds.), *Oxford Handbook of Modern Diplomacy*. Oxford University Press, Oxford, pp. 70–90.
Thakur, R., 2008. Conclusion: National Diplomacy and Global Governance, in: Cooper, A.F., Hocking, B., Maley, W. (Eds.), *Global Governance and Diplomacy: Worlds Apart?* Palgrave Macmillan, Basingstoke, pp. 288–299.
The Napoleon Series, 2008. Treaty of Paris 1814. Treaty of Paris 1814. www.napoleonseries.org/research/government/diplomatic/c_paris1.html (accessed 7.28.14).
Thematic Areas | G20 Argentina, 2017. www.g20.org/en/g20-argentina/thematic-areas (accessed 12.1.17).
Thomas, G., 2011. *How to Do Your Case Study: A Guide for Students and Researchers*. SAGE Publications; New York.
Tilly, C., Ardant, G. (Eds.), 1975. *The Formation of National States in Western Europe*. Princeton University Press, Princeton, NJ.
Towns, A.E., 2014. Carrying the Load of Civilisation: The Status of Women and Challenged Hierarchies. *Millennium* 42, 595–613.
Towns, A.E., 2010. *Women and States: Norms and Hierarchies in International Society*. Cambridge University Press, Cambridge; New York
Towns, A.E., Rumelili, B., 2017. Taking the Pressure: Unpacking the Relation between Norms, Social Hierarchies, and Social Pressures on States. *European Journal of International Relations* 23, 756–779.
Traub, J., 2005. The Statesman. The New York Times.
UK Government, 2013. G8 events. www.gov.uk/government/news/g8-events (accessed 7.27.14).
Urrestarazu, U.S., Hellmann, G., 2012. *Entering the Engine Room: Diplomacy, the Individual, and IR Theory*, Conferece Presentation, ECPR General Conference, Reykjavik 25-27 August 2011.
Van Rooy, A., 2004. *The Global Legitimacy Game: Civil Society, Globalization and Protest*. Palgrave Macmillan, Basingstoke; Hampshire, New York.
Vanessa, R.-M., 2009. The G20: A Practitioner's Perspective, in: Martinez-Diaz, L., Woods, N. (Eds.), *Networks of Influence?: Developing Countries in a Networked Global Order*. Oxford University Press, New York.

Vestergaard, J., 2011. The G20 and Beyond: Towards Effective Global Economic Governance (No. 2011:04). DIIS Reports / Danish Institute for International Studies.
Vestergaard, J., Wade, R.H., 2012. Establishing a new Global Economic Council: Governance Reform at the G20, the IMF and the World Bank. *Global Policy* 3, 257–269.
Villumsen, T., 2010. Capitalizing On Bourdieu: Boundary-Setting, Agency, and Doxic Battles in IR. Center for Advanced Security Theory, Research Seminar Presentation, University of Copenhagen.
Vincent, R.J., 1986. *Human Rights and International Relations*, Cambridge University Press.
Vincent, R.J., 1987. *Human Rights and International Relations*. Cambridge University Press, Cambridge; New York.
Vincent, R.J., 1984. Racial Equality, in: Bull, H., Watson, A. (Eds.), *The Expansion of International Society*. Oxford University Press, Oxford, pp. 239–254.
Volgy, T.J., Corbetta, R., Grant, K.A., Baird, R.G. (Eds.), 2011. *Major Powers and the Quest for Status in International Politics: Global and Regional Perspectives*. Palgrave Macmillan, New York.
Volgy, T.J., Corbetta, R., Rhamey Jr., P., Baird, R.G., Grant, K.A., 2014. Status Considerations in International Politics and the Rise of Regional Powers, in: Paul, T.V., Welch Larson, D., Wohlforth, W.C. (Eds.), *Status in World Politics*. Cambridge University Press, New York, pp. 58–84.
von Treitschke, H., 1916. *Politics*. Constable, London.
Waever, O., 1999. *Does the English School's Via Media Equal the Contemporary Constructivist Middle Ground?* Presented at the British International Studies Association Conference, Manchester.
Wallace, M.D., 1973. *War and Rank among Nations*. Lexington Books, Lanham, M.D.
Waltz, K.N., 1979. *Theory of International Politics*, 1st ed. Waveland Press, Inc., New York.
Warde, A., 2004. *Practice and Field: Revising Bourdieusian Concepts*, Centre for Research on Innovation & Competition Discussion Paper, The University of Manchester.
Washington Post Suggests Replacing Argentina with Chile at the G20, Merco Press, 23 April 2012, available online: http://en.mercopress.com/2012/04/23/washington-post-suggests-replacing-argentina-with-chile-at-the-g20.
Watson A., 1992, *The Evolution of International Society: A Comparative Historical Analysis*, Oxford: Oxford University Press.
Watson, A., 1992. *The Evolution of International Society: A Comparative Historical Analysis*. Routledge, London.
Watson, A., 1991. *Diplomacy: The Dialogue between States*. Routledge, London; New York.
Watson, A., 1982. *Diplomacy: The Dialogue between States*. Routledge, Abingdon.
Webb, E.J., Cambell, D.T., Schwartz, R.D., 1966. *Unobtrusive Measures: Nonreactive Research in the Social Sciences*. Rand McNally, Oxford.
Weber, C., 1998. Reading Martin Wight's "Why Is There No International Theory?" as History. *Alternatives* 23, 451–69.
Weber, M., 1922. *Economy and Society: An Outline of Interpretive Sociology*. University of California Press, Berkeley.

Webster, S.C., 1950. *The Congress of Vienna 1814–1815*, Later ed. Oxford University Press, London.
Weeden, K.A., 2002. Why Do Some Occupations Pay More than Others? Social Closure and Earnings Inequality in the United States. *American Journal of Sociology* 108, 55–101.
Weisensel, P.R., 1991. Russian Self-Identification and Travellers' Descriptions of the Ottoman Empire in the First Half of the Nineteenth Century. *Central Asian Survey* 10(4), 65–85.
Welch Larson, D., Paul, T.V., Wohlforth, W.C., 2014. Status and World Order, in: Paul, T.V., Welch Larson, D., Wohlforth, W.C. (Eds.), *Status in World Politics*. Cambridge University Press, New York, pp. 3–32.
Welch Larson, D., Shevchenko, A., 2014. Managing Rising Powers; The Role of Status Concerns, in: Paul, T.V., Welch Larson, D., Wohlforth, W.C. (Eds.), *Status in World Politics*. Cambridge University Press, New York, pp. 33–57.
Weldes, J., Saco, D., 1996. Making State Action Possible: The United States and the Discursive Construction of "The Cuban Problem", 1960–1994. *Millennium – Journal of International Studies* 25, 361–395.
Wendt, A., 1999. *Social Theory of International Politics*. Cambridge University Press, Cambridge.
Wendt, A., 1998. On Constitution and Causation in International Relations. *Review of International Studies* 24, 101–118.
Westlake, J., 1894. *Chapters on the Principles of International Law*. Cambridge University of Press, Cambridge.
Who are the Sherpas? G20 Mexico 2012. www.g20.org/index.php/en/who-are-the-sherpas (accessed 9.23.12).
Wight, C., 2006. *Agents, Structures and International Relations: Politics as Ontology*. Cambridge University Press, Cambridge.
Wight, M., 1991. *International Theory: The Three Traditions*. Leicester University Press/Royal Institute of International Affairs, Leicester.
Wight, M., 1977. *Systems of States*. Leicester University Press [for] the London School of Economics and Political Science. Leicester University Press, Leicester.
Wight, M., 1946. *Power Politics*. Leicester University Press, London.
Willetts, P., 2000. From "Consultative Arrangements" to "Partnership": The Changing Status of NGOs in Diplomacy at the UN. Global Governance 6, 16.
Wiseman, G., 2004. "Polylateralism" and New Modes of Global Dialogue, in: *Diplomacy*. Sage, London, pp. 36–57.
Wohlforth, W.C., 2014. Status Dilemmas and Interstate Conflict, in: Paul, T.V., Welch Larson, D., Wohlforth, W.C. (Eds.), *Status in World Politics*. Cambridge University Press, New York, pp. 115–140.
Woods, N., 2010. The G20 Leaders and Global Governance. Global Economic Governance Programme Working Paper, University of Oxford. Available online: https://www.geg.ox.ac.uk/news/g20-and-global-governance.
Xiao, R., 2011. The Moral Dimension of Chinese Foreign Policy, in: Xiao, R., Carlson, A. (Eds.), *New Frontiers in China's Foreign Relations: Zhongguo Waijiao de Xin Bianjiang*. Lexington Books, pp. 3–24.
Yukichi, F., 1885, *Theory of Leaving Asia*, in Jiji Shimpo, Japan.
Yonding, Y., 2004. *The G20 and China: A Chinese Perspective*. Presented at the the G20 at Leaders' Level? IDRC, Ottawa.

Bibliography

Zarakol, A. (Ed.), 2017. *Hierarchies in World Politics*. Cambridge University Press, New York.

Zarakol, A., 2010. *After Defeat: How the East Learned to Live with the West*. Cambridge University Press, Cambridge; New York.

Zhang, Y., 2014. The Standard of 'Civilisation' Redux: Towards the Expansion of International Society 3.0? *Millennium* 42, 674–696.

Zhang, Y., 1998. *China in International Society: Alienation and Beyond*. Palgrave Macmillan, New York. Print.

Primary and archival sources

Alexander, M. 1980. Political Discussion at the Venice Summit.

Amnesty International, 2008. "Anwar Ibrahim Continues Campaign despite Questionable Charges | Amnesty International." *Amnesty International*. www.amnesty.org/en/news-and-updates/news/anwar-ibrahim-continues-campaign-despite-questionable-charges-20080808, accessed July 27, 2014.

Armstrong, Robert. 1980a. "Record of a Meeting at the House of HM Ambassador, Vienna at Breakfast on 16 May." PREM19/188 f161. Margaret Thatcher Foundation Archive. At www.margaretthatcher.org/document/115741.

———. Letter. 1980b. "Quadripartite Meeting." April 15. PREM19/188 f198 (Note: Misfiled as 14 April 1980). Margaret Thatcher Foundation Archive. At www.margaretthatcher.org/document/115739.

———. Memorandum. 1980c. April 24. PREM19/188 f183. Margaret Thatcher Foundation Archive. At www.margaretthatcher.org/document/115750.

Armstrong, Robert, and Wade-Gery. 1980. "Quadripartite Meeting, Vienna, 16 May." PREM19/188 f156. Margaret Thatcher Foundation Archive. At www.margaretthatcher.org/document/115742.

Australian Cabinet. 1975. Resources Committee – Cabinet Minute – Economic Summit meeting – Without Submission.

Bayne. Memorandum to C.Q. Fogarty. 1975. "Giscard's Proposal for a Monetary Summit Conference." July 11. PREM 16/393. Margaret Thatcher Foundation Archive. At www.margaretthatcher.org/document/111524.

BBC News. 1998a. "Malaysia's Deputy Prime Minister Fired." *BBC*, September 2, sec. Asia-Pacific. At http://news.bbc.co.uk/2/hi/asia-pacific/163200.stm, accessed July 27, 2014.

———. 1998b. "Sodomy Charges Turn up Heat on Anwar." *BBC*, September 19, sec. Asia Pacific. At http://news.bbc.co.uk/2/hi/asia-pacific/175339.stm, accessed July 27, 2014.

———. 1998c. "Anwar Arrested amid Kuala Lumpur Protests." *BBC*, September 20, sec. Asia-Pacific. At http://news.bbc.co.uk/2/hi/asia-pacific/175896.stm, accessed July 27, 2014.

Bond UK. 2013. "About Us | Bond." At www.bond.org.uk/about-us, accessed April 17, 2013.

Bureau of Democracy, Human Rights, and Labor, US Department of State. 1999. "Indonesia Country Report on Human Rights Practices for 1998." *Indonesia Country Report on Human Rights Practices*. At http://fas.org/irp/world/indonesia/indonesia-1998.htm, accessed July 27, 2014.

Call on the Prime Minister by the Secretary-General of the Italian Foreign Ministry, 1976a.

———. 1976b.
Callaghan, James. 1977a. "Note by the Prime Minister of a Meeting at 10 Downing Street with President Giscard, President Carter and Chancellor Schmidt on Monday, 9 May, 1977, from 1000 to 1230." PREM 16/1223. Margaret Thatcher Foundation Archive. At www.margaretthatcher.org/document/111494.
———.Diplomatic Cable to James Carter. 1977b. "Economic Summit." February 21. PREM 16/1220. Margaret Thatcher Foundation Archive. At www.margaretthatcher.org/document/111505.
———. Letter to Gerald Ford. 1976, June 1. PREM 16/819. Margaret Thatcher Foundation Archive. At www.margaretthatcher.org/document/111520.
Callaghan, James, and Valery Giscard. 1977. "Conversation between the Prime Minister and President Giscard d'Estaing." PREM 16/1221. Margaret Thatcher Foundation Archive. At www.margaretthatcher.org/document/111501.
Canadian and Associated Press. 2014. "Stephen Harper Calls for Russia to Be Booted from G8 as U.S. Warns Vladimir Putin Likely Prepping for Invasion." *National Post*, March 23. At http://news.nationalpost.com/2014/03/23/stephen-harper-calls-for-russia-to-be-booted-from-g8-as-u-s-warns-vladimir-putin-likely-prepping-for-invasion/, accessed July 27, 2014.
Carter, James, and James Callaghan. 1977, February 25. PREM 16/1220. Margaret Thatcher Foundation Archive. At www.margaretthatcher.org/document/111506.
Carter, James. Diplomatic Cable to James Callaghan. 1977, February 12. PREM 16/1229. Margaret Thatcher Foundation Archive. At www.margaretthatcher.org/document/111504.
Civil20 Russia. 2014. "G8/G20 Sherpa List." *Civil Russia 2014*. At www.g20civil.com/sherpateam/sherpa-list.php, accessed January 1, 2014.
"Economic Summit." 1976. PREM 16/1220. Margaret Thatcher Foundation Archive. At www.margaretthatcher.org/document/111500.
Enders, Thomas. Diplomatic Cable to Henry Kissinger. 1976. "Canada and Next Economic Summit." November 26. 1976OTTAWA04687 / D760440-0624. US National Archives.
Erlanger, Steven. 1998. "The Fall of Suharto: The Legacy." *The New York Times*, May 22, At www.nytimes.com/1998/05/22/world/fall-suharto-legacy-suharto-fostered-rapid-economic-growth-staggering-graft.html, accessed August 4, 2014.
Ertel, Manfred. 2010. "Norway Takes Aim at G-20." *Der Spiegel Online*, June 22. At www.spiegel.de/international/europe/norway-takes-aim-at-g-20-one-of-the-greatest-setbacks-since-world-war-ii-a-702104-druck.html accessed April 18, 2013.
Ford, Gerald. Letter to James Callaghan. 1976a, May 5. PREM 16/819 (Note: Incorrectly labeled as 4 May 1975). Margaret Thatcher Foundation Archive. At www.margaretthatcher.org/document/111516.
———. Letter to James Callaghan. 1976b, May 30. PREM 16/819. Margaret Thatcher Foundation Archive. At www.margaretthatcher.org/document/111518.
———. Letter to James Callaghan. 1976c. May 31. PREM 16/819. Margaret Thatcher Foundation Archive. At www.margaretthatcher.org/document/111519.
———. Letter to James Callaghan. 1976d. June 1. PREM 16/819. Margaret Thatcher Foundation Archive. At www.margaretthatcher.org/document/111521.
———. Letter to James Callaghan. 1976e. June 5. PREM 16/820. Margaret Thatcher Foundation Archive. At www.margaretthatcher.org/document/111513.
G20. 2010. "The Seoul Summit Document." *G20 Research Group*. At www.g20.utoronto.ca/summits/2010seoul.htm, accessed July 27, 2014.

Bibliography

———. 2011. "G20 2011 Summit Communique." *G20 Research Group*. At www.g20.utoronto.ca/2011/2011-cannes-communique-111104-en.html, accessed July 27, 2014.

G20 Information Centre. 2014. "G20 Leaders Summit on Financial Markets and the World Economy: Delegations." *G20 Research Group*. At www.g20.utoronto.ca/2008/2008delegations1115.html, accessed July 27, 2014.

G6. 1975. "The Declaration of Rambouillet." *G8 Research Group*. At www.g8.utoronto.ca/summit/1975rambouillet/communique.html, accessed July 27, 2014.

Gates, Bill. 2011. "Innovation with Impact: Financing 21st Century Development." *GatesNotes*. At www.gatesnotes.com/Development/G20-Report-Innovation-with-Impact, accessed July 27, 2014.

Goodman, Lee-Anne. 2014. "Harper Ready to Urge G7 to Go Tougher on Vladimir Putin." *Global News*, March 24. At globalnews.ca/news/1226245/harper-to-urge-g7-to-go-tougher-on-putin/, accessed July 27, 2014.

Government of Australia. 1975. "Cabinet Minute: Resources Committee – Economic Summit Meeting." A5925 / 4130/CCR / 7500293. Australian National Archives. At http://recordsearch.naa.gov.au/scripts/Imagine.asp?B=7500293.

———. 1976. "Submission No 613: Tokyo Economic Summit Possible Australian Participation – Decision 1356." A12909, 613 / 7426768. Australian National Archives. At http://recordsearch.naa.gov.au/SearchNRetrieve/Interface/Details Reports/ItemDetail.aspx?Barcode=7426768&isAv=N.

Greenwald, Joseph. Diplomatic Cable to Henry Kissinger. 1975. "Reluctance of the Member States to Assume Community." October 30. 1975ECBRU09777 / D750377-0299. US National Archives.

Hillebrand, Martin. Diplomatic Cable to Henry Kissinger. 1975a. "Conversation with Chancellor Schmidt." September 25. 197 BONN 15731 251218Z / P850081-2126. US National Archives.

———. Diplomatic Cable to Henry Kissinger. 1975b. "German Press Comment on Rambouillet Summit." November 18. 1975BONN18880 / D750401-0754. US National Archives.

Hodgson, James. Diplomatic Cable. 1975. "Economic Summit." October 21. 1975TOKYO14951 / D750364-0303. US National Archives.

Hormats, Robert. 1975. "Memorandum of Conversation." www.fordlibrarymuseum.gov/library/docs.asp. Gerald R. Ford Presidential Library.

Hunt, John. Letter to James Callaghan. 1976. "Puerto Rico." June 16. PREM 16/821. Margaret Thatcher Foundation Archive. At www.margaretthatcher.org/document/111512.

———. Memorandum. 1978a. "Ref. A08541." December 12. FOI release (FOI249141) following Internal Review (IR251559). Margaret Thatcher Foundation Archive. At www.margaretthatcher.org/document/111528.

———. Memorandum to James Callaghan. 1977. "Preparations for an Economic Summit." January 19. PREM 16/1220. Margaret Thatcher Foundation Archive. At www.margaretthatcher.org/document/111499.

———. Memorandum to James Callaghan. 1978b. "Bonn Summit." May 29. FOI release 248745. Margaret Thatcher Foundation Archive. At www.margaretthatcher.org/document/111463.

Ingersoll, Robert. Telegram to US Embassy, Paris. 1975. "Giscard Favors Summit of Industrialized Nations." July 10. STATE 161902 TOSEC 060031 / D750237-1002. US National Archives.

InterAction. 2014. "About InterAction." At www.interaction.org/about, accessed July 27, 2014.

ITAR-TASS News Agency. 2014. "Italy Calls for Preserving Present G8 Format." *ITAR TASS*. At http://en.itar-tass.com/world/725097, accessed July 27, 2014.

Kissinger, Henry, and Helmut Sonnenfeldt. Diplomatic Cable to William Porter. 1975. "Presidential Letter to Prime MInister Trudeau." November 8. 1975STATE265536 / D750389-0725. US National Archives.

Kissinger, Henry. Diplomatic Cable to All US Diplomatic Posts. 1975a. "Economic Summit." October 10. 1975STATE241658 / D750352-0022. US National Archives.

———. Diplomatic Cable to All US Diplomatic Posts. 1975b. "White House Press Briefing on Economic Summit." October 11. 1975STATE243283 / D750354-0408. US National Archives.

———. Diplomatic Cable to US Ambassador Tokyo, US Ambassador London, US Ambassador Paris, US Ambassador Rome, US Ambassador Ottawa, and US Ambassador Bonn. 1975c. "Economic Summit." October 10. 1975SECTO16056 / D750363-0140. US National Archives.

———. Diplomatic Cable to John Volpe. 1975d. "Rumor's Complaint about Four Power Luncheon." July 31. 1975 SECTO 08081 311359Z / D750264-0498. US National Archives.

———. Diplomatic Cable to John Volpe. 1975e. "Italian Complaints about Rumors of Economic Meeting." August 1. 1975 SECTO 08101 011528Z / D750266-0362. US National Archives.

———. Diplomatic Cable to John Volpe. 1975f. "Secretary's Meeting with Italian Foreign Minister Rumor." September 30. 1975 STATE 232563 / D750340-0015. US National Archives.

———. Letter to Martin Hillebrand. 1975g. "Proposed Economic Summit." September 25. 1975STATE228933 / P850036-2037, N750004-0651. US National Archives.

———. Letter to William Porter. 1975h. "Economic Summit." October 9. 1975STATE241540 / P840178-2600. US National Archives.

Lunn, Susan. 2014. "Ukraine Crisis: G7 Leaders to Hold Summit in Brussels without Russia." *CBC News*, March 23. At www.cbc.ca/1.2583636, accessed July 27, 2014.

Margaret Thatcher Foundation. 2014. "Declassified G7 Files." *Margaret Thatcher Foundation – Large Scale Document Archive*. At www.margaretthatcher.org/archive/g7.asp, accessed July 28, 2014.

McGregor, Richard, and James Fontanella-Khan. 2014. "Russia Suspended from G8, but Not Expelled." *Financial Times*, March 24. At www.ft.com/cms/s/ef5a543e-b32b-11e3-b09d-00144feabdc0,Authorised=false.html?_i_location=http%3A%2F%2F

"Memorandum of Conversation." 1975. Gerald R. Ford Presidential Library. At www.fordlibrarymuseum.gov/library/document/0314/1553193.pdf.

Morris. Letter to Henry Kissinger. 1975. "Proposed Five Power Economic Conference." August 7. RU 07113 071239Z. US National Archives.

Morris, and Henry Kissinger. 1975. "Proposed Five Power Economic Conference." August 7. 1975 EC BRU 07113 071239Z / D750272-1178. US National Archives.

ONE. 2014a. "About." *ONE*. At www.one.org/international/about/, accessed July 27, 2014.

———. 2014b. "Annual Report." *ONE*. At http://one.org.s3.amazonaws.com/pdfs/oneannualreport2011.pdf, accessed July 27, 2014.

Pallister, Michael. 1980. "Political Discussion at the Venice Summit." June 6. PREM19/188 f124. Margaret Thatcher Foundation Archive. At www.margaretthatcher.org/document/115744.

Parry, Tom. 2014. "Stephen Harper Says He'll Push for Russia's Expulsion from the G8." *CBC News*, March 22. At www.cbc.ca/1.2583034, accessed July 27, 2014.

Percival. Diplomatic Cable to Henry Kissinger. 1976. "Economic Topics in Prime Minister's Discussion with President." July 21. 1976CANBER05242 / D760280-. US National Archives.

Porter, William. Diplomatic Cable to Henry Kissinger. 1975a. "Presidential Letter to PM Trudeau." November 10. 1975OTTAWA04210 / D750390-0967. US National Archives.

———. Diplomatic Cable to Henry Kissinger. 1975b. "Government of Canada Views on Rambouillet Exclusion and Future." November 14. 1975OTTAWA04265 / D750398-0684. US National Archives.

President, European Council. 2014. "The Hague Declaration." At www.consilium.europa.eu/uedocs/cms_data/docs/pressdata/en/ec/141855.pdf.

Price-Thomas, Stephen. Tweet to Lourdes Aranda. 2012a. "Invitation…" April 25. At https://twitter.com/stevept/status/195405107792318464, accessed July 27, 2014.

———. Tweet to Lourdes Aranda. 2012b. "Congrats…" April 26. At https://twitter.com/stevept/status/195701724315521024, accessed July 27, 2014.

———. Tweet to Lourdes Aranda. 2012c. "@lourdesaranda…'." April 26. At https://twitter.com/stevept/status/195706174438506497, accessed July 27, 2014.

———. Tweet to Lourdes Aranda and David Shorr. 2012d. "@mexiconsult…" April 26. At https://twitter.com/stevept/status/195701724315521024, accessed July 27, 2014. "Puerto Rico Summit Meeting." PREM 16/821. Margaret Thatcher Foundation Archive. At www.margaretthatcher.org/document/111510.

"Record of a Telephone Conversation between Chancellor Schmidt and the Prime Minister on Wednesday 16 March 1977." 1977. PREM 16/1221. Mar. At www.margaretthatcher.org/document/111497.

"Record of a Telephone Conversation between the Prime Minister and President Giscard d'Estaing on Friday 18 February 1977." 1977. PREM 16/1220. Margaret Thatcher Foundation Archive. At www.margaretthatcher.org/document/111495.

Rose, Clive. Memo. 1979. "Guadelope: Follow-up Action." January 12. FOI release (FOI249141) following Internal Review (IR251559). Margaret Thatcher Foundation Archive. At www.margaretthatcher.org/document/111527.

Sauvagnargues Calinet. 1975. "Sommet Monetaire." PREM 16/356. Margaret Thatcher Foundation Archive. At www.margaretthatcher.org/document/110973.

Save the Children. 2012. "Save the Children Says Pregnancy Kills or Injures One Million Girls a Year." At www.interaction.org/document/save-children-says-pregnancy-kills-or-injures-one-million-girls-year, accessed July 27, 2014.

Sonnenfeldt, Helmut, and Robert Ingersoll. Diplomatic Cable to US Ambassador Bonn, US Ambassador London, US Ambassador Paris, and US Ambassador Ottawa. 1975a. "Economic Summit." October 2. 1975STATE235072 / P84 0178-2645, N750005-0032. US National Archives.

———. Diplomatic Cable to US Ambassador Rome, US Ambassador Tokyo, US Ambassador Bonn, US Ambassador London, and US Ambassador Paris. 1975b. "Possible Economic Summit." October 1. 1975STATE233518 / P850036-2088, N750004-0727. US National Archives.

———. Letter to US Ambassador London, US Ambassador Bonn, US Ambassador Rome, and US Ambassador Tokyo. 1975c. "Possible Economic Summit." September 28. 1975 STATE 231096 / P850036-2076, N750004-0681. US National Archives.

UK Foreign and Commonwealth Office. 1976. "The Economic Summit Conference at Rambouillet: 15–17 November 1975." PREM 16/838. Margaret Thatcher Foundation Archive. At www.margaretthatcher.org/document/110959

———. Memorandum to James Callaghan. 1975. "Rambouillet: The French View." November 25. PREM 16/838. Margaret Thatcher Foundation Archive. At www.margaretthatcher.org/document/110958

UK Government. 1977. "Note of Discussion during the European Council Dinner for Heads of Government and President of the Commission at the Palazzo Barberini on Friday 25 March 1977." PREM 16/1254. Margaret Thatcher Foundation Archive. At www.margaretthatcher.org/document/111502.

Vile, M.J. 1979. "Guadelope Summit." FOI release (FOI249141) following Internal Review (IR251559). Margaret Thatcher Foundation Archive. At www.margaretthatcher.org/document/111525.

Volpe, John. Diplomatic Cable to Henry Kissinger. 1975a. "Possible Big Five MonetarySummit." July 29. 75 ROME 10839, 75 STATE 177516 / D750259-1006. US National Archives.

———. Diplomatic Cable to Henry Kissinger. 1975b. "Big Five Economic Directorate." July 30. 1975 ROME 10984 301447Z / D750263-0162. US National Archives.

———. Diplomatic Cable to Henry Kissinger. 1975c. "Press Reports on Colombo-Giscard D'Estaing Talks." September 13. 1974 [sic] ROME 12647 131807Z / D740256-1039. US National Archives.

———. Diplomatic Cable to Henry Kissinger. 1975d. "EC Foreign Ministers Meeting in Lucca: Economic Topics." October 22. 1975ROME15395 / D750367-0944. US National Archives.

———. Diplomatic Cable to Henry Kissinger. 1975e. "Ambassador's Meeting with Prime Minister Moro." October 27. 1975ROME15556 / D750372-0985. US National Archives.

———. Diplomatic Cable to Henry Kissinger. 1975f. "Italian Press on Results of Rambouillet Summit." November 19. 1975ROME16884 / D750402-0985. US National Archives.

———. Diplomatic Cable to Henry Kissinger, US Mission to Brussels, US Ambassador London, US Ambassador Paris, US Ambassador Ottawa, and US Ambassador Tokyo. 1975g. "Economic Summit." October 7. 1975ROME14518 / D750348-0427. US National Archives.

Wright, Patrick. Letter to James Callaghan. 1976., June 4. PREM 16/820. Margaret Thatcher Foundation Archive. At www.margaretthatcher.org/document/1115

Index

Abyssinia 98, 108
ActionAid 58, 95, 104
Adler-Nissen, Rebecca 17, 22, 34, 158, 173
Afghanistan 89, 125, 145
Aldo Moro 129
Alexander I of Russia 77
Algeria 51, 93
Andreotti, Giulio 140
Anghie, Antony 56
Apartheid 23, 76
Aranda, Lourdes 50, 91–93, 161, 166, 205
Argentina 62, 87, 91–93, 137
Armstrong, Robert 39, 124
Australia 41, 81; Failed G7 Bid 88–89, 123–126; Opposition to Spain in G20 81, 92–93, 123–124
Austria 64; Congress of Vienna 76–78, 117–118, 127–128
Austria-Hungary 46
Aznar, José María 88

B20 58–59, 79–80
Balance of Power 37, 77, 128
Balkenende, Jan Peter 90, 109, 110
Barriers 4–7, 19–32, 42–44, 53–71, 86–87, 138–142, 151–152; Achievable 5, 23, 27, 48, 53, 59, 60, 64–67, 151–153; Ostensibly Achievable 5, 27, 48, 53, 64–67, 152–153
Barroso, José Manuel 91
Bavaria 77
Beijing 57
Belgium 41, 65, 86, 139–140
Berlin 122, 125, 130
Berlusconi, Silvio 74
Bonn 122–123, 127, 130
Bonaparte, Napoleon 46, 76, 117–118, 128
Bono 79, 84, 95, 104

Boxer Rebellion 46, 57, 99
Boxer Protocol 57, 68
Bremmer, Ian 132
Bretton Woods 41, 119
BRICS 20, 74, 78
Brimelow, Thomas 131
British Overseas Aid Group (BOAG) 95
Brown, Gordon 94
Bull, Hedley 10–12, 37, 55, 64, 97, 160
Burning Bush 126, 163
Bush, George W. 89–90

Callaghan, James 120, 122–123, 127, 139–141, 163
Canada: G7 41–47, 88–89, 121–127, 131–132, 136–137; G20 93, 100
Carleton Group (See also, Library Group) 121, 127, 139
Carter, Jimmy 122–123, 140, 163
Castlereagh, Robert Stewart 128
Catholic Relief Services 79
Characteristics; Ascribed 4, 21–25, 30, 58–59, 79–83, 98, 117, 127, 135, 141, 152; Achieved 6, 19, 23–30, 36, 42–45, 53–66, 75–99, 117, 134–135, 142, 152, 160
China 44, 92–93, 102, 125, 133; Boxer Rebellion 46, 57, 99; Domestic Governance 61–62; Great Power Status 64–65; G-Summitry 136–137; Outreach 5 74, 78; Sino-Japanese War 81–82, 100–101; Treaty Ports 56
Christian Aid 95
Civil Rights 76
Clark, Ian 8
Clinton, William (Bill) 61
Closure Logics; Collectivist 3–5, 21–27, 33, 43–45, 53–67, 75–86, 103–104, 115–116, 133–141, 151–156; Individualist 20–30, 44–45, 53, 55,

60, 75–76, 135, 155; Functionalist 23–24, 32, 53–54, 86, 89, 96, 114–115, 128–132, 138, 141–143, 154–156; Functional Individualist 3–5, 26–27, 54, 59–67, 133, 152–156; Legal-Collectivist 4–6, 24–26, 33, 45, 53–59, 67, 104, 115, 138–141, 153–158; Legitimist 23–25, 56, 142
Colombo, Emilio 129–130, 139
Conference on Security and Co-operation in Europe (CSCE) 120
Congress of Vienna 66, 76, 98, 116–117, 121, 127, 131, 155
Credentialism 45–46, 75, 98–99, 132, 154
Crimea 40, 47
Cultural Representation(s) 40, 45, 54, 86–87 154–156
Czech Republic 44, 90

Decolonisation 9, 66, 75
Denmark 41, 77, 140
Dual Closure 27, 30
Dunne, Tim 9
Deference 12, 72–77, 87–88, 104–105, 124, 141, 152–155
Differentiation 5, 20–21, 30–33, 80–83, 97, 101–103, 152, 157
Diplomacy 8, 13–14, 37–43, 47, 55, 101–102, 137, 156

Egypt 93
Enders, Thomas 120
European Commission 39, 86, 92, 130–131, 138–141, 144, 169
European Community 41, 121, 138
European Union 42–43, 57–58, 89–92, 141, 16

Ford, Gerald 120, 126, 130, 163
Five, The Congress of Vienna 119–121; G-Summitry 86, 126
Four, The Congress of Vienna 76–78, 117–119; G-Summitry (See also: Guadeloupe Summit) 120–130, 164
Fowler, Robert 43, 167
France; Congress of Vienna 76–78, 80, 118, 128–129; G7 41, 43, 86, 88, 119–126, 131–132, 139; G20 89–90, 94; Great Powers' Club 46, 65–66, 99, 134
Franco-Prussian War 99
Frederick II of Prussia (The Great) 66
Froman, Michael 90–91, 93

G20 39–44, 58–63, 77–97, 115–116, 132–142, 154–156
G20 Summits; Antalya 164; Cannes 43, 58, 80, 95–96; Hangzhou 95, 137, 164; London 83, 86, 93–94, 96, 140, 166, 168–169; Los Cabos 58, 95–96, 164–166, 170; Pittsburgh 90, 93, 96–97; Seoul 43, 93, 95–96; Toronto 58, 79, 83, 93, 95–96, 164; Washington 62, 89, 94–96, 119, 126
G33 89
G5 41, 61, 74, 86, 102, 115, 121, 126, 131
G6 86, 131
G7 26, 39–44, 46–47, 54, 58, 61, 79–95, 121–127, 135–141, 160–169
G7 Summits; London 83–86, 93–96, 140, 166–169; Puerto Rico 88, 126–127, 139; Rambouillet 43, 86, 88, 120, 138–139; Venice 65, 124–125
G77 20, 136
G8 42–47, 61, 74–88, 94–95, 102, 132–138, 160–168
G8 Summits; Gleneagles 74, 84, 87, 132; Heiligendamm 132; L'Aquila 42, 102; Muskoka 42
Gates Foundation 7, 79, 95, 104, 167
Gates, Bill 95–96, 104
Geldof, Bob 84
Gender: masculine 21; patriarchy 23
Geographic Representation 63
Germany; Great Powers' Club 66; Nazi Germany 45–46; West Germany 41, 86, 119–122, 124, 126, 131–132, 139, 164
Giscard, Valéry 39, 41, 43, 92, 119–124, 129, 140–141
Gong, Gerret 7, 22, 60, 102
Gorbachev, Mikhail 61
Great Britain (See also: UK) 65, 118
Guadeloupe Summit 123–124

Habibie, B.J. 63
Hadley, Stephen 90
Hague, The 47
Haldén, Peter 55
Hanover 77
Harper, Stephen 89, 168
Helsinki 120–121, 129–130, 138, 164
Holland 46, 77
Howard, James 96, 168
Hu, Jintao 74
Hunt, John 88, 127, 139

Ibrahim, Anwar 62
Ichiro, Motono 134
Identity Adaptation 5, 29, 31, 72, 97
Indonesia 7, 61–63, 87, 93, 134
Informality 39, 41, 47, 140, 143, 162
InterAction 59, 78–79, 170
International Chamber of Commerce 80
International Labour Organization 96, 169
International Law 31, 37–38, 40–41, 47, 55, 60–61, 82, 100–102, 153
International Monetary Fund 41, 62–63, 85, 94, 119, 142
International Trade Union Confederation 96, 168
Ireland 41, 140, 149
Issue-Specific Regime 36, 38
Italy; Great Powers' Club 65–66, 98–99; G-Summitry 41, 44–47, 100, 120–127, 129–131, 136–141
Iwakura Mission 60, 101

Japan; International Society 47, 57, 60–61, 81–84, 97–103, 134–135; Great Powers' Club 75; G-Summitry 41, 88–89, 92–93, 119–121, 123–127, 137, 164
Jenkins, Roy 126, 140–141
Jones, Jim 91

Kahler, Miles 81
Keal, Paul 55, 98
Keene, Edward 9, 13, 25, 37, 55, 157
Kemal, Mustafa (Ataturk) 60
Kissinger, Henry 120, 129–131, 138

Labour 20 79–80, 96
Lamb, Geoff 95, 104
Lavrov, Sergei 47
León Gross, Bernardino 90–93
Levitte, Jean-David 90, 93
Levy, Jack 25, 64
Library Group (See also: Carleton Group) 39–41, 119–120, 163
Luxembourg 41, 139–140

Make Poverty History 84, 87
Malaysia 7, 61–63, 134
Manning, Charles 36, 160
Manuel, Trevor 39
Manzini, Raimondo 129, 131
Martin, Paul 26, 39, 43, 61–63, 74, 87, 132, 136, 161

Matthews, Lucy 104
McKinsey and Company 80
Merz, Hans-Rudolf 94
von Metternich, Klemens 117
Mexico 58, 74, 78, 90–96, 100, 137, 164–170
Mimicry 4–6, 29–32, 57, 65, 72–75, 83, 97–105, 131, 152–155
Mobility Dampeners 5, 28, 31, 40–48, 53–54, 67, 114, 151–152
Mondale, Walter 122
Moro, Aldo 129–130, 139
Multilateralism 8, 22
Murphy, Raymond 19, 25, 32

Napoleon (See: Bonaparte, Napoleon)
Netherlands, The 7, 43–44, 65, 89–94, 154, 157
Neumann, Iver 81–82, 97–98, 142
New Economic Partnership for African Development 43
Nigeria 7, 61–63, 87, 93, 134
Nixon, Richard 61, 119
Non-Governmental Organisations 7, 58–59, 76–97, 103–104, 137, 153, 160, 165
Non-State Actors 3–4, 7–10, 14, 24–26, 42, 54–59, 67, 78, 97, 103–104, 126, 131–142, 153–160
Normalisation 5, 31, 72, 88–89, 94–97, 152
Nuclear Security Summit 47

Obama, Barack 90–91
Oil Crisis 8, 41
Okagaki, Tomoko 56, 60, 82, 101, 133
Organisation for Economic Cooperation and Development 41, 58, 78, 137, 169
Ossala, Rinaldo 131
Ottoman Empire 47, 60–61
Outreach 5 42, 74, 78–79, 87, 91, 100–102, 132
Oxfam 7, 58, 84, 87, 95, 104, 166, 169

Palliser, Michael 126
Poland 44, 77, 90, 98, 127
Polish-Saxony Question 77, 106, 132, 146
Poltava, Battle of 75
Portugal 65, 77, 118
Primary Institutions 7–8, 36–38, 55, 59, 100
Prussia 7, 66, 71, 76–78, 117–118, 127–128

Index

Precedence 6, 28, 31, 40–48, 82, 88–97, 117, 136, 139, 154
Pragmatism 6, 40, 42, 88–89, 115, 117, 119, 154
Parkin, Frank 12, 19, 23, 26–28, 30, 155

Quadruple Alliance 118

Racism 42, 60, 133–134 153, 156
Rajoy, Mariano 91–92
Relational Strategies 29–33, 73–97
Reus-Smit, Christian 9, 15–17, 36–38, 48–49, 105–106, 134, 148
Robinet, Hervé 86, 139
Rudd, Kevin 89
Rumor, Mariano 129–130, 138–139
Russia; Congress of Vienna 117–118, 128; International Society 45, 60–61, 81–82, 97, 102–103; Great Powers' Club 46–47, 65–66, 75–78, 98–100, 134; G-Summitry 40, 47, 92–93, 127, 135–137

Sakue, Takahashi 82
Sarkozy, Nicolas 43, 80, 90, 94–95, 109, 196
Saudi Arabia 61–62, 87, 92–93
Save the Children 95
Saxony (See also: Polish-Saxony Question) 77, 127–128
Schmidt, Helmut 39, 120, 122, 140
Sherpa Group (See also: Carleton Group and Library Group) 39, 86, 88, 120, 124–127, 131, 137, 141–142
Shultz, George 39–40, 119, 161, 163–164
Siam 56–57, 103
de Silva, Lula 74, 102
Singh, Manmohan 74
Sino-Japanese War 47, 82, 102
Smithsonian Agreement 41
Social Closure Theory 19–33
Social Identity Theory 24
Solbes, Pedro 90
South Africa 20, 39 74, 78, 92–93, 157
Sovereignty 4, 6, 12, 22, 24, 26, 37–38, 47, 53–60, 65, 153
Spain; Congress of Vienna 76–77, 118–119, 128–129; G-summitry 44, 81, 88–94, 102, 154
Spanish Armada 75
Suharto 62–63
Summers, Lawrence (Larry) 26, 39, 61–62, 87, 161, 170

Sutrisno, Try 63
Sweden 46, 75, 77, 118
Switzerland 7, 44, 77, 90, 94, 154

Talbott, Strobe 61
Talleyrand, Charles Maurice 66, 76–78, 80, 98, 118, 128–129, 131
Think20 58–59, 165–168, 170
Thorn, Gaston 140
Tindemans, Leo 140
Treaty of Versailles 134
Treaty of Chaumont 118
Treaty of Geneva 82, 100
Treaty of Lisbon 91
Treaty of Nanking 56
Treaty of Paris 47, 76, 117, 118–119
Treaty of Portsmouth 102
Treaty Ports 57, 100
Triple Intervention 102
Trudeau, Pierre 43
Trump, Donald 65
Turkey 60–61, 87, 92–93, 137, 164

Unachievable 6, 27, 53–56, 65, 152–153
United Arab Emirates 93
United Kingdom (See also: Great Britain) 41, 122, 86, 89, 93, 119–125, 131, 139–141
United Nations 8, 42, 60, 95
United Nations Security Council 8, 81
United States 40–41, 47, 61–65, 78, 86–93, 101, 119–127, 129–132, 135, 139–140
Usurpation 5, 26–27, 29–30, 72–75, 105, 132, 152

van Rompuy, Herman 91
Volpe, John 129–130, 138

Webster, Charles 76, 80, 116, 128
Welsh, Jennifer 81, 97
West Germany (See: Germany)
Wight, Martin 11–12, 45, 98, 160
Wilson 39, 120, 140
Women's Suffrage 76
World Bank 142, 170
Wright, Patrick 140
Weber, Max 19, 21, 25, 151

Yukichi, Fukzawa 81

Zapatero, José Luis Rodríguez 89–92
Zarakol, Ayşe 6, 13, 99, 157, 163

Printed in Great Britain
by Amazon